LIVERPOOL & MANCHESTER
RAILWAY OPERATIONS
1831 – 1845

LIVERPOOL & MANCHESTER RAILWAY OPERATIONS 1831–1845

THOMAS J. DONAGHY

DAVID & CHARLES

NEWTON ABBOT

0 7153 5705 0

Set in Times New Roman
and printed in Great Britain
by Clarke Doble & Brendon Ltd Plymouth
for David & Charles (Holdings) Limited
South Devon House   Newton Abbot   Devon

For
MARY CATHERINE,
JAMES WILLIAM
and
HARRY J. DONAGHY, JR.

Foreword

Operations on the Liverpool & Manchester Railway, which were begun on 16 September 1830, proved to be one of the most significant developments in transportation history. The progress of the Liverpool & Manchester after its opening until its consolidation with the Grand Junction Railway Company in 1845 effectively demonstrated the L & M as truly the "Grand British Experimental railway". This evolution of the L & M, its growth, expansion and eventual consolidation, was typical of the majority of nineteenth-century British railways, which had, in many instances, imitated L & M theory and practice.

Many histories of the L & M have been written, but of these only one, that of C. F. Dendy Marshall, extensively covers the period of operations, growth and expansion, and Marshall's work is admittedly incomplete. In preparing our story of L & M Operations, a detailed analysis has been made of the minutes of meetings of the L & M Board of Directors, the L & M Sub-Committee, the L & M Proprietors, special L & M committees, and other Company records. In determining the expansion of the railway, the amending acts have been thoroughly explored as well as related sections of the Journals of the Houses of Commons and Lords. Contemporary newspapers such as the *Liverpool Mercury, Manchester Guardian,* the *Liverpool Mercantile Gazette,* and *The* (London) *Times,* have been used for a wider view of L & M activities, and to delineate public opinion on many phases of L & M operations. Many graphic descriptions and detailed technological explanations were found in contemporary periodicals and journals such as *Mechanics' Magazine, Herapath's Magazine, Gentlemen's Magazine, The Engineer,* and *The Railway Times.* Recently published journals such as *The Economic History Review, Railway World, Railway Age, Modern Transport,* and *The Engineering Journal,* provided some very useful information. Finally, biographical accounts of important men connected with the L & M such as George Stephenson, Robert Stephenson, Charles Vignoles and Henry Booth, were used at great length.

This work could not have been accomplished without the aid of several distinguished colleagues and institutions. The staffs of the following libraries and museums were most kind and helpful: British Transport Historical Records, British Transport Commission; Science Museum; University of Pittsburgh Library; Technology Department, Carnegie Library of Pittsburgh; Library of Congress; John K. Mullen Library, Catholic University of America; University of Pennsylvania Library; Yale University Library; Transportation Library, University of Michigan; New York Public Library; Library, Economics and Finance Department, Association of American Railroads; the John Crerar Library; Stanford University Library; Baker Library, Harvard University; and the David Leo Lawrence Library, La Salle College. Some years ago, Dr Robert E. Carlson, West Chester State College, suggested the writer investigate the L & M story. His sustained and helpful interest did much to bring this writing to completion. Moreover, I am indebted to Patrick Sheekey, F.S.C., G. O. Holt, and J. Allan Patmore for having read the manuscript in full and given many helpful suggestions. Edward Kline helped prepare the index. Responsibility for any errors rests with the author.

Finally, the writer is appreciative of sustained and cheerful encouragement on the part of his family and colleagues.

Thomas J. Donaghy, F.S.C.

Germantown
16 August, 1972

Table of Contents

List of Illustrations

CHAPTER I

Introduction

Operations on the Liverpool & Manchester Railway, which were begun on 17 September 1830, proved to be one of the most significant developments in transportation history. A new era was initiated, an era which was to see the railway remain the foundation of overland transportation for a century. The Liverpool & Manchester's policy of experimentation and expansion, so as to provide the maximum possible service, contributed much to establish its role in railway history. At the same time, the Company Directors accumulated a considerable body of information on operational theory and practice which was widely applied later. When one compares the operations of a modern railway with that of the L & M in the 1830s, the difference is striking. Yet, an examination of the development, expansion, and operations on contemporary railways demonstrates that many practices initiated by the L & M are still in use today. The enormous influence its example had on the projection, construction, and operation of other railways becomes evident in any study of railway history. In the final analysis, the story of the Liverpool & Manchester operations is one of continuing success. However, it was success won through the bitter, sometimes frustrating and dangerous, practice of "trial and error". It involved long-term investment in an unpredictable enterprise that did not always accord with public opinion. It meant developing types of construction never before attempted. Carrying people and freight at unheard of speeds was only one of the many risks involved. All these, and many other experiments, were necessary if the railway was to succeed. It is the purpose of this study to analyse and evaluate this success story.[1]

---

[1] Many accounts of the L & M's projection have been written, but most are incomplete. Only a few histories of the L & M cover its operations. See Henry Booth, *An Account of the Liverpool and Manchester Railway, Comprising a History of the Parliamentary Proceedings, Preparatory to the Passing of the Act, a description of the Railway, in an Excursion from Liverpool to Manchester, and a Popular Illustration of the Mechanical Principles Applicable to Railways. Also an Abstract of the Expenditure from the Commencement of the Undertaking, with Observations on the Same,* Liver-

In planning the L & M, its original projectors determined that a very definite need existed for an additional and improved system of transportation in Lancashire. Many factors contributed to the evolution of this need. Until the first half of the eighteenth century, Lancashire suffered economically from its geographical position and topography. But with the growth of Britain's western empire, ports along the Atlantic or ports which had immediate access to the Atlantic grew in importance. The port of Liverpool began to experience growth in both trade and population. These increases also had a stimulating effect on Manchester whose population and manufactures also began to expand after 1750. Lancashire's trade, population, imports and exports, factories, and coal mines, all grew apace, so that by the early nineteenth century, Liverpool and Manchester compared favourably with such centres as London and Birmingham.

Apart from seasonal inconveniences, transport of freight by road was extremely slow and costly. By 1800 the roads between Liverpool and Manchester could no longer handle the volume of freight, and even found it difficult to provide for travellers. The only other available transport was by water, via the Mersey and Irwell rivers and the Duke of Bridgewater's Canal. Inland water traffic in England dates back to the Roman occupation when the Fossdyke, connecting Lincoln with the river Trent, was constructed for drainage purposes. It was later developed for navigation. In 1564, the citizens of Exeter built a ship canal three miles long. Shortly afterwards, a two-mile section was added to link Exeter with the sea. In 1720, a group of Lancashire gentlemen acquired Parliamentary powers to improve the Mersey and Irwell rivers. They formed the Mersey & Irwell Navigation Company and for forty-two years monopolised water traffic between the two cities. Then,

pool, Wales & Baines, 1830; Joseph Kirwan, *A Descriptive and Historical Account of the Liverpool and Manchester Railway, from Its First Projection to the Present Time Containing All the Facts and Information That Have Yet Appeared on the Subject, with Numerous Interesting and Curious Original Details, Estimates of Expenses, &c, &c,* 2d ed, London, Simpkin & Marshall, 1831; C. M. Grieve, "A Short History of the Liverpool and Manchester Railway," in *The Book and Programme of the Liverpool and Manchester Railway Centenary,* Liverpool, 1930, pp 33–43; C. F. Dendy Marshall, *Centenary History of the Liverpool & Manchester Railway; (to which is appended a transcript of the relevant portions of Rastrick's Rainhill Notebook),* London, Locomotive Publishing, 1930; George S. Veitch, *The Struggle for the Liverpool and Manchester Railway,* Liverpool Post Printers, 1930; Robert E. Carlson, *The Liverpool & Manchester Railway Project, 1821–1831,* David & Charles, Newton Abbot, 1969; see also chapter 18 in Thomas Baines, *History of the Commerce and Town of Liverpool, and the Rise of Manufacturing Industry in the Adjoining Counties,* London, Longmans, 1852.

in 1791, the Duke of Bridgewater's Canal was opened to serve the Worsley coal district and Manchester. An extension of the Duke's canal ran as far as Runcorn Gap at the head of the Mersey estuary, and formed an independent means of transport between Liverpool and Manchester. At first, the Worsley–Manchester branch of the Duke's canal was to have used part of the Mersey & Irwell Navigation system, but this was avoided by the construction of a huge aqueduct to carry the Duke's canal over the Irwell into Manchester. Both waterways used flats which had a capacity of about twenty-eight tons, and when conditions were favourable, a one-way trip between Liverpool and Manchester took about eighteen hours. High rates and poor service offered by the navigation companies prompted the merchants and traders of Lancashire to investigate the possibilities of railways.

Railways were not unknown in Britain, having been in use for more than two centuries. During the first 175 years of its development, the railway never advanced beyond the horse-drawn colliery waggonway which was used to haul coal from the pit mouth to a nearby waterway. By 1587, over 300 such railways were operating in the coal districts of England, Scotland and Wales, and by 1776 railways were used as feeders and links in the canal system. By the beginning of the nineteenth century independent lines, such as the Surrey Iron Railway and the Oystermouth Railway, were put in operation. Finally, with the opening of the Stockton & Darlington Railway in 1825, a major step in railway development had been accomplished with the application of steam locomotion. The railways were not without their crusaders, and such men as William Jessop, Benjamin Outram, and Thomas Gray contributed much railway propaganda through their writings. Accordingly, by 1821–2, when the L & M projectors were initiating their plans for the railway, they found that the people of Lancashire were not entirely ignorant of the railway and its possibilities as a means of transportation.

With agitation for a new system under way, outstanding men were needed to lead a railway project. Such leadership was provided by William James, Joseph Sandars, and George Stephenson. William James was a unique individual—he seemed to possess a genius in many areas of technological endeavour, and in the early years of his life undertook several successful projects. For example, he was responsible for the draining and levelling of Lambeth Marsh, he drew up plans for a bridge across the Thames at London, and was responsible for the development of plans for several different railways. He was familiar with Trevithick's, Blenkinsop's, and Chapman's locomotives, and at one time was a colliery owner in South Staffordshire. James was also a prolific writer, and many of his statements in contemporary periodicals included suggestions for the development of the railway. James had favoured railways for about twenty years, and more particularly a railway that would link Liverpool and Manchester. It was obvious from his writings that he felt the steam locomotive would eventually bring the railway into its own. At the same time, James predicted that passenger traffic would contribute much to the success of a line between Liverpool and Manchester. In his first official connection with the L & M, James was employed to survey a route for the line, which he made in 1821 and 1822. The projected James line crossed Chat Moss and closely followed the ultimate L & M route. However, some business setbacks and a disastrous court case distracted him to the extent that, in spite of constant requests from the L & M provisional committee, he never put the results of his surveys into a presentable form. Accordingly, his connection with the L & M was ended. Nonetheless, James is given credit by many writers for his initial enthusiasm for the L & M project, and his name has its proper place in any account of the railway.

Joseph Sandars, sometimes called the 'Father of the Liverpool & Manchester Railway', was largely responsible for recruiting support, both financial and political, for the L & M. Among his business contacts and friends, Sandars set up committees in both Manchester and Liverpool. Out of these, a provisional committee was formed in the summer of 1822, and long-range plans were laid.

A meeting of the provisional committee on 20 May 1824 provided the necessary action which brought the L & M formally into being. A resolution was passed favouring the formation of a joint-stock company which was to be called the Liverpool & Manchester Railway Company. The committee felt that to obtain Parliamentary powers, construct the line and its works, purchase rolling stock, and set the railway in operation, £300,000 would be needed. This sum was to be obtained through the sale of three thousand shares, each at £100. Finally, the provisional committee selected George Stephenson as Chief Engineer. His first assignment was to draw up the necessary plans and sections for the new line. The committee was anxious to have these as quickly as possible so as to submit them to the next session of Parliament.

Stephenson began work immediately on his assignment. At the same time, a determined opposition was organised. Leaders in this opposition movement were such well-known men as the Earl of Sefton, the Earl of Derby, and Robert Haldane Bradshaw. In order to prevent the survey for the railway being made across their property, Sefton and

Derby used all their political and social influence, and even resorted to violence. They organised vigilante groups among their servants, and many violent struggles took place between the vigilantes and Stephenson's survey teams. In the meantime, Bradshaw, Superintendent of the Bridgewater Trust, had pamphlets distributed which succeeded in arousing public opinion against the surveys.

Despite the obstacles, Stephenson's first survey was completed in February 1825. The line suggested by him was to begin in the vicinity of the Prince's Dock, Liverpool. From there it went directly north to Vauxhall-road, then to Bootle, where the line curved directly east running through Fazakerly, Croxteth, Kirby, Knowsley, Eccleston, Windle, Sutton, Haydock, Newton-in-Mackerfield, Colborn, Lowton, Leigh, Pennington, Astley, Irlam, Worsley, Eccles, Pendlebury, Salford and Hulme parishes, 'to the neighbourhood of the westerly end of Water-street, Manchester.' The length of the line was about thirty-three miles, and it was estimated that an expenditure of about £400,000 would be needed to complete the railway. All the required evidence for the Bill having been compiled, the provisional committee turned it over to Thomas M. Sherwood, Parliamentary Agent for the L & M, whose duty it was to see that each clause of the Bill was properly stated, and in general, to guide the Bill through to royal assent. In March 1825, the L & M Bill received a second reading in Commons, and then the opposition became more pronounced. Appearing before the parliamentary committee on the Bill, canal interests and landowners testified against the desirability, usefulness, and economic prospects of the proposed railway. In defence of its position, the L & M brought in many merchants to speak in favour of a cheaper, quicker, and more efficient all-weather system of transportation for Lancashire. This manœuvre was offset by the opposition calling other Lancashire merchants and tradesmen who defended the adequacy of transport provided by the navigation companies and coach proprietors and carriers. In addition to this, the anti-railway forces gained advantage from George Stephenson's inability to testify precisely on the technical details of his estimate for the railway. Edward H. Alderson, counsel for the opposition, demonstrated that Stephenson did not know how wide the rivers were which the railway had to cross, the span of bridge arches, the height of the arches above the water, nor the depth of the Irwell. Stephenson was not certain of the levels of his cuttings and embankments, and he could not state how close the line would come to warehouses and other buildings owned by the waterways. The final blow to his testimony came when William Cubitt, an eminent civil

B

engineer hired by the provisional committee to check Stephenson's levels, stated that of the number he had examined, none was correct. This proved to be the turning point in the Parliamentary hearings. When all the evidence had been presented, the committee accepted the preamble by a vote of thirty-seven to thirty-six. When the individual clauses were voted on, the first two major clauses were defeated and the petitioners for the L & M Bill withdrew it.

Immediate plans were laid to submit another petition to the 1826 session of Parliament. These plans were devised in an atmosphere of encouragement from many wealthy and influential people. One such was William Huskisson, one of Liverpool's two MPs, who suggested that the provisional committee should stress the need for a railway due to constantly increasing traffic and should play down controversial issues such as the steam locomotive and monopoly. Naturally, several changes had to be made in the revised Bill. Because of the damaging effect Stephenson's testimony had had on the first Bill, it was decided, reluctantly, to dismiss him as engineer. The committee then hired John and George Rennie as chief engineers of the projected railway. The Rennies, in turn, hired Charles Blacker Vignoles as their chief surveyor. Vignoles began his survey in July 1825. He ran into the same type of opposition as had Stephenson the year before, but, although he had to do much of the work at night, he managed to complete the survey within the time prescribed by the committee. His proposed route differed from Stephenson's in that it left Liverpool through tunnels under the eastern section of the city and ran almost directly east through the parishes of Liverpool, Walton, Childwall, Huyton, Prescot, Winwick, Warrington, Leigh, and Eccles, and terminated in Salford near New Bailey Prison. The length of this route was approximately thirty-one miles, and was so laid out that the railway would skirt Sefton's property altogether, and went through only a few detached farm plots belonging to Derby. The clause in the original Bill calling for the use of steam locomotives was dropped. In the meantime, the committee enlisted the support of the Marquis of Stafford, principal Bridgewater trustee. The Marquis agreed to invest £100,000 in the project, and thus became a powerful figure in the Company, while at the same time he considerably blunted opposition to the plan. Since Bradshaw, as secretary of the Trust, worked to secure the £1,000 per day income the Marquis received, it would be very difficult for Bradshaw to oppose the railway interests too vigorously, since in so doing he would be endangering the Marquis's new investment.

Armed with a new line, new engineers, and increased confidence, the

Provisional Committee again presented a petition for an enabling Act to Parliament on 7 February 1826. This time the L & M Bill went through three readings in the House of Commons with ease; only in the Lords did the Bill encounter opposition, and this from Derby. Nonetheless, the enabling Act which brought the L & M into legal existence was given royal assent on 5 May 1826. The Act contained over two hundred sections, covering every facet of railway operation.

Almost immediately, Charles Lawrence, of Liverpool, was appointed chairman, and John Moss was appointed deputy chairman of the Board of Directors. The appointment of the principal engineer posed a problem. Because of the successful survey made by the Rennies and Vignoles, and the favourable impression made by George Rennie and Vignoles before Parliament, the directors felt the position should be offered to these men. When the Rennies were contacted the terms they asked proved unsatisfactory. The directors then decided to consult with either John Urpath Rastrick or George Stephenson as to general plans, and then see whether the Rennies would be willing to work with either or both of these engineers. As a result, George Rennie appeared before the directors to explain the circumstances under which he and his brother would take the position. Their plan excluded both Stephenson and Rastrick. The directors then rejected the Rennies and turned to George Stephenson, who it appears they had favoured all along. Many of the directors still had faith in Stephenson's ability as an engineer, and his promise to be at the scene of construction nine months a year convinced the directors they had found their engineer. Vignoles, who had already been working on the line, was left in a position that was never clearly defined. Stephenson thought Vignoles his assistant, and Vignoles felt he was Stephenson's equal. Eventually, misunderstandings between the two led to Vignoles' resignation in February 1827. Stephenson was then allowed to hire three assistants to replace Vignoles. He employed three able pupils of his: Joseph Locke, William Allcard and John Dixon. Locke was placed in charge of the tunnel to Crown Street and the western end of the line. Dixon was to supervise construction at the eastern end of the line, and Allcard directed activities in the intermediate section. Stephenson also secured the services of Thomas Gooch who prepared the drawings for the bridges, viaducts, inclines, tunnels, junctions, crossings and sidings. Having gathered what he considered a very capable staff, and recruited labourers from the north of England and Ireland, Stephenson pushed ahead with the construction.

Stephenson's plan called for putting the entire line under construction at once. In so doing, however, he did not spread his manpower evenly along the line. Few men were assigned to those areas which were level and, in general, required little preparation for laying the roadbed. Most of the labourers were allocated to three major projects, which Stephenson considered would consume the most time; they were the tunnels under Liverpool, the cut through Olive Mount, and 'floating' the line across Chat Moss. It was this last project that at one time caused great consternation among the directors, but Stephenson's plan for Chat Moss worked just when some directors and assistant engineers were ready to give up and look for a new route around the obstacle. While construction proceeded apace, Stephenson made the necessary preparations for stocking rails, sleepers, wagons, and other equipment.

Construction of the line was hardly under-way when the directors realised that the company would need more money. Accordingly, they applied to Parliament for amending Acts. Two such Acts were obtained on 12 April 1827 and 26 March 1828. These gave the railway power to borrow more money in order to complete construction of the line, and served to clarify many of the clauses in the original Act which had caused doubts in the minds of the directors. A third amending Act was secured on 14 May 1829. By it, the L & M was given power to carry its line directly into Manchester. Also, the directors were allowed to raise £127,500 by issuing £25 shares, the money so raised to be used to establish a Carrying Department with all its necessary buildings, locomotives, coaches, wagons, and equipment.

From the time the L & M project was first initiated, the directors had received many suggestions for the type of moving power to be used on the line. Each was given consideration, and in the last analysis it appeared as though the decision must favour either horsepower or the steam locomotive. In order further to acquaint themselves with the developments of the steam locomotive, the directors offered a prize of £500 in 1829 to the individual who would construct and operate to their satisfaction an 'improved locomotive'. In the meantime, the directors asked Robert Stephenson & Company to build a steam locomotive which was to be used on the line for experimental purposes. This locomotive, called *Twin Sisters*, was delivered on 25 July 1829.

To determine the winner of the £500 offered by the L & M, the Rainhill Trials were held during the first two weeks of October 1829. These trials were the subject for much comment and debate in contemporary newspapers and journals. Also, the public showed signs of great interest and the trials were attended in large numbers; it is

estimated that on 6 October 1829, as many as 15,000 persons gathered
at the Rainhill location. All four locomotive entries delighted the
crowds, but *Rocket* won the favour of the judges, and Robert
Stephenson was awarded the £500 prize because of *Rocket's* superior
performance under all conditions. The Rainhill Trials convinced the
L & M directors that the steam locomotive was best suited for their
purposes.

Tests and experiments with the locomotive on the L & M did not
end with the trials. *Rocket* and *Novelty*, the latter designed by John
Braithwaite and John Ericsson, continued to make test runs. These
proved more than profitable for the railway. The experiments revealed
that several locomotive details needed attention and improvement.
Fortunately, the railway had time to make the corrections before
beginning public operations. Also, the tests helped the public to become
used to locomotives running over the line and calmed some of their
fancied fears. Finally, the experiments and the many short excursions
arranged for company personnel along completed sections of the line
provided an instructional opportunity for railway employees in
operational theory and practice.

By mid-1830, Liverpool and Manchester were linked by rail, and the
first official trip over the entire line took place on 14 June 1830. In many
places the train had to run slowly because of the construction of
buildings, platforms, and bridges; in other places the directors stopped
the train to get a better look at the line. The running time for the
entire trip between Liverpool and Manchester was two hours and
twenty-one minutes. The experience for the directors was a gratifying
one, and it served to raise their hopes even higher for the success of the
enterprise.

Several delays in the arrival of equipment and the completion of the
works forced the directors to postpone the public opening of the line
from July to a later date. Finally, it was announced that the L & M
would open on 15 September 1830. People from all over Britain as well
as the Continent and America gathered in Lancashire for the great
event. The Prime Minister, the Duke of Wellington, was guest of honour.
Special trains carrying the guests started towards Manchester amid
great celebrations. Unfortunately, when the trains stopped at Parkside
for water, William Huskisson, who had left his coach, was struck by
Rocket coming along on the other line. Huskisson was rushed to Eccles
for medical attention, but died that evening. The shocked party continued to Manchester, arriving in the early afternoon. Later the trains
started their return journey to Liverpool arriving very late in the evening,

and the L & M was officially opened to the public. The next day, *Northumbrian* left Liverpool with several excursion coaches carrying about 130 people and returned the same evening from Manchester with approximately the same number. Full-scale operations commenced the following day.

CHAPTER II

The Permanent Way

A. *Maintenance*

From the time the first freight and passenger trains began operating on the L & M, all who were in any way responsible for the interests of the railway realised that maintenance of the new line was essential for successful and profitable operations. Accordingly, the organisation of the maintenance department was given the same priority as preparations for the public opening of the L & M. The men in this department would have to be experienced in railway construction, familiar with Lancashire weather conditions, and adept at handling employees. In this, the L & M was fortunate in having available such men as George Stephenson, John Dixon, Joseph Locke and William Allcard. As engineers it was their responsibility to keep the railway in such a condition that the public would always be assured of safe operations, and this was to be accomplished with the strictest economy. In all fairness, it must be stated that during the first few years of operations, which were probably the most difficult, Stephenson, Allcard and Dixon did an excellent job on the L & M. Unfortunately, in May 1833 all three men gave the directors notice of their intent to resign. Stephenson, recognised as one of the truly outstanding railway engineers of his day, had received several offers from other lines for his services, and this in part explained his reasons for wanting to move on. Allcard and Dixon had likewise received offers from other railways, but Allcard indicated his willingness to stay on if the company would raise his salary from £300 to £400 per year. Because of several projects already under construction such as the Lime Street Tunnel, and branch lines to Whiston Colliery and King's Dock, the directors were anxious to retain at least one of their experienced engineers. As a result, Allcard was granted the rise and he remained with the company. However, the directors stipulated that once the tunnel and branch lines were completed, they would have to let Allcard go. Dixon was also offered a rise, and when he saw Allcard was going to stay he followed suit. Special

23

arrangements were made for Stephenson. He was appointed consulting engineer for the entire line, at a salary of 100 guineas per year. This entitled the directors to write to Stephenson from time to time for his opinion and advice. If Stephenson's presence was needed on the line or before the Board, he would receive an additional seven guineas a day plus travelling expenses. Also, Stephenson continued as engineer of the Lime Street Tunnel, making the necessary checks on construction progress. The personnel situation in the maintenance department received another setback in July 1833, when Allcard suddenly resigned to take a position elsewhere. Dixon was temporarily assigned to take over Allcard's duties in addition to his own. Meanwhile, the directors informed Stephenson of Allcard's actions, but Stephenson made no offer to return to the L & M. A few months later, Dixon was offered a position with the London & Birmingham Railway at £600 per year. Immediately, the L & M Directors offered Dixon £600 plus travelling expenses, provided the L & B would release him from his signed contract. The chairman, Lawrence, was successful in having Dixon released, and he remained with the L & M. Shortly afterwards, Edward Woods was hired to superintend the Liverpool end of the line, and John Forsythe to assist Dixon at the Manchester end. In the end, Dixon remained with the L & M until its amalgamation with the Grand Junction. His experience in helping to build the L & M and his familiarity with the works and its needs served the company well.[1]

Compared to the first-rate engineers who directed the L & M maintenance department, the labour force employed in the department was, to say the least, wanting. A few platelayers and some navvies, who remained on after the initial construction of the line was finished, constituted the balance of manpower. The railway soon realised that much manpower and money would have to be expended to keep the line in good repair. In discussing the problem, it was suggested that 'Maintenance of Way' be let by contract. Although not unanimously received, the idea was given a try. The company engineers were asked to draw up typical contracts keeping in mind that the railway would supply the necessary materials. Thus, the contracts for maintenance would

[1] In January 1836, Dixon was appointed general superintendent of traffic, while remaining in charge of the Manchester maintenance department.—L & M Directors, *Minutes*, 4 Jan 1836. In 1839, Mr Woods's salary was raised to £800 per year. His assistant, Mr Green, was rehired for three years. Green's salary for the first year was £100, £120 for the second year and £150 for the third. In 1844, Mr James Rushton was hired to assist Woods at a much lower rate: £60 for the first year, with a £10 increase for each additional year.—L & M Directors, *Minutes*, 2 Dec 1839, 22 Apr 1841, 13 May 1844.

involve labour only. The first such contract was signed by John Dent in September 1833. But Dent, thinking he would deceive the company, did little more than make an appearance on the line. Accordingly, the directors cancelled his contract. The following month, a very satisfactory set of contracts was signed, this time with James Scott, who agreed to maintain the Liverpool end of the line at a charge of £250 per month, and John Cummings, who agreed to maintain the Manchester end at £252 10s (£252.50) per month. Scott, for an additional £10 per month, further agreed to maintain the Whiston branch line. These contracts were to be in effect for twelve months, and were renewable at the end of the year. The only change in the contracts for 1834 was that Scott received an additional 1s 10d (9p) per month. New contracts were drawn up for 1835. This time Scott agreed to take care of the Liverpool half of the line for £2,856, or £238 per month, and Cummings the Manchester half for £2,930, or £244 3s 4d (£244.17) per month. The directors ratified these terms provided 'there was to be no *extra charge* for supporting and securing bent and broken rails previous to their being replaced with sound ones'. However, Scott and Cummings refused to agree to this. Thus, when they submitted new proposals, Scott asked for an additional £60, and Cummings £200 for taking care of bent and broken rails. Scott's tender was accepted without change but the treasurer was directed to negotiate with Cummings for the best possible terms. In 1836, Scott provided maintenance for the Liverpool half for only £2,600 per year, and Cummings charged £2,800 per year for the Manchester end. However, in the meantime the L & M had decided to provide ballast wagons; previously Scott and Cummings had to hire their own. This in part explains the difference in contract prices. In all contracts for maintenance it was understood that they would be performed under the direction of the L & M engineers. Naturally, there were frequent arguments between the engineers and contractors, but for the most part the contracts were carried out faithfully. When the depression of 1837–8 forced the railway to inaugurate a drastic economy over the entire system, maintenance of way by contract was dropped, and the work was performed by L & M employees. This policy was continued until 1842, when the directors again considered the possibility of contracting for maintenance. The company advertised for bids from contractors who would maintain the way and 'uphold bridges and fences, with the slopes of cuttings and embankings'. Of the few replies received, the most favourable was that of John J. MacDonnell, former engineer on the Great Western Railway. He proposed to maintain the entire line for £130 10s (£130.50) per mile per year. Although the treasurer was instructed to invite MacDonnell to inspect the line, there is no indication that a contract was ever let. Apparently, the directors felt it would be cheaper to allow company labour to continue the work.

A major problem in maintaining the line was proper drainage. Accumulated water from rain and melted snow often blocked the way, washed out embankments, and sent tons of earth and rock over the main line. At Edge Hill, particularly, there was almost constant flooding of the line. To overcome this, culverts were built to drain the huge cut there. Unfortunately, the railway had to allow the culverts to empty on to their own land behind the engine shops at Edge Hill; consequently their shops were frequently flooded. To keep some embankments along the line from washing away young 'Forest Trees' were planted. Where feasible, however, stone blocks were laid over the entire area of a bank and the water drained down over the stones to gutters alongside the lines.[2] In 1833, the directors became increasingly concerned over the drainage problem. As a result, they issued orders to the engineers to draw up plans for more efficient draining of the system, 'especially of the tops of the slopes of the cuttings'. The directors contacted a Mr Studholme of London, who had successfully experimented with and developed a new method of draining. He was asked to inspect the L & M line and give his suggestions. After his inspection Studholme recommended that two or three men should be taught his method of 'Tile Draining'. The tile drains were set into the slopes and embankments that needed it most. For a section twenty-two yards wide, the cost of materials would be about 50s (£2.50) for each drain. If manuring and sowing of grass were needed, an additional 17s (85p) was added. The directors felt it worth their while to have all the slopes and embankments provided with the tile drains and ordered the engineers to proceed on the project without delay.[3] Except for extraordinary amounts of rain and snow, drainage on the L & M was well taken care of after 1834, and train delays due to flooding were a rarity.

[2] L & M Directors, *Minutes*, 19 Sep, 26 Sep 1831 and 22 Apr 1833.
[3] On Chat Moss, a wide marshy area where the track bed had been floated on a series of different types of fill, during heavy rains the swift flowing water in gutters alongside the roadbed threatened to undermine it. To prevent this Dixon devised a method of building perpendicular arms or dams fifty yards wide and a few hundred yards apart. This stopped the rapid flow of the water and consequent trackbed washouts.—L & M Directors, *Minutes*, 2 Jul 1832. Some seepage was experienced in the tunnels due to the porous stone and special arrangements had to be made with the owners of the surface land for the installation of drains. Since the droppings rotted the tunnel ropes, the Directors spared no expense or trouble in this matter.— L & M Directors, *Minutes*, 5 Jun 1843.

Winter weather was always a cause for concern along the railway. Frequently the freezing and thawing process would cause damage to retaining walls, bridges, culverts, and drains. In 1841, the retaining wall along the south side of Parkers cutting bulged so much due to a sudden thaw that it threatened the operations along the main line. The directors periodically warned the engineers to be on the lookout for 'slips or other failures of the works' once the snow was melted. In general, the problems of drainage at all seasons were effectively settled early in the history of the L & M. With little or no experience to go on, the directors were willing to try anything until they came up with the right answers. This 'experimental willingness' served the company well throughout its history.

Except for gas lamps attached to the wall of the tunnel to Wapping, little other attempt was made by the railway to light any part of the line before 1831.[4] A suggestion was made by C. E. Rawlins that the L & M light the entire length of the line between Liverpool and Manchester. He volunteered to undertake the project, but failed to submit any estimates as to cost and the type of light that would be used, and so the matter was dropped. Actually, lights were needed only at busy terminal points and junctions. In October 1832, the first light was put on the main line at Edge Hill opposite the siding where loaded freight wagons stood. Employees moving in and out of the area were in constant danger of being struck by the trains, and the light was installed as a safety measure. Eventually, naptha lamps were installed at most terminals and junctions.[5]

The proper maintenance of the line was the first major step taken toward safe operations, and the L & M directors were always insistent that their line be in the best condition. They frequently inspected the line and did not hesitate to issue orders and instructions to the engineers when their inspection trips were completed. Here however two principles clashed; the line should be maintained in the best possible condition at all times in the interest of safety, but this work could not be done on Sunday. The puritan mind frowned on Sunday travel, and to have gangs of men working along the railway on Sundays was more than Lancashire would tolerate. The directors did allow some work to be

[4] In 1834, the L & M carried out experiments in Wapping Tunnel with gas lamps fixed to the wall compared with lamps placed on the trains and moved back and forth. The fixed gas lamps remained in use, and the movable lamps were later used to light passenger coaches in the Lime Street Tunnel.—L & M Directors, *Minutes*, 10 Nov 1834; 'Cable Operation at Liverpool and London,' *The Railway Magazine*, LXXVIII (May-Jun, 1942), 174.

[5] L & M Directors, *Minutes*, 19 Aug 1839.

done, but only in case of 'urgent necessity'. In all such cases a special report had to be submitted to the directors indicating the work done and the reasons for doing it on Sunday.

One of the major construction projects along the L & M line, after it was in operation, was the building of the 'new tunnel' from Edge Hill to Lime Street in the centre of Liverpool. The main purpose of the tunnel was to bring passengers nearer the heart of Liverpool. The directors felt the expense of the tunnel would be offset by an increase in passenger traffic. At the same time, the freight station at Crown Street would be relieved of much congestion once the passenger traffic was removed from that area. At first, the directors were not quite sure where to locate the new terminus, but they felt it should be in the general area of Dean and Charlotte Streets. The Cattle Market was finally chosen as the most logical spot for the station. In August 1831, the directors ordered George Stephenson to prepare a plan of a tunnel to run from the engine shops near Edge Hill to the Cattle Market, Lime Street, Liverpool. Within the month the plans were completed, and the L & M chairman was appointed to apply to the Common Council of Liverpool for their consent. The reply of the Council was favourable; it would approve the tunnel provided it was used for passengers only.[6]

Actual construction of the tunnel presented many problems. Excavation meant finding a place to deposit the earth. Mr Leigh, a representative of Lord Salisbury, offered the company two fields in Crown Street for a period of three years at £300 per year rent, to be used only for excavated material. The directors, not being sure the tunnel would be completed within three years, agreed to take the land if they could have it for four years, and Mr Leigh granted this concession. John Moss, Robertson Gladstone and John Cropper were appointed a sub-committee to purchase the necessary land and premises for the tunnel according to the provisions of the enabling Act; they were also to make

[6] The reaction of the *Liverpool Times* to the 'new tunnel' was as follows: 'When this arrangement is completed it will be a great accommodation to the public; and we have no doubt it will meet with the support of the authorities of the town. The frequent arrival and departure of so many Omnibuses were sure to be found a great inconvenience in the streets through which they had to pass. And we believe the Directors have been desirous of remedying it'.—quoted in *Manchester Guardian*, 17 Sep 1831, p 3. The tunnel was to be '1⅓ miles long; 25 feet high; 22 feet wide; lit by gas; ventilated so the temperature is the same as the outside; and the roof of the tunnel will be coated with Roman Cement'.—*Manchester Guardian*, 1 Oct 1831, p 2. The Directors considered the possibility of a third tunnel to carry freight from the railway to the north end of Liverpool. But this was not accomplished until 1849 with the opening of Victoria Tunnel to Waterloo Dock.

agreements for passing under certain properties. The final amended specifications of the tunnel were lithographed and sent to the directors and proprietors, and advertisements for construction contracts were published.[7]

The contract for the tunnel construction was awarded to McKenzie, Longworth & McLeod. The total cost was set at £38,156, but if brick was used instead of stone on the interior, it would be an estimated £12,018 less, which then was to be deducted from the total. The L & M accepted the latter arrangement, and the construction was to be completed within two years. A few weeks later, Longworth and McLeod withdrew from the contract and the entire project was put into McKenzie's hands.

During the construction of the tunnel, Joseph Locke reported that the line of direction was off by about two feet, two inches, between the Asylum shaft and the Crown Street shaft. The report suggested an immediate drift to connect the two shafts, which the directors ordered to be done immediately. At the same time, the directors demanded an explanation from Stephenson and Allcard. Stephenson attributed the mistake to the compass, which he claimed was affected by the iron pipes used to keep out water. He definitely stated it was not Allcard's fault and that the deviation would hardly be noticeable once the tunnel was completed. Although the construction work on the tunnel did not proceed as rapidly as had been hoped, little other difficulty was experienced in the construction.

It was not till 15 August 1836 that the Lime Street Tunnel was opened. Trains using the tunnel descended to Lime Street by gravity, but were controlled by two brakemen in an open 'brake-van' on the front end. Trains leaving the Lime Street station were drawn up the tunnel by ropes. The ropes were kept tight by a 'tightening carriage running on rails, attached to a rope passing over a pulley down to a counterweight in a well sixty feet deep, containing water in which the weight was immersed'. It took the trains about five minutes to go up the tunnel, compared to the three minutes needed for going down. It was very important, both for operations and safety, that the ropes in the tunnel be in good condition. Accordingly, the sub-committee

---

[7] In advertising their intent to make a tunnel to Lime Street, the L & M had inadvertantly informed the real estate speculators, who in turn bought up the property they knew the railway would need. Thus, the company had to pay larger sums than they had expected for the land.—L & M *Minutes*, 26 Sep 1832.

advised Allcard to see to it that the tunnel ropes were kept safe and in good order. They likewise suggested experiments with wire cables, since these were already in use in Wapping Tunnel. Shortly afterwards, wire cable was installed.[8]

In order to keep the line clear of pedestrians, animals, wagons and other road traffic, the L & M built many bridges, overpasses, footpaths, fences and gates. Also, guardrails were constructed along the line where there was any danger that the coaches or wagons would be thrown against the deep cuts. In 1832, Dixon and Allcard were requested to submit a report to the directors of the number of lineal yards of guard-rail which would be required to 'render every part of the Line perfectly safe'. Where the line was constructed on top of embankments, there was great danger that the train would jump the rails and roll down, and with the increased speed on the railway, this kind of accident was more likely. In 1836, Colonel Shaw Kennedy suggested that safety mounds be constructed on top of all embankments that were more than ten feet high. These mounds would tend to prevent the trains from going over the side, or at least lessen the velocity at which they would go over. This suggestion was adopted and the mounds proved very effective.[9]

Gates along the L & M were quite numerous. Every station, whether it was at a road crossing or not, had its gates to keep the people off the line. Each farm along the way had gates opening on to the line where the residents needed access to their property on the other side. In this last case, the responsibility for the opening and closing of the gates rested with the property holders. Those who did not shut their gates after passing through were subject to a fine of £10.

The most important gates were those placed where the roads and railway crossed on the level. When first constructed, the gates were placed directly across the railway. The directors soon felt that the gates should be built across the roads rather than across the railway. After a thorough study of the matter, Dixon suggested that the railway apply to the highway authorities in Wavertree and West Derby Townships for permission to change the position of the gates. The permission was readily granted, and the gates were then built on either side of the

[8] C. F. Dendy Marshall, *One Hundred Years of Railways From Liverpool and Manchester To London Midland and Scottish*, London, London Midland & Scottish Railway Company, 1930, p 23; *Manchester Guardian*, 30 Jul 1836, p 2, and 20 Aug 1836, p 3; L & M Directors, *Minutes*, 2 Jun 1842.
[9] L & M Directors, *Minutes*, 20 Feb 1832 and 20 Jun 1836.
[10] 1 William IV, *c*. li, 22 Apr 1831.

railway, across the road.[11] In general, this idea was followed throughout the line, and the practice of leaving the gates across the railway soon disappeared. In 1839, Parliamentary powers granted to the L & M strengthened the railway's position as to the building of gates at road intersections, but extra protection for road travellers was required. Where gates were already in use, they were always to be kept closed except when road traffic required passage. In those places where the road crossed the L & M on the level, and gates had not been built, the railway was required to build them immediately. Since the gates were locked across the roads at night, bells were installed at all the gates at this time so that travellers could rouse the gatekeepers. Where the railway ran close to the turnpikes, protective screens had to be built in order to keep road travellers off the railway, and to prevent sparks from the locomotives from damaging turnpike vehicles.[12]

Bridges frequently were used on the L & M to great advantage to cross roads, streams, and rivers. When the company obtained powers to build an extension line to Hunts Bank, they were required to cross all streets in Salford by means of bridges or viaducts, all of which were to be built of stone, brick, or iron. The railway was also required to 'make substantial Arches or Culverts of Brick or Stone over all gas pipes'. The exact dimensions of the bridges and viaducts were set down in the 1839 enabling Act. Further, the railway had to pay for any damages done to pavements or roads in the process of raising or lowering them.[13]

From time to time, the railway received requests from citizens of various localities for an under- or over-bridge. Sometimes the railway was expected to carry the entire financial burden. In Eccles, some of the people donated money to the project, while the L & M paid the major portion of the bill. These donations on occasion took the form of land grants for the construction of the bridge. Although the citizens acted as a body, there were frequently individuals who held out against both

[11] Gates were impossible in the congested Liverpool streets. Once when the L & M received permission to lay a line across Wapping and Ironmonger Lane to the company's yard at King's Dock, they could allow only four wagons at a time to cross the streets and the safety of the people in the streets was the railway's responsibility.—L & M Directors, *Minutes*, 12 and 22 Oct 1832.

[12] 2 Victoria, *c.* xli, 14 Jun 1839; L & M Directors, *Minutes*, 23 May 1842. The gatemen kept the gates in good repair and were required to paint them when needed. The railway supplied the paint.—L & M Directors, *Minutes*, 11 Jul 1833.

[13] 2 Victoria, *c.* xli, 14 Jun 1839. The viaduct over Great Ducie Street was limited to a sixteen-yard width, and the viaduct over the Irwell was to be 110 feet wide and the arch was to clear the water at a height of eighteen feet and a width of ninety feet. The railway was responsible for the care and maintenance of all its bridges and culverts.—*Manchester Guardian*, 1 Jun 1842, p 3.

the railway and the citizen group, and the railway found itself in un-
ending and complicated legal negotiations. Still, in all cases the
railway appeared to be anxious to do more than its part to remedy a
situation where the road crossed the railway on the level.[14]

B.   Development of the Rail

A very important aspect of early railways was the development of the
rail. Without good tracks, the railways would not have been able to
develop their operations to such an extent that they would be able to
surpass the roads and waterways. The basic idea in using rail was to
give greater mobility to the rolling stock. If the rail impeded the mobility
of the coaches, locomotives or wagons, then it did not serve its purpose.
Besides aiding mobility, the rail had to withstand the great pressure
exerted with the passing of heavy trains, and stand up for a considerable length of time under the adverse weather conditions. As with
most of the original features of the L & M, the first rails were experimental and eventually had to be replaced.

These first rails 'were rolled iron, fifteen feet long, weighing 35 lb per
yard'. This light rail soon proved inadequate; the weight of the rolling
stock, especially the locomotives, was too much for the rails.[15] As early
as 1832, the assistant engineers were constantly reporting broken rails
throughout the entire line. The directors knew that if the railway was to
remain operational they would have to have a stronger rail. Consequently, Stephenson was called in and asked to consider the possibility
of new rails and report his findings.

From 1832 on, the L & M became a veritable experimental laboratory
for testing various types and kinds of rail. In one instance, the engineers
were ordered to take two rails from the north line and one from the
south line of the Whiston inclined plane and determine the comparative
wear on each. In another experiment, malleable iron rails fifteen feet
long, weighing about 177 pounds, were laid down; they were taken up on

[14] L & M Directors, *Minutes*, 9 Apr, 21 May, 28 May, 30 Jul 1838, 2 Sep 1839,
and 10 Feb 1840. In 1843, the L & M numbered all bridges and culverts beginning
at the Liverpool end. Numbers were painted on the battlements and corresponding
numbers were kept in a book. After inspection, the engineer would made an entry
about each construction and include the date of inspection. The book was to be
available to the directors at all times.—L & M Directors, *Minutes*, 7 Aug 1843.

[15] Marshall, *Centenary History*, p 36; Nicholas Wood, *A Practical Treatise on
Rail-Roads, and Interior Communication in General. Containing Numerous Experiments on the Powers of the Improved Locomotive Engines: And Tables of the Comparative Cost of Conveyance on Canals, Railways and Turnpike Roads*, 3d ed, London,
Longmans, 1838, p 582.

10 February 1833, and it was found they had lost 18½ ounces per rail. During that time 600,000 tons had passed over the rails. The actual annual loss was only 1/268th of the original weight, and it was computed that it would require 100 years or more to reduce the rail to half its original weight. Cast-iron rails were laid on the south side of the main line for a period of eighteen months. During that time the rails lost 1 pound 8½ ounces, again with approximately 600,000 tons having passed over the rails. But, when the directors ordered new rails in 1833, they did not specify malleable iron; instead heavier rolled iron rails, weighing fifty pounds a yard, were bought.[16]

Shape played an important part in the development of the rail. The original rails on the L & M were fish-bellied,[17] but in 1834 the directors decided to lay part of the line with parallel shape rails. The two down lines were to be laid half with fish-bellied and half with parallel rail. For a period of a year, the rails were to be kept under close observation and a detailed report submitted to the directors. After having made a thorough study of these and other types of rail in use on other railways, Dixon submitted a detailed report in June 1835. In general his conclusion was that 'Fish Belly form gives greatest strength with the least weight of Iron'. Dixon felt that a fifty-five pound fish-bellied rail was equal in value to a sixty-pound parallel rail, although he admitted the latter had more practical conveniences. Parallel rail was better on curves since the supports could be kept nearer on the inside rail and further apart on the outside rail. Also, the fish-belly rail was inconvenient when cuts had to be made at crossings and junctions, and it required a variety of chairs. What Dixon was saying was that he would prefer the parallel rail if it were heavier. He felt the 'T' shape rail with a web base was impracticable, because of the difficulty of attaching it to sleepers. Spaces had to be left in the grooves and these spaces caused the rails to come loose in a short time, which was quite dangerous. Also, the 'T' rails required heavier chairs and were harder to attach to the points and turntables. Dixon concluded the report on rails with the following statements:

> A good strong parallel rail with a plain stalk that just drops into a
> plain grouve in the chair is in my opinion the best. . . . I feel

[16] L & M Directors, *Minutes*, 10 Sep 1832, 5 Aug, and 25 Nov 1833; Wood, *Treatise*, p 729.
[17] A fish-bellied rail had a solid round base which tapered up towards the flat surface of the rail. The parallel rail had a plain straight stalk which supported the top flat surface, which in turn had straight edges on either side. The 'T' rail was similar to the parallel except that it had rounded edges on the top flat surface, and a web on the bottom. The stalk, connecting the top surface and the web, was straight.

confirmed in my opinion that the Plain Shanked Fish Belly Rail
and the chair to suit it may be obtained of the greatest strength for
the least money per mile of any Rail that I have yet seen[18]

Dixon had made his case; the most important factor in the rail was not
convenience, but strength.

Realising that the entire line would have to be laid with stronger
rails, the directors made preparations for the project in November
1835, and were ready to lay the rail in January 1836. The cost was high,
and during the relaying process the disbursements in the maintenance
department increased by about £1,500 per month.[19] At first progress
was slow, but the prospect of having North Union and Grand Junction
trains running over the L & M main line caused the directors to decide
'to relay the whole way more rapidly' than originally contemplated.
Even though their intentions were good, the directors were delayed by
financial problems. The cost of iron had gone up considerably due to
the increased demand made on the manufacturers by the several
railways under construction. In order to cope with the increased cost,
the directors, with the consent of the proprietors, decided to apply to
Parliament for powers to raise money to relay the line. The Act was
obtained in 1837, and the relaying of the entire line with heavier rail was
completed that same year.[20]

All the problems with the rail were not settled with the relaying of the
line. The railway remained in the trial-and-error state as regards the
rail for several more years. In 1838, the down lines of the Sutton and
Whiston inclines were reported in very poor condition. Woods felt a
parallel, as opposed to fish-bellied, rail with a three-foot bearing would
stand up better in these spots. The directors approved the relaying of
the inclines and the treasurer was to take into consideration the use of
sixty-pound rails with three-foot bearings, or seventy-five-pound rails
and five-foot bearings. At the same time, the Lime Street Tunnel's

[18] Report from John Dixon, Railway Office Manchester, 29 June 1835, to
Chairman of the Grand Junction Railway; hereinafter cited as Dixon Report.

[19] *Manchester Guardian*, 6 Feb 1836, p 3.

[20] 7 William IV, *c*. xxvii, 5 May 1837. Some claimed that the L & M used seventy-
five pound rails to relay the line. Others said seventy, sixty-two, sixty, and fifty-
pound rails were used at different spots along the line.—*Manchester Guardian*, 10
May 1837, p 2; Francis Whishaw, *The Railways of Great Britain and Ireland Practically Described and Illustrated*, London, John Weale, 1842, p 191; C. E. R. Sherrington, *A Hundred Years of Inland Transport 1830–1933*, London, Duckworth, 1934,
p 212. At first, the new rails cut into the flanges of the train wheels. To prevent this,
the inner edges of the rails were rounded, which in turn brought the rails ¼ inch
nearer but did not in any way affect the position of the wheels.—*Herapath's
Magazine* III (January, 1841), 26.

down line was relaid with sixty-pound rails. It was reported that the rails in the Parkside area had been forced out of line due to the heat. When laid, the rails had been set too close together, and the directors ordered that this was to be avoided when the new rails were laid.[21] This was the type of survey, research, and experiment which continued with rails on the L & M down to the time of its amalgamation of interests with the Grand Junction in 1845.

Other than the development of the best possible type of rail, a smooth railway required a very special type of cushioned bed. For the most part, the trackbed was made up of ballast. Once the terrain was dug out and smoothed to the desired level, then the ballast was laid to form a cushion for the rails. Besides providing a smooth ride, the ballast also enabled the engineers to lay the rails more evenly. Ballast on the L & M consisted of broken stone, small coal mixed with earth, and small coal alone; 'which last is indeed the best description that can be used, being compact, yet, sufficiently porous to admit of free percolution of the water'.[22]

On top of the ballast cushion, wooden or stone sleepers were placed. Wooden sleepers were used only over thirteen miles of the line in places subject to some settlement such as Chat Moss, Parr Moss, and the embankments, where stone sleepers would sink. The rails were set in chairs or clamps which were bolted to the sleepers; this held the rails in place when the trains passed over them. The undulating motion which the ballast allowed with the passage of the trains would have pulled the rails out of place if they were not securely fastened to the sleepers. At first, the L & M used oak sleepers. The problem of rotting had to be considered in view of safety and economy. After much experiment, Dixon and Allcard recommended that the L & M switch to larchwood sleepers. This was done gradually, and by 1839 they were in use throughout the entire length of the L & M. Still, the larchwood sleepers needed treatment to prevent rotting. The L & M purchased a licence for the use of Ryan's Patent Process, in which the sleepers were soaked for several days in a chemical solution which Ryan had experimented with and found effective.[23] Where stone sleepers were used, the rails were clamped to the stones, which for the most part were diamond shaped. They were set about two feet apart, but because of their shape their corners just about touched one another. The stone sleepers were not

[21] L & M Directors, *Minutes*, meetings of 28 Mar, 2 Apr, 1 Oct 1838, and 4 May 1840.

[22] Whishaw, *Railways*, p 191.

[23] L & M Directors, *Minutes*, 8 May 1837 and 17 Dec 1838.

looked upon too favourably since they often sank into the ballast, and it proved costly to shore them up. Although stone sleepers were used on the L & M until 1838, whenever new sleepers were needed, wooden ones were installed.[24]

Another problem the L & M engineers encountered was the space at the joint where two rails were laid end to end. When the trains passed over these rails, a very loud noise was made along with a very uneven ride. In 1836, the L & M experimented on the line by filling these spaces with small pieces of wood called keys. These were the answer to the problem, and a smoother, quieter ride was the result of their use. In order to keep them from rotting and having to be frequently replaced, the keys were put through 'Bramah's hydrostatic press after being dipped in palm oil'. It took four men an entire day to make 700 six-inch keys by the Bramah's process, but the directors felt the time and expense well worth the results obtained.[25]

The crucial point, then, in the development of the rail on the L & M was the directors' bold decision to relay the entire line. It was done at great expense and at a time when the price of iron was increasing. Any other decision might have caused the collapse of the entire railway. Light rail would have prevented the use of heavier and more developed locomotives. Finally, if the L & M rail had not been able to handle heavier rolling stock, those companies which formed branches and junctions with the L & M might have constructed parallel lines and offered better service.

C. Buildings

As a carrier of freight and passengers, the railway was of necessity obliged to construct many buildings along its line. Stations for passengers were necessary both as a convenience and as a safety measure. At first, L & M stations consisted of a series of ground-level platforms along the line where passengers were expected to wait for the trains. As the passenger traffic increased, more extensive accommodation was provided. Before 1840, the L & M had built sheltered waiting places at Newton, Kendricks Cross (Rainhill), Patricroft, Bury Lane,

[24] Dixon Report. The platelayers had the habit of breaking sound stones, and hacking into wooden sleepers when the week's work appeared to be falling short. It was easier to injure the stone sleepers, and this conduct in part militated against their use. The directors ordered that anyone found damaging the sleepers was to be dismissed and brought before a Magistrate.—L & M *Minutes*, 13 Jun 1833.

[25] L & M Directors, *Minutes*, 26 May 1836; Whishaw, *Railways*, pp. 195-6.

Flow Moss, Kenyon Junction, and North Union Junction. By 1841, plans for larger waiting rooms were drawn up for Rainhill, St Helens Junction, Bury Lane and Patricroft. In these same plans, arrangements were made to build platforms or 'stages' in order to make it easier for passengers to get in and out of the coaches.[26]

Passenger accommodation at the ends of the line was much more elaborate. With the cutting of the 'new tunnel' it was necessary to plan and construct a new passenger station in Liverpool. The L & M negotiated with the Common Council of Liverpool for the purchase of the Cattle Market which was to be the site of the new station. The railway had to pay £9,000 for the site, plus 4 per cent interest. The price included all the buildings of the Cattle Market, but did not include the weighing machinery. Since the new station would occupy such a prominent place in Liverpool, the directors decided to make the façade a work of art, and persuaded the Liverpool Council to contribute £2,000 to the project.

The end result was a rather large station constructed of wood and iron framework topped with a slate roof. The station contained many offices which were used by the L & M and some rented to other companies. Opened on 15 August 1836, it became the centre of travel in Liverpool and was the harbinger of the great masterpieces as well as monstrosities of architecture that have served the railway world as terminals.[27]

A proposal was made to remodel the station at the Manchester end of the line in 1835. The idea was to provide an arrival station for coaches of all railways entering the city. At the same time, facilities for handling the London & Birmingham traffic were to be built in conjunction with the extended station. The L & M accepted William and Henry Southern's contract to carry out the improvements at a cost of £7,999. The station was not to be as elaborate as Lime Street, and it was nearly all wood construction. A little less than seven months after the contract was signed, the Manchester extensions were opened.

Another large station was built at Hunts Bank in Manchester in 1843; however, this was a joint project sponsored by the L & M and the Manchester and Leeds Railways. It served the L & M after the

[26] L & M Directors, *Minutes*, 1832–8, *passim*. In some cases, separate waiting rooms were provided for ladies.—L & M Directors, *Minutes*, 7 Mar 1831.

[27] The Liverpool station became the nerve centre for the L & M's clerical operations. Other railways occupying offices in the station were the Grand Junction and the North Union.—L & M Directors, *Minutes*, 19 Dec 1836, 8 May 1837, and 24 Sep 1838.

completion of the extension line to Hunts Bank. The station, planned to be called Hunts Bank, was opened in 1844 as Victoria.[28]

As a carrier of freight, the L & M had to build several warehouses for the convenience of its customers. Since material shipped by railway is not always picked up on the day it arrives at its destination, the railway had to accept partial responsibility for freight until claimed by a consignee. It was both impractical and uneconomical to leave freight in the wagons until called for, hence the necessity of investing in warehouses. Also, the canals had provided limited storage space for their customers, and if the L & M was to compete effectively with the canals, it would have to offer the same service.

The two largest concentrations of warehouses on the L & M line were at Wapping in Liverpool, and Water Street in Manchester. The original construction of warehouses in Manchester cost £13,900. Before the range was finished it was necessary to plan and add an additional floor to one of the warehouses. In order to handle heavy freight, several cranes were built at the same time the warehouses were constructed. In 1834, a moveable 'Waggon Crane' was installed at Manchester to handle the large increase in bulk materials. Several years later more cranes were installed along with a weighing machine having a twenty-ton capacity. Actually, the Manchester warehouses never proved to be sufficient for the amount of traffic on the railway except during depression periods. In many instances, when freight volume proved too heavy the L & M had to pay rent for warehouse space elsewhere.[29]

The warehouses originally built at Wapping in 1829–30 were soon outdated. Many of the old open sheds were walled in and the floors flagged to provide more space. This proved to be a saving in expense for a while, but other arrangements had to be made because of the upsurge in traffic. In 1833, several new buildings were added to those already at Wapping and additional storeys were added to the original buildings. In 1837, a two-storey stable was built, the second floor being used for the storage of old company files. Between 1838 and 1842, several more additions were made at Wapping. To load and unload trunks and stone, a 'very large' crane was added in 1831. The following year, a crane operated by steam was introduced to speed up the transfer of goods from warehouse to wagon. The steam crane was replaced in

[28] L & M Directors, *Minutes*, 8 Jan 1844. For detailed description of Victoria station, see Appendix F.

[29] L & M Directors, *Minutes*, 6 Jun, 4 Jul, 18 Jul 1831, 22 Dec 1834, 1 Aug 1839, and 15 Jan 1844; The original weighing machine at Manchester had a capacity of fourteen tons.

1839 with a large hoist worked by Hagues Patent Pneumatic Engine, sometimes referred to as a vacuum engine. In spite of these mechanical aids, the porters and warehousemen still had a tremendous amount of backbreaking work in the storage departments.

In 1843, the entire storage system at Wapping was threatened with stifling restrictions by a Bill which the Liverpool Town Council had presented in Parliament. The purpose of the Bill was to further fire prevention in Liverpool. It contained many 'objectionable restrictions' covering the construction and use of the railway's warehouses. The directors sent a petition to Parliament asking to be heard against the Bill. At the same time, they let it be known that they would rather deal with the town clerk and work out their differences with him than go into Parliament. Accordingly, the town agreed to private negotiations, and the railway was able to protect its interests. The issues having been settled favourably for the railway, the L & M accommodation at Wapping continued to grow; larger turntables to handle the Grand Junction wagons were installed, a new warehouse was built in Crosbie Street, and the land between Wapping and Ironmonger Lane was roofed over for more space.[30] The tremendous outlay for essential buildings in the freight department was balanced by the steady flow of freight traffic over the L & M throughout its existence. Freight receipts paid for the expansion of the freight department and, at the same time, the L & M was able to show a fair profit in that department.

Several special arrangements were made for the convenience of the L & M freight customers. At Manchester a timber wharf, along with the necessary cranes to handle large quantities of wood, was constructed. A special platform for loading and unloading horses was built at New Bridge station. In 1834, the railway built a coal depot, along with several small offices, at the King's Dock, Liverpool. The offices were rented to coal agents shipping coal via the L & M. The Liverpool Dock Committee gave the L & M permission to appropriate one of the quay berths in the King's Dock, Liverpool, the quay to be used exclusively by vessels carrying freight to or from the railway. This encouraged shipping companies to persuade their clients to send freight directly to Manchester via the L & M.[31]

The railway was forced to construct cattle docks at various places along the line due to the frequent requests made to carry animals. In

[30] When L & M freight traffic on branch and junction lines developed, the railway had to rent warehouses for goods received from other railways.—L & M Directors, *Minutes*, 1 Apr 1844.

[31] L & M Directors, *Minutes*, 20 Jan 1835, 5 Feb 1844.

some cases, farmers along the way agreed to build these on their own property, or allow the railway to do so, if it proved convenient to the neighbourhood. Cattle docks were built at Cunningham's Bridge, on the north side of the railway at Oldfield Lane, on George Jones's land in Salford, and on company property at Broad Green. Actually, cattle traffic was never impressive, and as late as 1842 the railway tried to encourage this trade by improving the Broad Green cattle dock. On the other hand, traffic in pigs was quite profitable. Few loading places for pigs were needed along the line, since most of the pig traffic originated in Ireland. Pig pens were built in the Crown Street yards, Liverpool, to handle the incoming trade. In 1841, the Crown Street facilities were enlarged because of an increase in traffic, and separate pens and loading platforms for the L & M and the Grand Junction were provided. Two years later, large pig-handling facilities were built at Manchester in such a way that it would be very easy to enlarge them. This proved a wise move since they had to be enlarged just two months after being completed. Before the year was out, the treasurer reported that 'the Piggery just opened four months was yielding considerable above 10 per cent on the outlay'. Here was another example of an L & M investment well made.

Because of inadequate housing for L & M employees in the rural areas between Liverpool and Manchester, the company attempted to provide homes. Cottages were built at places convenient to the various works along the line; for example, several were built at Brickfield for those who worked in the locomotive shops. Many of the stations had cottages for their clerks or policemen, and there were cottages at nearly every crossing where a watchman was required. The cottages were in no way pretentious. At most, they consisted of two or three rooms, unfinished on the inside and having dirt floors. The rent varied from place to place. For example, a cottage with a garden at Sutton was rented for 3s 6d (17½p) per week, while a 'Wood Cottage on the Line' went for 2s (10p) per week. Occasionally, when the railway found its cottages unoccupied, it would advertise the sale or rent of the cottages to the public.

In order to protect its locomotives from the elements when they were not in use on the line, the L & M built a variety of shelters for them. Perhaps the most unusual engine sheds in Lancashire were those at Edge Hill drilled out of rock. Mrs Earle, whose property bordered the L & M's, made known her intention of making arches in the rock which separated the two properties, and the directors persuaded her to let George Stephenson engineer the job so that the arches could be used to shelter the locomotives. Wooden sheds did not prove substantial in high winds and the railway made most of their locomotive sheds out of stone. Locomotive sheds were built at Crosbie Street, Brickfield station, at the bottom of Sutton incline, and at Wavertree Lane station. The sheds at Brickfield station were used by both the L & M and the Grand Junction companies.

The operation of a railway required a variety of other buildings aside from those already mentioned. Coachmakers' shops were set up at Lime Street and Great Nelson Street. To protect the coaches from the weather, several coach sheds were built at various places along the line. The railway built its own coke ovens to carry on experiments in the development of a cheaper coke for use in the locomotives. Also, a small iron foundry was built to serve the general purposes of the railway. Smithy shops, store rooms for iron produced by the company, tool sheds, storage sheds for coal and other fuels, water tanks, and various offices and shelters along the line complete the array of buildings required for an efficient and successful operational railway.[32]

Having noted the varied maintenance problems of the Liverpool & Manchester Railway, it becomes evident that attention to the multitude of seemingly petty details involved formed a major contribution to the overall success of the railway project. On the other hand, if these same details had not been carefully worked out with much zeal and patience, it is likewise evident that just a few little details handled poorly or clumsily might have ruined the chances of success for the L & M. It is to the credit of the L & M directors that they were alert and interested enough to see the necessity of attending to such things as proper drainage, guardrails, gates, bridges, culverts, experiments with improved types of rail, ballast, sleepers and the great variety of buildings involved in the system. All these things were important to the eventual success or failure of the company, and the L & M directors proved that in the long run the efficient and intelligent handling of what some might think the 'small problems' of the railway, paid for themselves more than once over. Having conquered the problems of maintenance, and built a decent right of way, the problem of providing an equally efficient rolling stock confronted the railway.

[32] L & M Directors, *Minutes*, 16 Jan 1832, 21 Jan 1833, 26 Oct 1835, 20 Mar and 22 Jun 1837.

CHAPTER III

Rolling Stock

A. Locomotives

Although triumphant at the Rainhill Trials, *Rocket*, the product of collaboration among George and Robert Stephenson and Henry Booth, soon proved inadequate for the job that had to be done on the L & M. True, *Rocket* remained in operation for many years, but Stephenson more than anyone else recognised it was only the beginning. It was a good beginning, but greater strides had to be made in locomotive construction and development. When building several *Rocket*-type locomotives for the L & M, Robert Stephenson & Co made many alterations in the original design and as a result they developed a new class of locomotive. *Meteor* exemplified these alterations. Its cylinders were lowered to such an extent that they were nearly in a horizontal position. The driving wheels were enlarged to a five-foot diameter, the length of the tubes increased from eighty-eight to ninety-two inches and the diameter of the tubes increased by two inches. A further development of the *Meteor* class locomotive was *Northumbrian* which had its firebox placed inside the boiler and thus became the first example of the modern locomotive boiler.[1]

Late in 1830, George and Robert Stephenson developed a new type of locomotive, the *Planet*, which contained all the improvements and changes the Stephensons had developed since first building *Rocket*. Overall the locomotive was more sturdily constructed, and combined the following improvements—the blast-pipe, the tubular boiler, horizontal cylinders inside the smoke-box, cranked axle, and the firebox fixed to the boiler. The directors of the L & M were more than satisfied with *Planet's* construction.[2]

[1] Ernest Leopold Ahrons, *The British Steam Railway Locomotive 1825–1925*, London, Locomotive Publishing, 1927, p 17; L.T.C. Rolt, *George and Robert Stephenson, The Railway Revolution*, London, Longmans, 1960, p 162.

[2] Marshall, *Centenary History*, p 85; John Rowland, *George Stephenson, Creator of Britain's Railways*, London, Odhams, 1954, p. 210; Samuel Smiles, *The Life of George Stephenson and of His Son Robert Stephenson; Comprising Also a History of the Invention and Introduction of the Railway Locomotive*, New York, Harper, 1868,

Robert Stephenson & Co, which supplied most of the early loco-motives to the L & M, continued to make improvements on the *Planet* class. For example, all four driving wheels were made equal in diameter and coupled together. This principle was demonstrated in *Samson* and *Goliath* which were built to handle heavy freight trains on the inclined planes. By coupling the wheels, 'adhesion on the rails was more effectually secured, and thus the full hauling power for the locomotive was made available'. By 1832, *Planet* class locomotives were proving so satisfactory that the L & M directors ordered that future locomotives purchased from Robert Stephenson & Co be of that construction.[3]

One of the disadvantages of the newer *Planet* class locomotives was their increased weight as compared with *Rocket* class. The L & M directors, concerned over the condition of the track, ordered that 'no engine weighing above Eight Tons will be allowed to traverse the Road'. Actually, this order was in a sense too late, since locomotives such as *Samson* and *Goliath*, which were already on the line, weighed as much as ten tons.

It was obvious to all interested in the construction of locomotives that there was a need for more power, but it was generally agreed that more power meant more weight. Robert Stephenson, in his *Patentee*, tried to solve the power and weight problem by adding an extra pair of wheels for power, while omitting the flanges from the drive wheels to cut down on weight. *Patentee* was also fitted with a steam brake, in which a separate cylinder was provided, and when steam was applied the actuating rods pressed several shoes against the driving wheels. Although the theory was correct, practical applications were lacking, and the L & M eventually abandoned the steam brake in favour of the hand brake. However, *Patentee* became the prototype of express train loco-motives for the next fifty years.[4] At this time, Stephenson also attacked the problems of excessive rocking motion in the locomotives. *Swiftsure*, built in 1834, had four fixed eccentrics placed on the driving axle in order to actuate the valves by four separate gab end eccentric rods. This provided for two forward gears and two reverse gears. Finally, a change in position of the throttle along with the other changes effected less rocking motion on the locomotive.[5]

By 1835, L & M engineers felt it would be more feasible to build

p 335. 'The *Planet* may be taken as the true progenitor of the modern locomotive'.— 'Links in the History of the Locomotive , *The Engineer*, XCVI (March, 1881), 192.

[3] Ahrons, *Railway Locomotives*, p 21; S. Smiles, *Life of George and Robert Stephenson*, p 335; L & M Directors, *Minutes*, meeting of 12 Mar 1832.

[4] Marshall, *One Hundred Years*, p 27.

[5] 'Links in the History of the Locomotive', *The Engineer*, XCVIII (March, 1883), 160.

smaller locomotives to work the inclines. It was suggested that the 'bank' engines, as they were called, should be no larger than ten or eleven tons, having four coupled wheels and a fifteen-inch cylinder with an eighteen-inch stroke. Actually, this was only a reduction of one inch off the cylinder compared with *Samson* and *Goliath* which had been used as bank engines.[6]

After much observation and experiment, engineers in the L & M locomotive department determined that passenger locomotives would gain more power through using a shorter stroke. Thus, in ordering eleven passenger locomotives in 1836, the L & M directors asked Tayleur and Co, R. & W. Hawthorn, and Mather Dixon & Co, to build the locomotives with a twelve-inch stroke. Although the L & M reduced the stroke on its locomotives, there were many engineers on other railways who were convinced that the power of a locomotive did not depend solely on the amount and pressure of steam developed. Another popular theory was that the heavier the locomotive, the more powerful it would be. The defenders of this assumption said the additional weight caused greater adhesion to the rails and a resulting superior performance.[7] Having just completed the relaying of their line, the L & M directors were hesitant to approve another increase in locomotive weight. Hence, they were quick to favour the idea that a shorter stroke would provide the same amount of power as an increased weight in the locomotive.

With the many improvements and changes made in both freight and passenger locomotives, it became more and more difficult for the locomotive manufacturers to determine just what features the railways preferred in their locomotives. Accordingly, the L & M published a report entitled *Specifications for a Locomotive Engine*,[8] which contained all the improvements on locomotives up to 1836. After this date, when a

[6] L & M Directors, *Minutes*, 8 Jun 1835.

[7] Ahrons, *Railway Locomotive*, p 31. It is doubtful whether or not the L & M ever actually reduced the stroke to twelve inches. In citing the usual proportions for L & M locomotives, de Pambour writing in 1836 lists the stroke as being sixteen inches. He also lists the wheels as being four feet in diameter, but it has already been demonstrated that the directors ordered larger wheels for the passenger locomotives, and the smaller wheels used on the bank engine were never that small.—F. M. Guyonneau de Pambour, *A Practical Treatise on Locomotive Engines Upon Railways. . . . With Practical Tables, Giving at once the Results of the Formulae; Founded Upon a Great Many New Experiments Made on a large scale in a daily practice on the Liverpool and Manchester Railway, with many different Engines and Considerable trains of carriages*, New York, D. K. Minor and George C. Schaeffer, 1836, p 14.

[8] In many instances exact measurements are missing in the *Specifications*, which makes it very difficult to resolve any doubts as to the precise size of locomotive parts on the L & M.

company contracted to build a locomotive for the L & M, it was required to follow the *Specifications* as nearly as possible. These requirements remained in effect until the L & M began to build locomotives in its own shops in the early 1840s. This did not mean that improvements developed between 1836 and 1841 could not be used on L & M locomotives; this was not the way in which the 'Grand British Experimental Railway' worked. The directors were more than anxious that any new discoveries be applied to their locomotives. So it was, when *Lion* came on the L & M in 1838, it contained several recent improvements in boiler construction.[9]

Once steam pressure had been built up in early locomotives, one of the main problems was to prevent it escaping. If the steam escaped through the various valves due to poor construction, a loss of both power and fuel occurred. On the L & M, trouble was experienced with the valves until 1838, when several improvements were made on them and demonstrated in *Lightning*. These changes proved profitable for the railway, since it could operate with a 25 per cent reduction in fuel consumption and, at the same time, attain higher speeds. Two years later, John Dewrance, then in charge of the engine shops at Edge Hill, fitted *Rapid* with valves which enabled a still better performance.[10]

Having been successful in containing steam within the locomotive, the next step forward in locomotive construction was to make more steam available. To do this without increasing the size of the boilers was

[9] William Henry Boulton, *The Railways of Britain, Their History, Construction and Working*, London, Sampson Low, 1950, p 269. 'According to the specification for new boilers for the Liverpool and Manchester Railway, dated October 1838, the barrels were to be made of four narrow Low Moor iron plates, each the full length of the barrel, that is, about 7′ 6″ to 8′. The plates were lap jointed with longitudinal seams only. Thus, the material worked under the worst conditions, for not only were there four logitudinal lap seams in (such) boilers . . . but the grain of iron was placed so that the maximum stress acted across it .—Ahrons, *Railway Locomotive*, p 36. The usual pressure at this time was 50 lb per sq in, and the new specifications did not change this. It was felt that this pressure was the maximum for safety. Although Woods said he felt 70 lb per sq in perfectly safe, the directors would not approve such an operation on the L & M, feeling that it was not perfectly safe.—L & M Sub-Committee, *Minutes*, meeting of 9 Sep 1841.

[10] George Stephenson reported that engine chambers on the L & M varied from one inch to an inch and a half. He pointed out that the chambers on the *Rocket* were three inches, but he found more steam could be made by diminishing the diameter and getting more surface.—Great Britain, Parliament, *Report from the Select Committee of the House of Lords Appointed to Consider the Bill Entitled: An Act to repeal such Portions of all Acts as imposes prohibitory Tolls on Steam Carriages, and to substitute other Tolls on an equitable Footing with Horse Carriages*, 19 Jul 1836, p 57; Gerald Francis Westcott, comp., *The British Railway Locomotive. A Brief Pictorial History of the First Fifty Years of the British Steam Railway Locomotive, 1803–1853*, London, Her Majesty's Stationary Office, 1958, p 7.

difficult, but the addition of a second dome solved the problem.
Regulators were set in the first dome near the chimney, so the L & M
engineers decided to build a similar dome above the fire box, the
entire space in the extra dome being used to store steam. In this aspect
of locomotive construction, the L & M was far ahead of other
locomotive manufacturers.[11]

The process of reversing a locomotive on the line remained a
complicated one until 1842. Up to that time the mechanisms required
for putting a locomotive in reverse were crude and cumbersome. The
two methods in use before 1842 are described as follows:

> Some engineers used the so-called 'gab' motion in which there
> were two huge V-shaped members or 'gabs', one for forward
> running and one for reverse; the driver engaged the reversing rod
> actuating lever into one or other of the V's, which in turn were
> oscillated backwards and forwards by the motion of eccentrics on
> the driving axle of the locomotive. This oscillation was transmitted
> through the gabs to the valve spindle and the valves were opened
> and closed as required. There was a simpler mechanism that needed
> two levers to operate it; one to de-clutch, so to speak, and another
> to effect the actual reversal. The trouble with this device was that
> the two levers on the engine footplate were oscillating backwards
> and forwards while the engine was in motion, and as such were a
> great nuisance to the driver.[12]

William Howe developed the following process which made reversing
much easier:

> [He] connected the rods from the forward and reverse eccentrics to
> either ends of a single curved link. This link had a central slot in
> which could be slid, upwards and downwards as required, a die
> block to which the valve spindle was connected by links. This
> proved to be the most simple reversing device up to that time.[13]

Some parts of the locomotive caused more concern in their development and use than did the majority of the mechanisms involved. The
fire box, in particular, became the centre of a controversy on the L & M.
Mr Bury, a locomotive manufacturer, felt that a round fire box was
best for working a locomotive. Opposition to this idea on the part of
L & M engineers caused the directors to seek outside help. A report
from Mr Farey and Mr Field, both of London, favoured the square fire

[11]Ahrons, *Railway Locomotive*, p 35.
[12] O. S. Nock, *The Railway Engineers*, London, Batsford, 1955, pp 138–9.
[13] *Ibid.*

box. Their statements upheld George Stephenson's contention that the round fire box was very dangerous.[14] Because of the strong objections on the part of Bury, the directors asked Stephenson and Bury to write their views on the subject and again submit them to Farey and Field. After a second study, Farey and Field submitted another report to the directors:

> We are of the opinion that the square-sided fire-boxes with stays are decidedly preferable to, and safer than, the circular-sided fire-boxes without stays.

Farey and Field likewise pointed out that the round fire boxes were not safe from explosion since they did not give any warning that they were wearing out as did the square fire boxes. Despite this setback, Mr Bury took immediate steps to develop a square fire box for his locomotives so that they would be satisfactory for the L & M.[15]

For a considerable time there was some doubt on the L & M as to what material was best suited to line the fire boxes. Dixon opted for copper and in 1833 all new fire boxes and all those to be relined were to have copper linings. It was soon found that the copper did not withstand the tremendous wear and pressure exerted when a locomotive was in full operation. In an attempt to strengthen these linings, they were to be painted and covered with a 'hard coating of Solder or Brass'. At the same time, the engineers were told to consult Bury to determine how useful iron fire boxes had proved. Finally, the directors ordered a fire box to be made of plate steel, 'if it appeared to the engineers that it could be done'.[16]

Locomotive wheels, which were extremely important for economy and

[14] Stephenson felt circular fire boxes dangerous because they could not be strengthened by cross-stays and the effects of their bursting would be disastrous.

[15] *Report of John Farey and Joshua Field: Respecting Boilers for Steam Engines*, Liverpool, E. Smith, 1833, p 1. The *Report* indicated that a square fire box enabled the total length of the engine to be shorter and the circular box weighing more had a greater tendency to break the rear axle.—*Ibid*, pp 2–3.

[16] L & M Directors, *Minutes*, 7 Apr 1834; L & M Sub-Committee, *Minutes*, meeting of 12 Jun 1834. The final specifications for fire-boxes on the L & M were as follows: 'copper plate 7/16ths inch thick—Plate in which tubes are inserted ¾ inch thick—roof thickened with cross bars and sides with copper stays tapped and riveted ... a clear water space between inner and outer Box of 3 inches except immediately under tube ends where waterway must be 4½ inches, the bottom of the Firebox outside to be 20 inches clear from rails when engine on wheels'.—*Specification for a Locomotive Engine*, 1836. The importance of the fire box is described as follows: 'It is in fact, in the fire-box and boiler that resides the real source of power of the engine. From thence results all the effects produced. The cylinders and other parts are the means of transmitting and modifying the power; but what could be their effect, if that power did not exist?'—de Pambour, *Treatise*, p 11.

safety of operations, were likewise involved in a minor controversy before a definite policy was established on the L & M. Not only were the wheels of necessity a precision instrument, which could either detract from or add to the power of the locomotive, but from a mechanical point of view they also determined the safety of the train in motion. In 1831, Bury asked permission to try *Liverpool*, which had six-foot wheels, on the L & M. Although Stephenson felt that its six-foot wheels would be injurious to the road, and were less than safe, he consented to the trial and agreed to submit a report on the performance to the directors. During the trials, *Liverpool* overturned and the fireman and engineer were killed. The accident was blamed on the construction of the wheels, and the *Manchester Guardian* promptly took issue with the L & M Directors for having allowed *Liverpool* to be tested on their line.[17]

Stephenson nevertheless continued to study the advantages and disadvantages of several different types and sizes of wheels. In reporting the results of his studies to the L & M directors, he indicated that he was opposed to any diameter larger than five feet. After considering Stephenson's report the directors, being concerned with safe operations on the L & M, established a bylaw which stated that 'in the future no Engine shall be allowed to be introduced on the Railway with wheels of larger diameter than 5 feet'. The new bylaw was printed and sent to all locomotive manufacturers who dealt with the L & M. It remained in effect throughout the history of the L & M and contributed much to the L & M safety record which was one of the best in Britain.

The size of the wheels being settled, the directors in 1832 then tackled the problem of the number of wheels. George Stephenson recommended that all locomotives have six wheels, and the first six-wheeled locomotive built by Charles Tayleur & Co, was tried on the L & M in 1833. But the wheels rubbed the side check rails and the wooden point levering and were therefore not considered safe. In the meantime, Robert Stephenson & Co developed a six-wheeled locomotive, *Patentee*, and its trial runs

---

[17] L & M Directors, *Minutes*, 20 Jun 1831. Bury was told after the accident that any locomotives he had for sale with wheels larger than five feet in diameter would be rejected.—L & M Sub-Committee, *Minutes*, meeting of 10 Oct 1832. The *Guardian*'s comment was as follows: 'Indeed we think the directors of the Manchester and Liverpool railway, or their servants, were, in some degree blameable for allowing it (Liverpool) to run upon their line at all in the condition in which it is stated to have been. They ought to exercise the power vested in them by their Act, of preventing any engine from running on the line which, in the opinion of their engineer, is at all unsafe . . . but the preservation of human life is a matter of too great consequence to be neglected, merely on account of the gossip of idle people, or the complaints of interested parties'.—*Manchester Guardian*, 30 Jul 1831, p 3.

on the L & M proved very successful. The following demonstrates the advantages of the six-wheeled locomotive:

... the additional wheels were not intended to relieve the driving wheels of any great part of their load, but to check the pitching of the Engine by taking a part of the weight, at the time of the plunging. The trailing springs therefore carried a very light load.

This was the beginning of the type of locomotive that would be used on English railways more than any other till 1894.[18] After 1835, the L & M Directors reserved the right of requiring any locomotive working on the line to have six wheels.

There were many who were not in favour of six-wheeled locomotives, claiming that they were the cause of several accidents. The safety record of the six-wheeled locomotive was questioned in a letter of 9 October 1840, from the chairman of the Eastern Counties Railway to Lieutenant-Colonel Thomson, who had made a report on the new type of locomotive. It read in part as follows:

A comparison of the accidents, from failure of the machinery, which have occurred upon railways where six-wheeled engines are in use (such as the Liverpool and Manchester, the Grand Junction etc.) shows that they are most disastrous both in number and extent; while on the London and Birmingham, the North Union, the Midland Counties, and several other railways, where four-wheeled engines are exclusively used, many millions of passengers have been carried without a single instance being known in which an engine has run off the lines, or a single fatal accident has occurred, in consequence of the failures of any part of the machinery.[19]

The opinions expressed in the above letter cannot be taken for fact. The main cause of engines running off their lines, aside from objects having fallen or been placed on the line, was due to the motion of the locomotive. The three basic motions of locomotives[20] during this period

[18] L & M Directors, *Minutes*, 6 Feb, 5 May 1834; Ahrons, *Railway Locomotive*, p 22.
[19] Great Britain, Parliament, *Return: Reports, Returns, etc. Relative to Railways*, 8 Mar 1841, p 2, Supplementary Paper.
[20] The three basic motions of locomotives are: (1) oscillating or rocking motion caused by differences in the levels of two rails; (2) horizontal oscillation, transverse to the line of rails, caused by flanges of wheels striking against the rails, in consequence of changes in direction of the road, and by the cone of the wheels constantly correcting the effects of this action and of that arising from small deviation in gauge of rails; (3) vertical or pitching motion, produced by the preceding motions, by the deflection of the rails, by sinking of any small portions of the road, and by inequalities at the points of junction of several rails.—*The Times* (London), 15 Oct 1841, p 6.

D

would indicate that there was no reason for an engine with six wheels to be more apt to leave the rails than one of four wheels. On the contrary, the six-wheeled engine would have more stability. If the 2–2–2 locomotive was so prone to accidents, it would not have remained so long on the railways of the country.

Maintenance of the locomotives in good running condition was the chief function of the engine department of the L & M. Its staff handled all minor repairs on company locomotives which the manufacturers were not responsible for. As early as 1832, the L & M shops could handle such jobs as installing new tubes, new boilers, new fire-boxes, reboring cylinders, repairing gauges, and keeping the locomotives in 'good clean condition'.[21] Because of limited space, not all engines that needed repairs were dealt with in the company shops. Some were sent to local locomotive manufacturers who contracted to do the work. This frequently proved to be cheaper for the railway, especially in cases where locomotives needed extensive repairs.[22] When locomotives showed signs of wear in an abnormally short time, the directors would send them back to the manufacturers and demand that they be repaired without charge to the railway.[23]

The L & M locomotive department became more and more proficient in repair work. This, along with the great expense involved in the purchase of locomotives, brought forward the suggestion that the L & M construct its own. In 1838, when the treasurer stated that four new locomotives would be needed to carry the expected increase in traffic for 1839, the directors ordered that wheels, axles, framing and engine gears be made at the company's works and that the boilers, fire boxes

[21] L & M Directors, *Minutes*, 13 Jun, 6 Aug 1832, 10 Apr, 15 May, 5 Sep, 1833, 27 Jun 1834.

[22] *Milo, Ajax* and *Saturn* were sent out to undergo complete repairs. When *Milo* was sent back on the line, Bury informed the directors that he refused to repair any more L & M engines 'on account of the difficulty of giving satisfaction to the Foremen and Enginemen of the company'.—L & M Directors, *Minutes*, meeting of 13 Oct, 1 Dec, and 8 Dec 1834.

[23] L & M Directors, *Minutes*, 2 May 1836. The Board demanded that *Eclipse* and *Star* be repaired by Tayleur & Co without charge. The locomotive department proved to be one of the most expensive to operate on the L & M. Besides the purchase of new locomotives, the many repairs required by locomotives operating under great pressure was very costly. When brass tubes were substituted for copper the expenses dropped, but compared to other departments the outlay remained high throughout the history of the L & M.—*Directors' Reports to Proprietors and Accounts-printed*, 5 Jan 1832, 23 Jan, 23 Jul 1833, and 23 Jan 1834, hereinafter cited as *Directors' Reports*. The credit for what little saving the L & M affected on the use of brass instead of copper for boiler tubes must go to John Dixon.—Robert Young, *Timothy Hackworth and the Locomotive*, London, Locomotive Publishing, 1923, p 385.

and tubes be contracted for. The actual construction would then be completed at the company shops. Mr Melling, who directed the shops, was not completely satisfied with this arrangement, since he wanted to build a complete locomotive in the shops. Melling finally obtained permission to build such a locomotive 'when *Swiftsure, Atlas, Ajax* and *Pluto* were completely repaired'. With the appointment of John Dewrance as locomotive superintendent in 1840, the programme of building locomotives in the L & M shops was pushed to its fullest extent. Nearly all the locomotives that came new on the L & M line between 1841 and 1845 were produced in the shops under the direction of Dewrance.[24]

> The 2–2–2 engines of the Liverpool and Manchester Railway designed by John Dewrance were noted for their neatness . . . all were built in 1841–4 at the company's own works at Edgehill, Liverpool. They were comparatively small with 12 in by 18 in cylinders, 5 ft driving wheels, and 3 ft 6 in. carrying wheels. Their chief feature was the solid forged wrought iron wheel centres . . . the fire box side stays were not riveted over inside the box, but had long projecting heads shaped like the frustrum of a pyramid . . . the average weight of these engines in working order was $15\frac{1}{2}$ tons.[25]

The first locomotives turned out of the L & M shops actually cost £400 less than had been charged by local manufacturers for similar engines. But, in the long run, the project proved to be more expensive because of the cost of materials and labour and, in the opinion of one observer, 'lost the advantage of improvements, and of the division of labour'.[26]

One of the additional burdens of the locomotive department was the cost of fuel. The L & M used coke for the most part in order to get a greater heat in a shorter time and to cut down on the amount of smoke given off by the locomotives. From the outset of L & M operations, the company kept periodic records of the amount of coke used by the

[24] Marshall, *One Hundred Years*, p 28. Apparently Dewrance was an expert on valves: 'Even the vast increase in efficiency realisable from the use of valves with long laps had been discovered as early as 1840 by Dewrance, on the Liverpool and Manchester Railway'.—Oswald S. Nock, *British Trains, Past and Present*, London, Batsford, 1951, p 31.

[25] Ahrons, *Railway Locomotive*, p 50.

[26] Braithwaite Poole, *The Economy of Railways as a Means of Transit, Comprising the Classification of the Traffic, in Relation to the Most Appropriate Speeds for the Conveyance of Passengers and Merchandise*, London, William Clowes and Sons, 1856, pp 15–16.

different locomotives.[27] The directors and engineers used the records to determine the most economical type fuel or locomotive, whichever the case might be. Little information was gained from the first reports, so it was decided to record the weight of the loads pulled along with the amount of coke used.[28] Even with the additional information, the directors felt the accounts were 'not appearing to afford any instructive result', so they were dropped. But the problem of uneven and expensive fuel consumption continued to plague the L & M. A new plan was inaugurated in which two different types of fuel were used at different ends of the line. Gas coke was used in all locomotives put on the line at Parkside, and Worsley coke in the locomotives put on at Manchester. After keeping records on the two types of coke, the L & M decided to use Worsley coke in all its locomotives since it was not consumed as quickly as Gas coke. The railway continued to use Gas coke when experimenting with new locomotives just in case a new type of locomotive construction would prove more satisfactory with it.[29]

Anthracite coal, calcined or baked, was tried in 1838. Although less coal was consumed on a trip between Liverpool and Manchester, it did not give as hot a fire as coke and, as a result, the trip took twenty-seven minutes longer. Coke was retained as the major fuel on the L & M, and the railway continued to keep fuel records from time to time just in case there might be some change. Between 1840 and 1844, when nearly the entire fleet of L & M locomotives was renewed, there was a slight drop in fuel consumption. However, between 1831 and 1845 there was never really any major change in the amount of fuel consumed.

[27] The first account was as follows:

Engines	Lb Coke Used	Trips	Miles	Lb Coke Per Trip	Lb Coke Per Mile
North Star	18,990	22	660	861	28 3/6
Phoenix	8,005	10	300	800	27
Planet	9,464	16	480	592	19 3/4
Arrow	7,896	11	330	718	24
Meteor	11,104	17	570	653	22

The account was for one week, each engine pulling four coaches. L & M Directors, Minutes, 22 Nov and 13 Dec 1830.

[28] L & M Directors, Minutes, 24 Jan 1831. New accounts gave the following information: Planet: 1,744 tons conveyed 30 miles. Coke—25,180 lb—0·48 lb per ton per mile or 839 lb = 7.1.27 per trip.—L & M, Minutes, 11 Jul 1832.

[29] L & M Directors, Minutes, 22 Aug 1833. In September 1833, Sun and Etna consumed 826 and 806 pounds of Worsley coke per 30-mile trip, excluding getting up steam. Using Gas coke, Sun and Etna consumed 921 and 917 pounds respectively per trip. When Gas coke was first used, the dust was not taken out and this caused increased weight. So, the next time Sun and Etna used Gas coke they consumed only 834 and 833 pounds per trip respectively. However, this was still more pounds per trip consumed than Worsley coke.—L & M Directors, Minutes, 16 Sep, 23 Sep, and 30 Sep 1833.

Increased speed led to an increase in fuel consumption and this would explain in part why there was such a slight drop in fuel consumption in the locomotives built in the 1840s as compared to those built in the early 1830s. At the same time, it does point to an improvement in construction of the locomotive.[30]

Shortly after the Rainhill Trials, when the L & M made its decision to use steam propulsion, a storm of public criticism of the locomotive again broke out. It was up to the L & M, in a sense, to prove the critics wrong. The performance of the various locomotives on the L & M soon silenced the critics, for the work done by them during the first years of operations was without precedent. It was not long before all, except a few diehards, were convinced that the steam locomotive was the best source of power for railways.

On 26 February 1831, the *Manchester Guardian* reported that *Samson* pulled '107 tons 5 cwt at 20 mph' between Liverpool and Manchester and completed the trip in two hours and twenty-one minutes. The *Guardian*'s editor then noted:

> We imagine that the performance yesterday will, at any rate, put an end to the system of petty detraction which has been so long and so incessantly levelled at Mr Stephenson and his engines, by a little knot of pseudo-mechanics. . . . We are anxious to see how this and other recent occurrences will be treated in the *Mechanics' Magazine*, the organ of the party to which we have alluded.[31]

The L & M locomotives continued to perform well. Between 1832 and 1834, the average locomotive on the L & M travelled about 20,000 miles per year, and there were some that covered as many as 30,000 miles. Most of these locomotives made the trip between Liverpool and Manchester in less than two hours. This was done with less weight than *Samson* carried on its epoch-making trip, but it was still a great accomplishment for the locomotive manufacturers of the day.[32]

One of the advantages of the railway over the canals and the turnpikes was speed. As long as it was consistent with safety, the directors were always glad to approve any acceleration for both freight and passenger trains. It was not unusual for locomotives with a few

[30] L & M Directors, *Minutes*, 30 Jul 1838 and 1 Aug 1842; Ahrons, *Railway Locomotive*, p 65.

[31] *Manchester Guardian*, 26 Feb 1831, p 3. The following month *Mechanics' Magazine* acknowledged *Samson's* performance.—'Steam Carriage Performances on the Liverpool and Manchester Railway', *Mechanics' Magazine*, XV (Mar 1831), 36–7.

[32] Wood, *Treatise*, p 592; L & M Directors, *Minutes*, 11, 16, 23 Apr, and 30 Jul 1832.

passenger coaches attached to attain speeds up to thirty miles per hour on level parts of the line. In some instances, the trip between Liverpool and Manchester was made in less than one hour. Of course, L & M trains were not scheduled to run that fast. In general, the first-class trains made the trip between Liverpool and Manchester in one hour and thirty minutes, and the second-class trains made it in about one hour and forty-five minutes. But this was still far below the time required when travelling by coach on the turnpike, or via canal barge. Therefore, it is not surprising to find the directors reporting a tremendous increase in the passenger business in 1837. 'The means employed to attain this end have been principally a larger and superior class of Locomotive engine'.[33]

Compared with motive power in use before the coming of the railway the performances of the locomotives on the L & M gained, both for that railway and other railways throughout Britain, a tremendous prestige. Never before had people and freight been transported in such comfort and speed. Since locomotive performance determined in great part railway operation, the steam locomotive proved a vital factor in the great railway venture made by the original investors of the L & M.

One of the main factors contributing to the development of the locomotive on the L & M was the maintenance of the original spirit of the railway's projectors. The 'Grand British Experimental Railway' continued to be the research laboratory of the early British railway system. The directors were always receptive to new suggestions for the operation of any phase of the line. Many individuals, locomotive manufacturers, neighbouring railways and foreign railways benefited greatly from the experiments carried out on the L & M. As long as the interests and safety of the line were protected, the directors were more than happy to extend their facilities to experiment. As a result many applied for, and received, permission to run new locomotives on the L & M. These locomotives were allowed on the line for many months or for as long as the inventor or builder saw fit.[34] Needless to say, the

[33] L & M Directors, *Minutes*, 27 May 1833; Great Britain, Parliament, *Second Report from the Select Committee of the House of Lords Appointed to Inquire and Report whether Any Danger Is Likely To Arise from Locomotive Engines being used on Railroads passing through narrow Streets*, 7 Jul 1836, p 72; *Directors' Reports*, 26 Jul 1837, p 1.

[34] L & M Directors, *Minutes*, 27 Jun, 19 Sep 1831, 2 Apr, 16 Jul, 1 Sep, 1 Oct 1832, and 18 Jul 1842. In one case, the directors agreed to lend Lord Dundonald wheels and spare parts that he needed in order to try his engine on the line. In 1839, an American locomotive, *Victoria*, was tried on the L & M, and Woods reported that it appeared to be about the same as engines already on the line. Unlike other locomotives used experimentally, *Victoria* seems to have been taken into L & M stock, but later 'replaced.'

L & M sometimes benefited from the results of tests carried out on its own line by other people.

Other experiments were carried out by the L & M on their own locomotives with a view to utilising the inventions or suggestions which the railway received by the hundreds. A *Phoenix* class locomotive was set aside in 1832 for the use of the sub-committee 'in such ways as they might consider advantageous to the concern'. Many suggestions and inventions came from the employees. Dixon and an unidentified workman developed an improved form of slide valve which, because of its construction, freed the valves from very heavy pressure. Henry Booth, treasurer, was credited with the suggestion for an improved type of lubrication for the locomotives. It was Booth's opinion that there was great waste on the railway in the use of oil on the journals and other moving parts of the locomotives. He felt the grease used on the axles of the coaches would accomplish the same purpose, and do so at a much lower cost. Melling, foreman of the locomotive department, made several contributions such as the hollow double straight axle which allowed one wheel to travel faster than the other on curves; the adhesion wheel; the coupling wheel, which made for an easier and safer connection between the locomotive, tender and coaches; and the 'Patent Link Gearing', the most successful of all of his inventions. Because of Melling's position in the locomotive department, the L & M felt it was entitled to the benefit of any patents taken out by him on locomotive improvements.[35]

On many occasions, the directors extended the courtesy of their equipment to inventors who wished to try out their schemes. A. H. Houldsworth, MP, interceded for A. M. Perkins, inventor and engineer, and asked that he be allowed to place one of the Perkins's Patent Boilers on a company locomotive. The directors granted the permission on the understanding that the railway was not to withstand any expense or inconvenience. Some of the inventors offered to pay for the use of L & M equipment, as was the case with Mr Ogle and Mr Summers. They first offered the L & M the use of their Patent Boiler for £10,000. During the trial period, they were willing to pay the company £1,000 for using the locomotive. Since this was nearly the price of a new locomotive, the railway could not lose. In 1834, the directors agreed to allow Lord Dundonald to experiment with his revolving engine on *Rocket*. He felt the expense would not exceed £30, and if it did he would pay any amount over that. The directors allowed John Gray £300 in

[35] L & M Directors, *Minutes*, 1834–8, *passim*.

expenses in order to try his two inventions on the line. The first was a double-grated fire box for burning coal and coke, and the other was a series of improvements on valve gearing. The valve gearings proved to be useful in saving on the amount of fuel consumed by the locomotives. In the end, Gray offered the railway free use of his patented improvements at the rate of £20 per locomotive for any locomotive on which the directors used the valves.[36]

Several inventions eventually used on the L & M after trial on that line should be mentioned in passing. A Mr Reynolds, of London, had a patent on a new rotary engine which he tried on the L & M and which proved to be very successful. In 1838, a model 'cow catcher' was inspected by the directors. Its purpose was to remove obstructions from the rails by using the force of the locomotive. Although put under consideration, the 'cow catcher' was not immediately adopted on the L & M. Finally, an invention from America was tried with great success. Babbit's 'Improved Britannia Metal bearings' when used on locomotives produced a saving of 75 per cent on oil and, because of less wear and tear, a great saving in labour. Babbit offered the unrestricted use of his bearings to the L & M for £500 for which he included some other minor improvements.[37] In general, it can be stated that anyone who presented his cause to the L & M received at least a hearing. If the proposed suggestion or invention seemed at all possible and calculated to improve the locomotive, a trial was permitted, sometimes with financial assistance on the part of the railway.

At the beginning of operations on the L & M many manufacturers in Lancashire were anxious to supply the railway with locomotives, and the Rainhill Trials enabled the company to get the best possible choice of locomotive. Many accused the L & M of co-operating in a monopoly with Robert Stephenson & Co. Since George Stephenson was the resident engineer on the L & M, and his son Robert built locomotives, the immediate conclusion of many was that the railway was playing

[36] It was calculated that Gray's gearing system enabled the company to save two to three cubic weight of coke per day.

[37] L & M Directors, *Minutes*, 16 Nov 1843. There were two other important discoveries during our period which were used on the L & M, but there seems to be no evidence that they were first tried on the line. A precision instrument called Mr Milne's dynamometer enabled engineers to correct theories of resistance, correct form and shape of wheels, axles, rails, the effect of curves and inclines. A patent by Mr. Thomas Banks for renewing engine tyres was developed. It 'is accomplished by the application of steel to the peripheries of either old or new wheels in such a manner, that increased durability is ensured at an inconsiderable cost in the first production, and a permanent economy in the ultimate result'.—*Manchester Guardian*, 15 Aug 1838, p 3; 25 Jun 1842, p 2.

favourites. Between 1830 and 1833, the L & M purchased thirty-two locomotives, twenty-six of which came from Robert Stephenson & Co, and this statistic was the basis of the claims of favouritism. In reply, the L & M Directors published a letter received by them from Braithwaite and Ericsson, dated 18 January 1831:

> We consider it our duty to report to you that we have, during the [Rainhill] trials of our locomotive engine the latter days, fully ascertained its properties and capabilities; and we feel great pleasure in expressing our gratitude for the attention we have experienced during the experiments, which have been facilitated by every assistance on the part of the company.[38]

Yet the controversy continued outside the company. The editor of the *Mechanics' Magazine* accused the *Manchester Guardian* of favouring the Stephensons and using lies to cry down the Stephenson rivals.[39] Of course, the whole thing was not necessarily a question of favouritism. There was every possibility that the directors felt certain the performance of *Rocket* in the Rainhill Trials proved beyond a doubt that Stephenson's locomotive was the best at the time. When other local manufacturers met the requirements set up by the L & M, the directors were quite willing, and often did purchase many locomotives from foundries other than Robert Stephenson & Co. In August 1831, Edward Bury contracted to build two locomotives for £730 each. Between 1832 and 1838, the L & M purchased locomotives from the following manufacturers: Galloway Bowman & Co, Fenton & Murray Co, Hick & Co, Sharp Roberts & Co, George Forrester & Co, the Vulcan Foundry which was owned by Robert Stephenson and Charles Tayleur jointly, Tayleur & Co, the Horseley Iron Co, Mather Dixon & Co, the Haigh Foundry, Todd, Kitson & Laird, and Thomas Banks & Co, of Manchester. Naturally, there was competition among the various companies and it was suggested by Farey that another premium for the most improved locomotive should be offered by the L & M.[40] This suggestion was not followed through. It was not really necessary, since each company knew that it was already involved in a highly competitive field, and would therefore endeavour to produce the best locomotive possible in the hope that the railway would buy it.

[38] L & M Directors, *Pamphlet Reply-Edinburgh Review*, Liverpool, 1831, p 12; Young, *Timothy Hackworth*, pp 262–3.
[39] 'Steam Carriage Performances on the Liverpool and Manchester Railway', *Mechanics' Magazine*, XV (March, 1831), 38–9.
[40] L & M Directors, *Minutes*, 1831–8, *passim*.

The L & M was able to purchase its first locomotive from Robert Stephenson & Co for as little as £400. But an advance in the cost of labour and materials, along with a sharp rise in demand, caused the price of locomotives to increase considerably. In 1832, the company paid £800 for *Caledonian* with a spare set of 'strong wheels' thrown in. In 1834, although the directors were not entirely satisfied with *Experiment*, built by Sharp Roberts & Co, they agreed to purchase it for £700. Ten months later the railway paid George Forrester & Co £860 for a locomotive having an eleven-inch cylinder, an eighteen-inch stroke, and a copper fire box. At the same time, *Titan* and *Orion* were purchased from the Vulcan Foundry at £950 each. In 1835, Mather Dixon & Co agreed to build two 'bank engines' for £800 each. Charles Tayleur & Co was paid £1,050 for a locomotive having a fourteen-inch cylinder and a twelve-inch stroke. When the L & M purchased ten new locomotives in 1837, it did not pay less than £1,000 for any one of them, and the maximum price was £1,350. Bury, testifying before Parliament in 1838, stated that the cost of his first passenger locomotive was £700. His price for passenger locomotives in 1839 was £1,250 and for freight locomotives £1,400. It was at this time that the L & M decided to investigate the possibilities of building their own locomotives as has been discussed above.[41]

Having paid full price for their locomotives, the L & M directors saw to it that they received their entire worth. Where locomotives broke down before they had been in operation very long, the directors asked the manufacturers for reimbursement. Of all the locomotive manufacturers with which the L & M dealt, Robert Stephenson & Co had more claims made against it than any other.[42]

When the locomotives wore down to a condition beyond repair, they were broken up, and if any parts could be salvaged they were taken and stored at the Edge Hill locomotive shops. Others were sold for scrap. Finally, some locomotives, for which the L & M no longer had any use, were sold to other railways or individuals. Apparently, a used locomotive was not a hard thing to sell at this time. *Sans Pariel* was the first locomotive sold by the L & M, since 'this Engine will not work with

[41] L & M Directors, *Minutes*, 1832-7, *passim*; Great Britain, Parliament, House of Commons, *Second Report from the Select Committee on Railways Together with Minutes of Evidence*, 9 Aug 1839, p 321.
[42] *Vestra, Milo* and *Atlas* were found to be inferior and the L & M sent them back to Robert Stephenson & Co and asked for reimbursement. The same company also received a bill for several cracked locomotive wheels and a cracked axle on *Pluto*. After 1833, the L & M required a twelve-month guarantee on all locomotives.— L & M Directors, *Minutes*, 23 Apr, 18 Jun, 9 Jul 1832 and 3 Jun 1833.

coke, and is therefore unfit for the L & M line'. It was purchased by the Stockton & Darlington Railway in October 1831. Even *Rocket* was not safe. It was sold, along with its tender, to James Thompson of Carlisle for £300. However, before it went off the line the directors had a 'good drawing' made in order to show the first type of locomotive used by the L & M. Thompson used *Rocket* for three years at Kirkhouse Colliery. After lying dormant for several years, it was sent to Robert Stephenson and Company to be overhauled and demonstrated at the Great Exhibition of 1851. For reasons unknown to Thompson, *Rocket* remained at Newcastle until 1862 when it was presented to the Science Museum in a partly dismantled condition. It is still to be seen in the Museum today.[43] In this respect the L & M did not set a precedent. Many railways have kept as a prized possession the first locomotive to run on their line. At the same time, such an action demonstrates a shrewd, detached financial policy on the Liverpool & Manchester.

B. Coaches

Passenger rolling stock on the L & M was extremely important. The locomotive department had to provide the type of motive power the public wanted, while the passenger department had to provide an equally desirable means of passenger conveyance. Since the passenger receipts constituted a major source of income on the L & M, it was very important that the best possible type of passenger accommodation be created.

A railway coach was an entirely novel conception in 1830. The coal wagon served as a model for the idea of a railway truck, but that was not enough. Here a coach had to be built on a strong frame, supported with springs in order to prevent rough jolting when starting and stopping. The first L & M coaches were not too well constructed. They were extremely short, having a length of only seven feet between the wheel centres. This produced a pronounced see-saw motion while the train was on the line, especially when stopping and starting, and when the train picked up speed. At first, the wheels were made of iron and crudely shaped. Because they were constantly breaking, George

---

[43] Mr McKenzie, the tunnel contractor, purchased *Comet* for £250 and *North Star* for £275. *Goliath* sold for £100. *Sun* was sold for £200 and *Etna* for £250. Mr Locke of the Grand Junction company paid £500 for *Experiment*. *Meteor* was sold for £240. Mr Edward Cropper purchased *Caledonian* for the London & Birmingham Railway for £400. *Liver* was sold for £700 to Mullins and McMahon, contractors on the North Union Railway. p 181 n—L.T.C. Rolt, *George and Robert Stephenson*.

Stephenson ordered wooden spokes made for them. The coaches were connected with chains which caused a great deal of jolting when they came together as the train stopped or started. Added to this, Henry Booth testified in Parliament that for the first two years of operations L & M coaches were completely without buffers. In the summer of 1831, a spring was substituted for the chains and it was suggested that 'a bell should be rung, or the guard should sound his horn, a moment or two before the train is set in motion'. In this way the passengers could more or less brace themselves for the start.[44]

The L & M operated two classes of passenger coaches. First-class coaches were enclosed, and had three separate compartments. They resembled four coach bodies mounted on springs attached to trucks. The interior was elegantly decorated with buttoned upholstery. On both sides of each compartment, there were three seats separated by armrests. No provisions were made for lighting the coaches until 1834, when only one compartment on each coach was lighted. The exteriors of the coaches were painted in bright colours, and a name was given to each coach.[45] The ultimate in first-class travel by rail was on the mail coaches. The *Manchester Guardian* describes them as follows:

> They have four seats in each compartment; and the contrivance by which one of the compartments is convertable into a bed carriage . . . is a very desirable one to the invalid or valetudinarian, whom necessity obliges to travel. The backs are taken out of the seats on one side, opening into a sort of boot, lined with black leather and cushioned, and are then laid down across the space between the back and front seats, into which they fit, thus forming a complete

[44] L & M Directors, *Minutes*, 11 Oct 1830; C. Hamilton Ellis, *Nineteenth-Century Railway Carriages In the British Isles—from the Eighteen-thirties to the Nineteen-hundreds*, London, Modern Transport Publishing, 1949, p 13; Great Britain, Parliament, House of Commons, *Report from the Select Committee on Railways appointed to consider whether it is desirable for the Public Safety to vest a Discretionary Power of issuing Regulations for the Prevention of Accidents upon Railways, in the Board of Trade; and if so, under what Conditions and Limitations; Together with the Minutes of Evidence Taken Before Them*, 27 May 1841, p 34; *Manchester Guardian*, 30 Jul 1831, p 1, quoting the *Liverpool Times*. In 1833, the Sub-Committee ordered all the Blue Coaches to be 'filled up with Drawing and Buffer Springs'.—L & M Directors, *Minutes*, meeting of 14 Jan.

[45] *The Railway Companion, Describing An Excursion Along the Liverpool Line, Accompanied with a Succinct and Popular History of the Rise and Progress of Railroads*, London, Effingham Wilson and James Fraser, 1833, p 25; Ellis, *Railway Carriages*, p 14; Charles Dollfus and Edgar de Geoffry, *Histoire de la Locomotion Terrestre Les Chemins de Fer*, Paris, 13 rue Saint-Georges, 1935, pp 102–3. Dollfus suggests that the style and design on L & M coaches was copied by nearly every railway, and that present-day design evolved directly from the L & M.

bed. The cushions on the opposite seats are buttoned up and form a pillow; the legs are put into the boot, and the passenger may thus sleep or recline comfortable.

Second-class coaches were open wagons with wooden seats four abreast, separated and numbered. At first, these coaches, like those of the first-class, were constructed without buffers. But in 1833, buffers were put on all coaches. Second-class passengers, besides being subjected to the elements, were sometimes burned by sparks from the locomotives. Because of this, the L & M decided to enclose all of its coaches; however, the second-class coaches did not have windows or lights, which made for rather uncomfortable travel. Yet, compared to the trip by stage coach, it was smoother, quicker, cheaper and safer.[46]

The question of third-class coaches was broached by the L & M directors in 1839. Currie told the directors that third-class coaches on the Manchester & Leeds Line consisted only of wagon bases boarded up, and having no seats. But the L & M directors were afraid that if such cheap coaches were introduced, many of the first- and second-class passengers would use them as was the case on the M & L. Railway transport was cheaper than stage coach, and since there was no law requiring third-class coaches till 1844, it was not until that year that a third-class service was introduced on the L & M. Even after the Act was passed requiring a 'cheap train each way daily', the directors pointed out that it did not directly affect the L & M since their rates of fare were lower for second-class coaches than the Act would allow them to charge for open coaches at third-class rates. Still, the L & M did introduce the third-class service.[47]

From time to time the directors anticipated an increase in passenger traffic and initiated construction of more coaches. In December 1833, Mr Wordsell, in charge of the L & M coach shops, was ordered to build four new first-class coaches and have them ready for summer travel the following year. Also, the Blue Coaches (or second-class coaches) were to be repainted. At times the L & M coach shops could

[46] Great Britain, Parliament, House of Commons, *First Report from the Select Committee on Railways, Together with the Minutes of Evidence*, 26 Apr 1839, p 33; Great Britain, Parliament, *Second Report from the Select Committee of the House of Lords Appointed to Inquire and Report whether Any Danger Is Likely To Arise from Locomotive Engines being used on Railroads passsing through narrow Streets; With the Minutes of Evidence*, 7 Jul 1836, p 46.

[47] L & M Directors, *Minutes*, meeting of 7 Oct 1839; 7 & 8 Victoria, *c.* lxxv, 8 Aug 1844.

not keep up with the increasing traffic, and coaches were purchased elsewhere. In 1836, the treasurer bought six first-class coach bodies, but the L & M shops added the frames and other necessary equipment. With the opening of the North Union Railway, there was a corresponding increase in passenger traffic on the L & M, and eight first-class and four second-class coaches had to be built at the company shops. In 1840, an additional £2,000 had to be spent on new passenger coaches for the same reason.[48]

After about ten years of carrying passenger traffic, the L & M began to make some improvements in their coaches. In 1841, at the request of several corn merchants, blinds were placed in all the first-class coaches. In 1844, the directors decided to improve the second-class coaches by installing glass windows, thus giving greater protection against the elements. Finally, since there was no second-class accommodation for servants who accompanied their masters, it was decided to appropriate the first compartment of the first-class coaches for the servants. In all such cases, the servants were charged only the second-class fare.

As with the other departments of the L & M, many experiments were carried out in the coach shops and several new devices were tried out on the company's coaches. For a short time, George Stephenson's self-acting brake was used on the L & M, but it was not too effective and it gave way to the hand brake. In 1833, Henry Booth devised an additional set of springs with double hanging shackles which were used on the first-class coaches. The 'buffing apparatus', which consisted originally of rods and levers acting on something like elliptical carriage springs, was replaced in 1835 by Bergin's device, which was a combination of a coiled spring with rods from end to end of the coach 'and is more effectual in preventing the concussions in stopping or starting'. In one case, a locomotive going at fifteen miles per hour was run against a set of coaches having Bergin's device, and neither the coaches nor the locomotive suffered damage.[49] A combination coupling screw and spring buffer was invented by Henry Booth. This type of coupler remained in use on most railways throughout Britain till 1869. Finally, Booth invented a lubricant for the coach axles, using a compound of

[48] L & M Directors, *Minutes*, 9 Dec 1833, 15 Sep 1836, 12 Oct 1837, 10 Feb 1840. The second-class coaches were painted blue in order to distinguish them from first-class vehicles, and were commonly called 'Blue Coaches'.

[49] S. Smiles, *Life of George and Robert Stephenson*, pp 334–5; L & M Directors, *Minutes*, 10 Jul 1833; Pangborn, *World's Railways*, p. 105; L & M Directors, *Minutes*, 7 Dec 1835.

Russian tallow, palm oil, soda and water. Although Booth did not request compensation for his inventions, he was offered 150 guineas by the L & M for their use, which he graciously accepted.[50]

Patent brakes were offered to the L & M by Mr William Stewart and Mr Thomas Smith, but neither proved satisfactory. For its own part the railway, under the direction of Woods, carried on experiments designed to determine the best possible way of braking the trains when on the inclines.[51]

The development of passenger coaches on other railways was, to a great extent, influenced by L & M coach construction. Such railways as the Manchester & Leeds, the Grand Junction and the London & Greenwich actually modelled their coaches on those built by the L & M. The railway was quite liberal in allowing other railways to use plans and sections from its coach shops, and to make periodic inspections of L & M coaches to learn of any improvements. Coach builders in Lancashire likewise used L & M coach design in supplying other railways with rolling stock.[52] The attitude of the L & M directors in spreading their knowledge and experience is summed up in the following report to the proprietors:

Engineers and scientific men from different parts of the world are not infrequent visitors at the company's workshops, which are at all times accessible for the benefit of the public—whether for the purpose of scientific research, or of practical information.[53]

Whatever the L & M had that would be of benefit to other railways, they were quite willing to share. It was this spirit that exemplified the L & M throughout its history, and enabled it to attain such a model position in the development of the British railways system.

[50] Robert Smiles, *Memoir of the Late Henry Booth of the Liverpool and Manchester, and Afterwards of the London and North-western Railway*, London, Wyman, 1869, pp 42–3; L & M Directors, *Minutes*, 13 Mar 1837.

[51] L & M Directors, *Minutes*, 1837–8, *passim*. The L & M accepted Mr Isaac Babbitt's offer of the use of his Patent Metal Steps and Axle Boxes for their locomotives and coaches for the payment of £500.

[52] L & M Directors, *Minutes*, 15 Sep 1834, 12 Oct 1835, 5 Jul 1838; Ellis, *Railway Carriages*, p 14. 'It was left to the Manchester and Liverpool Company to demonstrate the practicability of a well-equipped steam railway which made passenger transportation a leading feature of its labours'.—'Fiftieth Anniversary of the Opening of the First Steam Passenger Railway', *The Railway World*, VI (Oct 1880), 963.

[53] *Directors' Reports*, 23 Jan 1835.

C. Wagons

Goods rolling stock on the L & M consisted of several different kinds
of wagons. This was necessary because of the variety, as to size, shape
and construction, of the freight the railway was expected to handle. Aside
from horse wagons, freight equipment was rather simple. Horses
carried on the L & M at first rode in better conditions than did second-
class passengers, horse wagons being built to carry two horses in separate
stalls. The enclosed wagon was completely padded on the inside and
had a bin for food to be consumed during the journey. A side section of
the wagon dropped down and was used as a ramp to load the horses.
Each wagon had four windows with swinging shutters, and on both
ends, near the roof, slits were provided for ventilation. A treadled floor
completed the interior. Because of the short distance between Liverpool
and Manchester, the L & M built only a few such horse wagons, since it
was found elaborate accommodation was not needed. It was a common
sight on the L & M to see a horse standing in an open wagon, and
covered with canvas during inclement weather. However, when the
Grand Junction began operating over the line, horse wagons were a
more common sight.[54]

Ordinary freight wagons were of a much simpler design. They
consisted merely of a heavy floor laid on two sets of trucks with very
small wheels. No springs were used and the wagons were of the crudest
possible construction. In some instances, where certain items required
it, the sides were built up to as much as five feet. Since the freight
wagons were open, sparks from the locomotives caused frequent fires
on the freight trains. To overcome this, heavy canvas sheets were tied
over the freight, and this same canvas served as protection during
inclement weather.[55] It was this type of wagon that served the L & M
for freight traffic throughout its history. There was little need for any
more elaborate accommodation and, of all the wagons used on the
L & M, these were the most numerous.[56]

[54] Two horse wagons were built for the L & M in 1833, but after that no more
were built.

[55] L & M Directors, *Minutes*, 7 Feb 1833.

[56] In 1833, the L & M took a survey of the number of wagons on the line. The
survey disclosed 301 wagons on the various lines and the highest number painted on
any wagon was 312. The difference in numbers had been explained by three wagons
having been burnt, and others had been so thoroughly repaired they appeared to be
new, and higher numbers were painted on them. In 1833 and 1835, the L & M had
fifty wagons built. When the survey was taken there were fifty on order and were not
included, so that by 1836 there were about 462 freight wagons on the L & M.—

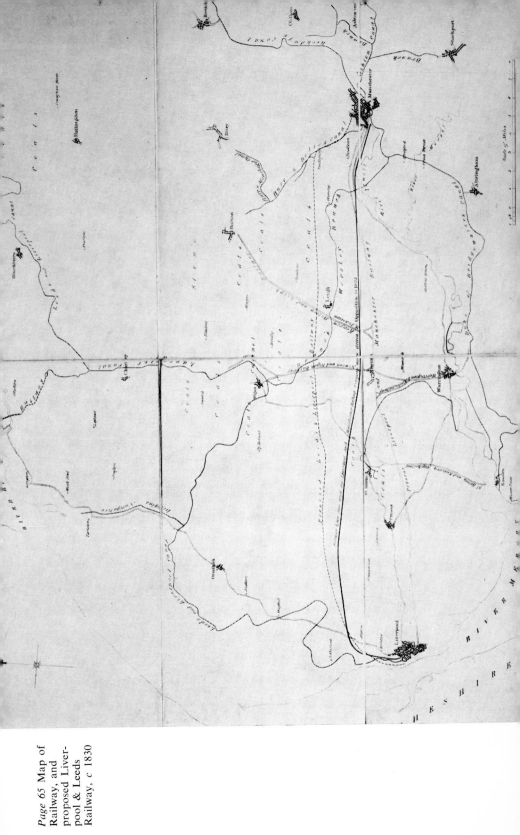

Page 65 Map of Railway, and proposed Liverpool & Leeds Railway, *c* 1830

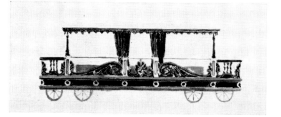

Page 66 Opening day guest list, and drawings of special carriages for opening day

L & M passenger train arriving in Manchester

When the L & M began hauling timber, it found that the freight wagons were too short to handle it, so special wagons had to be built for this purpose. Whishaw describes the design as follows:

> Timber placed on two trucks—cross pieces of timber, curved towards middle, higher than the sides by about 2″; above these are cross-timbers 12″ by 8″, and curved upwards as to their ends, which are four inches above the fixed cross pieces. Each piece turns on a swivel fixed in the middle of the cross timber.[57]

Actually, the only thing necessary for the transport of timber was the availability of trucks, which the L & M stored at various places along the line in case of an emergency in the freight department.

The L & M developed another type of wagon for coal traffic, which was little more than a slight improvement on the coal carts used at the collieries. The coal wagons built by the railway were of two kinds. Those used at the Manchester end of the line had bottoms that would open out and let the coal drop into storage bins. At the Liverpool end, the boxes had to be lifted from the trucks and transferred to carts. Other than this distinction, the coal wagons were not much different from the wagons used along the line to convey freight. Many of the collieries that used the L & M to transport coal had their own wagons, which made for a conglomeration of coal wagons in use. The only restrictions placed on coal wagons belonging to others dealt with weight requirements and the proper placing of wheels. For many years little care was taken of the coal wagons and the directors became concerned over their condition. In 1841, Woods was ordered to clean up any wagons on the line belonging to the L & M, and to inform other companies which had wagons in poor condition to do the same. Of the three major traffics on the L & M, coal provided the smallest income. It seems that the inattention bestowed on the coal wagons was matched by the poor income of coal traffic.[58]

Wherever possible, the L & M carried animals (other than horses) in the regular freight wagons. At first, there was little call for transport of animals, but as the demand grew an attempt was made to provide better accommodation. The L & M built a special type of wagon for sheep. It had a flat bed placed on trucks, and was slatted to about a

L & M Directors, *Minutes*, 10 Sep 1832, 21 Sep, 23 Dec 1833, and 23 Nov 1835. In 1835, the L & M decided to list and value the rolling stock each year. The results were to be entered in a 'Stock Book'.—L & M Directors, *Minutes*, 19 Jan and 2 Feb 1835.

[57] Whishaw, *Railways*, pp 203–5.

[58] In 1831, a coal wagon box cost the railway only £5.

E

height of four feet. In bad weather a tarpaulin was stretched across the top. But the sheep traffic never provided sufficient income, and the directors refused to replace any of the sheep wagons when they wore out. A similar type of wagon was built for the pig trade. Instead of slats, the flat bed was surrounded with vertical rails about four feet high. Eventually, sheep, cattle and any other animals were conveyed along the L & M in the pig wagons. These were more available and in greater numbers than the others, due to the large import trade in pigs from Ireland via Liverpool.[59]

Several ballast wagons remained on the line after the completion of the works. For the most part, they were used to carry tools, materials and workmen along portions of the completed line during construction. Some few were kept for maintenance purposes, but the majority were sold to other railways and contractors during the first few years of operations. By 1834, the entire stock of ballast wagons was ordered to be sold at auction.[60]

There was little done by way of experiment on the L & M with the freight and other wagons. For a while, a disagreement arose over the use of wooden or cast-iron wheels, and Edward Woods made several experiments with the different types. Woods felt that wooden wheels were best but the L & M, instead of using wooden wheels, developed a combination cast-iron wheel with a wrought iron tyre.[61]

The story of rolling stock on the L & M was one of constant development and experimentation. As the influence of the railway grew, the demand for increased service grew apace. The L & M had to meet this demand or fall behind in the competition. And it realised that the development of the locomotive was a prime factor in keeping ahead. Again, the willingness of the L & M directors to experiment with improvements, devices and inventions served the railway well. The contributions of the locomotive manufacturers of Lancashire were likewise a great boon to the L & M. There would have been little use in keeping pace with locomotive development if the railway did not intend to do the same with the remainder of the rolling stock. As has been demonstrated, the L & M provided the acme of transportation

[59] L & M Directors, *Minutes*, 25 Feb 1839. The pig reeve rode on the wagons with the pigs at no extra charge.

[60] L & M Directors, *Minutes*, 3 May 1832. In 1834, the treasurer was authorised to sell 100 large and 300 small ballast wagons to the Dublin & Kingstown Railway.— L & M Directors, *Minutes*, 16 Jun 1834.

[61] L & M Directors, *Minutes*, 3 Oct 1842. Not being sure of an automatic disengaging device, the directors ordered it to be tried out on two coal waggons.— L & M Directors, *Minutes*, 21 Feb 1831.

facilities available during that time, and provided the basic design for future development of the passenger coach.

Having invested heavily in providing a safe and efficient right of way, along with a highly developed rolling stock, the proprietors of the L & M were rightly anxious to have their investment prove worthwhile. As with the other departments of the railway, the L & M directors were pioneers in the handling of modern railway finance, and their performance in this sometimes difficult and complicated task added prestige to their venture.

CHAPTER IV

Finances of the Liverpool & Manchester Railway

A. Income

In studying the finances of any enterprise, it is important to determine from the outset whether or not a working capital was available to the company and, if so, what were the capital sources. In the case of the Liverpool & Manchester Railway, ample capital was available from the beginning of operations. Not only was the railway able to declare a dividend for its first six months of operations, but the credit of the L & M was sound, and the company was able to meet all financial obligations. Once operational, aside from loans and the issue of new shares, the main sources of income were receipts from carrying passengers, freight and coal. Of the three, the passenger receipts proved to be the largest source of income.

According to the enabling Act of 1826, the L & M was permitted to make the following charges on passengers:

	s	d	
Any distance not exceeding 10 miles	1	6	(7½p)
Any distance exceeding 10 but not 20 miles	2	6	(12½p)
Any distance exceeding 20 miles	4	0	(20p)[1]

However, in determining passenger fares such things as time, place, demand, cost of operation, wages and service provided, all had to be considered. As a result, when circumstances changed, passenger fares on the L & M fluctuated. During the first months of operation, first-class passengers between Liverpool and Manchester were charged 7s (35p) one way. Passengers travelling second-class paid 4s (20p). Fearing that the volume of passengers would drop once the novelty of the railway wore off, the directors ordered a fare reduction, effective from 1 January 1831. First-class fares were set at 4s 6d (22½p), plus 6d for omnibus service, and second-class fares dropped to 3s 6d (17½p) including omnibus service.[2]

[1] 7 George IV, *c.* xlix, 5 May 1826.
[2] L & M Directors, *Minutes*, 8 Nov and 13 Dec 1830; C. F. Dendy Marshall, 'The Liverpool and Manchester Railway', *The Railway Gazette*, LIII (September, 1930), 364. Omnibuses carried train passengers from strategic points in Liverpool and Manchester to the train stations.

As the demand for an even better type of passenger accommodation arose, the L & M provided a first-class service in coaches containing four passengers compared to six in the regular first-class coaches. The one-way fare for these between Liverpool and Manchester was 7s (35p).[3]

Although the income from passenger travel had been more than the directors had expected, they felt it necessary to raise the fares in 1832. Increased cost of operating locomotives and an advance in the government tax on passenger receipts were the reasons given for this increase. Fares between Liverpool and Manchester were increased to 6s 6d (32½p) in the Royal Mail coaches, 5s 6d (22½p) in first-class coaches, six inside, and 4s (20p) in second-class coaches. The fares for intermediate stations were as follows:

(*Manchester to Liverpool*)

Down Trains	*1st*			*2nd*[4]		
	s	d		s	d	
Wavertree Lane	1	6	(7½p)	1	0	(5p)
Broad Green	1	6	(7½p)	1	0	(5p)
Roby Lane Gate	1	6	(7½p)	1	0	(5p)
Huyton Lane Gate	1	6	(7½p)	1	0	(5p)
Rainhill	2	0	(10p)	1	6	(7½p)
Sutton	2	6	(12½p)	2	0	(10p)
St Helens Junction	2	6	(12½p)	2	0	(10p)
Collins Green	2	6	(12½p)	2	0	(10p)
Warrington Junction	3	0	(15p)	2	6	(12½p)
Newton Bridge	3	0	(15p)	2	6	(12½p)
Parkside	3	0	(15p)	2	6	(12½p)
Bolton Junction	3	6	(17½p)	2	6	(12½p)
Bury Lane	4	0	(20p)	2	6	(12½p)
Barton Moss	4	0	(20p)	2	6	(12½p)
Patricroft	4	6	(22½p)	3	0	(15p)
Eccles	5	0	(25p)	3	6	(17½p)
Cross Lane	5	6	(27½p)	4	0	(20p)

(*Liverpool to Manchester*)

Up Trains	*1st*			*2nd*		
	s	d		s	d	
Cross Lane	1	6	(7½p)	1	0	(5p)
Eccles	1	6	(7½p)	1	0	(5p)
Patricroft	1	6	(7½p)	1	0	(5p)
Barton Moss	1	6	(7½p)	1	0	(5p)
Bury Lane	2	0	(10p)	1	6	(7½p)
Bolton Junction	2	6	(12½p)	2	0	(10p)
Parkside	3	0	(15p)	2	0	(10p)
Newton Bridge	3	0	(15p)	2	6	(12½p)
Warrington Junction	3	6	(17½p)	2	6	(12½p)
Collins Green	3	6	(17½p)	2	6	(12½p)

[3] L & M Directors, *Minutes*, 10 Jan 1831.
[4] *Manchester Guardian*, 6 Oct 1832, p. 3; L & M Directors, *Minutes*, 26 Sep 1832.

St Helens Junction	3	6	(17½p)	2	6	(12½p)
Sutton	4	0	(20p)	2	6	(12½p)
Rainhill	4	0	(20p)	3	0	(15p)
Huyton Lane Gate	4	0	(20p)	3	0	(15½p)
Roby Lane Gate	4	6	(22½p)	3	6	(17½p)
Broad Green	5	0	(25p)	3	6	(17½p)
Wavertree Lane	5	6	(27½p)	4	0	(20p)

Shortly after these were published, there was a noticeable drop in the number of passengers using the L & M, a general trend which continued for some time. Also, by 1835, the passenger receipts showed a decrease in profits since July 1831.

		Charge			*Each Passenger Cost*			*Profit*		
		s	*d*		*s*	*d*		*s*	*d*	
1831	Jul	4	7¼	(23p)	2	0¼	(10p)	2	7	(13p)
	Dec	4	6½	(22½)	2	0¼	(10p)	2	6¼	(12½p)
1832	Jun	4	7¼	(23p)	2	6¼	(12½p)	2	1	(10½p)
	Dec	4	8½	(23½p)	2	7¼	(13p)	2	1¼	(10½p)
1833	Jun	5	1¼	(25½p)	2	10½	(14p)	2	3	(11½p)
	Dec	5	1¼	(25½p)	2	6¾	(13p)	2	6½	(12½p)
1834	Jun	5	0¼	(25p)	2	10¼	(14p)	2	2¼	(11p)

Considering every twelve passengers to constitute one ton, over the entire period, the charge increased 9½ per cent, the cost of transport increased 40 per cent and the profit decreased 14¾ per cent.[5] Despite this drop in profits, passenger receipts nevertheless continued to provide the major source of income for the L & M.

Another fare change was contemplated in view of the completion of the new tunnel to Lime Street, Liverpool, and the increased convenience it would provide for the passengers. A minority of the directors felt that the fares should be raised rather than changed according to scale. But the majority opinion was that 'a liberal policy toward the public will eventually be beneficial to the Proprietors'; the fares were not raised.[6] This policy was destined to guide the directors of the L & M throughout its history. Many other railways utilised this liberal yet beneficial attitude.

Periodically, circumstances arose which forced the L & M directors to raise passenger fares when no increase had been contemplated by them. On one occasion, the St Helens Railway gave the L & M notice that it would raise the fare from Liverpool and Manchester to St

[5] *Abstracts of Printed Reports of the Directors*, 23 Oct 1835.
[6] *D rectors' Reports*, 27 Jul 1836.

Helens by 6d. In order to absorb this charge, the L & M treasurer was authorised to raise the whole fare between St Helens and Liverpool and Manchester also by 6d.

Between 1835 and 1845, the L & M experienced two periods of recession in the passenger department. In 1837, the quarterly report for the period ending 30 September showed a large decrease in passenger receipts. It was during this quarter of the year that most of the holiday travel took place, and the depression had practically eliminated that luxury. After 1837, passenger traffic remained relatively stable until 1841, when there was another noticeable drop. England was again going through a period of depression and, as a result, merchants and dealers had little reason to travel between Liverpool and Manchester. Other reasons advanced for the cutback in travel were the severity of the winter of 1841, and the introduction of the penny post which enabled more people to carry on their business by mail.[7] Other than the two above-mentioned periods, there was little fluctuation in L & M passenger receipts.

Another fare increase was contemplated by the L & M in 1844 in order to balance the tremendous outlay of funds made for the construction of the extension line to Hunts Bank. This news was not too well received by some passengers, but their complaints were quickly answered in the *Manchester Guardian*:

> With respect to the proposed increase of fares, it must not be forgotten that the line now in progress is constructed, not merely for the purpose of effecting a junction with the Leeds line, but also with a view of bringing passengers to a more central point in Manchester—a service which may fairly deserve some additional remuneration.[8]

An increase of 6d on all classes of trains was to be put into effect as soon as the Hunts Bank line was completed. The fares would then be 7s (35p) in the mail coaches, 6s 6d (32½p) first-class, and 5s (25p) second-class. In spite of the increase and the complaints, the number of passengers carried after the new fares came into effect varied little.[9]

As mentioned above, the L & M had made no provisions for third-class travel before 1844. When the sub-committee suggested an

---

[7] *Directors' Reports*, 24 Jan 1838, 27 Jan 1841, and 25 Jan 1843. Passenger receipts dropped at the Warrington and Rainhill stations due to the introduction of a very fast omnibus providing a service to Liverpool.—L & M Directors, *Minutes*, 30 Nov 1843.

[8] *Manchester Guardian*, 7 Feb 1844, p 3.

[9] L & M Directors, *Minutes*, 4 Apr 1844.

improvement in the second-class coaches, they also agreed to establish third-class trains. The third-class fare was set at 3s 6d (17½p) for the trip between Liverpool and Manchester,[10] but a few months later it was reduced to 2s 6d (12½p). With this step came the suggestion that all fares be reduced. The explanation given was that the opening of the Hunts Bank line had increased the traffic on the L & M, and there had been a general revival of trade throughout the country. The directors approved the reduction, and the new rates of 6s (30p) first-class and 4s (20p) second-class were put into effect on 21 October 1844. These rates were again reduced by 20 per cent on 1 January 1845 for the same reasons.[11]

Realising that it would be to the advantage of the railway to keep all available rolling stock in operation at all times, the L & M provided extra passenger services whenever the occasion demanded it. For example, in 1839, the Election Committee hired the 'Duke's Train of Carriages' and were charged £21 each way, and again, between 120 and 150 Sunday School teachers hired the Blue Coaches to go from Manchester to Liverpool and return, the charge being £20. Special trains were run to the Newton races. There is little indication of the fare to Newton on the race trains, but on trains returning from the races, the fare to Rainhill was 2s (10p), and 3s (15p) for 'places nearer Liverpool'. Extra trains were also put on for Whitsuntide Week and for the Grand Exposition. In both cases the round trip fare between Manchester and Edgehill was 5s (25p).[12]

The L & M made special arrangements with the government to carry troops. The first charge was 2s 6d (12½p) per man between Liverpool and Manchester. The government objected and the charge was lowered to 2s 2d (11p), no charge being made for women 'belonging' to a regiment as long as the number of women did not exceed the proportion of ten women to every 100 men. Military baggage was carried for 8s (40p) per ton. These prices remained in effect till 1841 when the government asked the railway to carry officers for 2d per mile. This the directors agreed to, but since other railways had lower rates the government requested another revision of fares. The new agreement was comparable to that which the London & Birmingham Railway had made with the

[10] Even when this service was inaugurated, the L & M was still below the scale of fares on the principal railways of Britain.—*Directors' Reports*, 24 Jul 1844.

[11] L & M Directors, *Minutes*, 14 Oct and 21 Oct 1844; *Directors' Reports*, 29 Jan 1845; *Liverpool Merchantile Gazette*, 21 Oct 1844, p 4. In 1844 the gross receipts in the passenger department increased by £8,000.

[12] L & M Directors, *Minutes*, 22 Nov 1830, 9 May 1831, 11 Jun 1835, 22 Nov 1841, 5 May, 9 May, 6 Jun 1842.

government; the fare was 2⅛d per mile for officers and 1⅛d per mile for soldiers. Heavy baggage was carried for 3d per mile.[13] This agreement with the government did not last long. After the passage of two Acts in Parliament pertaining to railways, the L & M 'agreed' to carry soldiers for 1d per mile and officers for 2d per mile.[14]

Beginning on 10 November 1830, mail was carried on the L & M for the Post Office at a charge of 1½d per mile 'on each mail'. During the 1837 depression the Post Office made it known that they felt the charge for carrying mail was too high on all railways. To effect greater economy the Post Office had Mr Henry Labouchere introduce a Bill into Parliament which, if passed, would allow the Post Office to run its own trains on railways free of charge. The L & M, supported by the *Manchester Guardian* and the other railways in Britain, objected so vigorously that the Bill failed to get passed.[15] As a result, the agreement the L & M had already reached with the Post Office remained in effect. Some slight changes were made as the Post Office requested additional or less service. In 1844, the same Act which required the railways to provide better service for troops also required 'Railway Companies to afford additional facilities for the Transition of Mails'. This in effect meant the charges for carrying mail were to be revised downward.[16] Accordingly, the L & M directors drew up a new agreement which provided that the railway would:

> . . . convey the Mail Guard and his Letter Bags, by all or any of the regular Trains for £1000 per annum. The Railway Company reserving to themselves that control over the Times of departure and the speed of Transit which they at present enjoyed.

After a long delay, the Post Office agreed to this final arrangement. Each quarter of the year the L & M received £250, the only change in the contract being that the 7.30 pm train from Liverpool would make connections with the southbound North Union train at Parkside and carry the 'North mail' to Manchester.

When considering the income of the L & M on its passenger traffic, it is necessary to note that the railway was taxed on such an income.

[13] L & M Directors, *Minutes*, 18 Oct, 30 Oct 1830, 21 Jun, 28 Jun, 9 Aug, and 23 Aug 1841.
[14] 5 & 6 Victoria, *c.* lv, 30 Jul 1842; 7 & 8 Victoria, *c.* lxxv, 9 Aug 1844. Under the new regulations it was to a greater advantage of the L & M to carry troops on special, independent trains.—L & M Directors, *Minutes*, 11 Nov 1844.
[15] *Manchester Guardian*, 20 Jun 1838, p 2. This was another example of the full-flegded support the editors of the *Guardian* gave the L & M throughout its history.
[16] 7 & 8 Victoria, *c.* lxxv, 9 Aug 1844.

Rather than pay a per-capita tax, the L & M was able to come to an agreement with the government to pay a fixed sum. The agreement was short-lived due to a proposed new tax in 1832 which would amount to £15,000 per year on the L & M. Since the new tax would be levied on every coach, whether full or empty, a delegation of directors called on the Minister of Tax at London and asked him to set aside the provisions of the new tax law which would hurt the company. The group met with some success, since the new tax was lowered to $\frac{1}{2}$d per mile for four passengers or 1s 8d (8$\frac{1}{2}$p) per mile per passenger. This duty remained in effect from 1832 to 1842, when another appeal was sent to the Chancellor of the Exchequer requesting a commutation of the 'present passenger duty into a percentage tax on Gross Passenger Receipts, provided such percentage did not exceed 5 per cent'. The L & M was not alone in this request, and a *Times* editorial suggested that Parliament listen to the request of the railways, although the editor's argument was in favour of the people rather than the railway. The requests were heard, and a new passenger tax came into effect on 1 August 1842. It called for a 5 per cent duty on all gross passenger receipts.[17]

The second largest source of income on the L & M came from the freight traffic. When the early estimates for the company had been drawn up, it was thought that freight would provide the major source of income. But, the initiation of freight operations proved a financial disappointment and remained such.

After a very slow start, the L & M Directors reported in 1831 that freight traffic was increasing. The railway had carried 35,865 tons of freight between Liverpool and Manchester, and 6,827 tons between Liverpool and Bolton Junction (otherwise Kenyon Junction) by September 1831.[18] Original estimates for freight traffic indicated three times as much traffic would have passed over the line by that time.

In October 1831, an increase in sheep traffic proved to be the harbinger of a general freight increase on the L & M. Special arrangements were even made to handle sheep traffic as follows:

> ... a clerk from the railway will attend throughout the day, and on each succeeding Monday, at the Cattle Market, London Road, to book sheep in lots, according to priority of application, and to give written orders for the conveyance of the same to Manchester that evening, or the following day if preferred.

[17] L & M Directors, *Minutes*, 4 Apr 1842; *The Times* (London), 2 May 1842, p 7. Under the old tax system, the railways' profit increased on first-class passengers, and so they tended to increase first-class and cut back second- and third-class service.
[18] *Directors' Reports*, 28 Sep 1831.

The charge for carrying sheep on the railway was about 8d per head, which was twice the cost of driving sheep via road.[19]

Whenever possible the railway provided the type of freight service requested. In its third year of operations, the L & M added several services to the usual freight traffic. Burnt lime was carried from Manchester to Sutton at 4s (20p) per ton, and 5s (25p) per ton to Liverpool. Scrap iron conveyed between Liverpool and Manchester went at 8s (40p) per ton. The railway agreed to carry manure between Manchester and Chat Moss for 1s 6d (7½p) per ton, with the parties involved loading and unloading this bulky matter. Stable manure carried between Manchester and Kenyon cost 2s 6d (12½p) per ton. Farm products shipped from Chat Moss to Liverpool went at 5s (25p) per ton. All freight to and from the Rainhill Glass Bottle Works was charged at 3s 6d (17½p) per ton with the understanding that the L & M was not responsible for damage. Coal shipped between Wigan and Liverpool went at 3s 6d (17½p) per ton. Horses shipped via coach trains were charged 10s (50p) for one horse, 18s (90p) for two, and 22s (£1.10) for three. Slates carried between St Helens Junction and Manchester were charged 2s 6d (12½p) per ton if sent in L & M wagons. Finally, the L & M agreed to carry the London Stage for the Warrington Company between Liverpool and Warrington Junction; the charge for the service was 5s (25p) each way.[20] These charges for freight shipments were not permanent. When traffic in a particular category declined, or when petitioned by a customer, the railway usually made some reductions.[21]

Depressions made great inroads on the freight side. In 1837, traffic in manufactured goods for export, timber for building purposes, and general goods destined for Manchester dropped considerably. The L & M found little consolation in the misfortune experienced by the

---

[19] *Manchester Guardian*, 8 Oct 1831, p 1; L & M Directors, *Minutes*, 19 Sep 1831.

[20] L & M Directors, *Minutes*, 1832, *passim*.

[21] Examples of reductions and/or changes in freight rates are as follows: in 1833, lime sent between Liverpool and Manchester was reduced from 5s (25p) to 4s (20p) per ton. At the same time, charges on the Wigan coal trade were reduced from 4s 6d (22½p) to 4s 4d (21½p) per ton. The charge for sheep was changed to 30s (£1.50) a wagon in 1836. In 1839 the cost of shipping horses was raised to 14s (70p) for one horse, £1 for two horses, and 24s (£1.20) for three horses. A special charge for shipping horses was made to the War Department—4d per mile per horse, if the distance was less than 50 miles; 3½d per mile per horse, if the distance was less than 100 miles; and 3d per mile per horse, if the distance was more than 100 miles. In order to protect its interests in the freight department, the railway posted large sign boards with the freight rates listed. These boards also carried 'notice restrictive of the company's liability, as carriers, and also the Rate of Charge for Insurance of hazardous Goods'. Silk, for example, had to be insured when shipped via rail and

canals frozen during a hard winter.[22] The depression which hit England in 1840–1 slowed freight traffic on all railways. In order to fight the depression, the L & M hired a special agent for the freight department at Manchester whose duty it was to contact various merchants in the city in order to stimulate freight business. Also, arrangements were made with the Manchester & Leeds Railway to inaugurate a through service to the Yorkshire area, which it was hoped would then increase the freight traffic on the L & M.[23]

As the depression of 1841 gradually faded there was a general increase in L & M freight traffic. At the same time, the company began to experience increased competition from several new railways in the Lancashire area. This explains the fluctuating charges for freight and coal on the L & M which changed three times between 1842 and 1844. Also, with the opening of an extension line to Hunts Bank in 1844, L & M customers had several new areas of trade opened to them. In order to effect a better freight service through co-operation with the Manchester & Leeds Railway, a special committee was appointed to draw up new freight rates and submit them to the L & M for its approval, The new rates were to be in effect between Liverpool and such towns as Oldham, Rochdale, Todmorden, Wakefield, Leeds and Hull. Freight was divided into classes, and charges were made accordingly. First-class freight, consisting of grain, flour, iron and timber, was to be carried at 6s 6d (32½p) per ton. The charge on second-class freight was 8s (40p) per ton and this included cotton, wool, dyewoods, sugar and coffee. Wine, spirits, indigo, tea and silks were considered as third-class, the charge for which was 10s (50p) per ton. The 'speed' or down goods were charged higher rates: first- and second-class down goods went at 9s (45p) per ton, but the third-class down goods remained 10s (50p) per ton.[24]

In considering the L & M freight charges and traffic volume it becomes evident that the opening of the railway produced an impact on existing freight carriers. This was particularly true of the canals, which were forced, once the L & M became operational, to lower their rates on general freight between Liverpool and Manchester from 15s (75p)

the charge to the sender was 1s (5p) on every £100 worth of silk. No package of silk could be insured for less than 1s (5p). An increased demand on the L & M to carry packages less than freight encouraged the company to extend its parcel facilities. This developed into the twentieth-century Railway Express service. The rates were from Liverpool to Manchester, 1s 6d (7½p) to Rainhill Gates, and Bury Lane Station, 9d, and beyond Bury Lane 1s (5p). Parcels from Manchester went at the same ratio.— L & M Directors, *Minutes*, 1833–43, *passim*.

[22] *Directors' Reports*, 24 Jan and 25 Jul 1838.

[23] L & M Directors, *Minutes*, 10 Aug 1840, 4 Oct 1841, and 20 Jun 1842.

[24] L & M Sub-Committee on Carrying Arrangements, *Minutes*, 4 Apr 1844.

to 10s (50p) per ton.[25] This does not mean that the railway took a major portion of freight traffic from the canals. The canals continued to carry on much the same as they had before the railway opened, but the presence of the railway provided the competition which forced the canals to revise their rates. Consequently, a running battle developed between the L & M on the one hand and the Old Quay Company (the Mersey and Irwell Navigation Company) and the Duke of Bridgewater's Company on the other. The resultant cut-throat competition was often the cause of quick, drastic reductions in freight rates on both the canals and the railway.

To compete effectively with the canals, in February 1831 the L & M lowered its rates on cotton from 11s (55p) to 10s (50p) per ton. Shortly afterwards the navigation companies went still lower with their rates, at the same time increasing their efforts to obtain business. The railway followed suit by having Mr Sandars, Mr Tayleur and Mr Earle canvass the area for business. These men were given the power to 'grant reasonable accommodation' where they thought necessary. In other words, they were given blanket powers to lower rates on cotton at will. The railway began to receive complaints that their rates on other freight were too high. To offset these complaints, the directors ordered that all freight rates be the same as those charged on the Duke's canal.[26] As long as the rates of freight were the same on the navigation companies and the railways, all parties seemed satisfied. Arguments ensued when one company provided more advantage than another.

In 1834, a new dispute broke out with the navigation companies over charges made for warehouse rent. Except in certain cases,[27] the L & M did not make any charge for the use of their warehouses by the customers. This particularly irked the Old Quay Company and it threatened again to lower its rates unless the railway made such a charge. The L & M directors eventually agreed to charge rent, but the Old Quay Company and the Duke's Company could not come to an agreement on freight

---

[25] John H. Clapham, *The Early Railway Age, 1820–1850* (Vol I of *An Economic History of Modern Britain*), Cambridge, University Press, 1926. pp 396–7.

[26] In December 1832, the L & M came to terms with the Leeds and Liverpool Canal as follows: 'charges-Merchandise-cotton, corn, flour, timber, sugar, coffee, groceries, wine & spirits, manufactured iron, oil & tallow: To Bolton delivered 10s per ton, To Leigh delivered 6s per ton, To Fieldsley Bank delivered 9s per ton, To Chowbent delivered 8s 6d per ton. Charge on clay, pig iron, slates at option'.— L & M Directors, *Minutes*, 6 Dec 1832.

[27] Sometimes merchants left their grain and flour in the L & M warehouses, and in the meantime would use canal facilities for transporting other goods. Only in such cases did the L & M charge rent for storage.—L & M, Directors, *Minutes*, 18 Jul 1832.

rates. This in turn caused Mr Southern, of the Duke's Company, to refuse to be a party to any agreement involving warehouse rent. The two navigation companies, after much discussion, cleared away their difficulties and all the companies involved, including the L & M, agreed to charge the same rate for warehouse rent after the goods shipped or received had remained in storage for one month. Freight rates were also agreed.

It was now the turn of the railway to object to certain 'unfair' practices used on the canals. The L & M argued that the canals were allowing several small carriers to transport freight on the canal at lower rates and without requiring warehouse rent. Being convinced that their suspicions were correct, the directors threatened to end the agreement for charging rent for the use of warehouses if both the Duke's canal and the Old Quay Company could not prove them wrong. The reply of the Old Quay Company was both disappointing and direct. It consisted of an advertisement of a large reduction on all freight rates via the canal, plus a 10 per cent discount on all goods shipped from Liverpool if the consignees removed the freight from canal property and paid the full charges within three days of the freight's arrival at Manchester. At the same time, the Duke's Company informed the L & M that all agreements were at an end. Hoping to save its position, the railway appointed a sub-committee which was to contact the Old Quay Company. The committee was given power to make any change in rates, if it did not succeed in its attempts to conciliate the canals. The Old Quay Company would not budge, and there was little the railway could do since this company controlled the navigation of the rivers and therefore the other carriers. It was this company alone that could compete effectively with the railway, and after 1836 it continued to carry freight at lower rates between Liverpool and Manchester than the railway.[28]

A drop in freight traffic in 1840 on the L & M was blamed by the railway on the Old Quay Company. The L & M started another price war with the canal, claiming that the railway was not receiving its proper share of the freight traffic. Rates were lowered twice by both groups before the Old Quay Company asked the railway for another meeting in order 'to avoid if possible the evils of a direct collision'.[29] Before the meetings of the two companies got under way, Mr Hargreaves told the L & M directors that the Old Quay Company, working with

[28] L & M Directors, *Minutes*, 6 Jul and 13 Jul 1835; James Wheeler, *Manchester: Its Political, Social and Commercial History, Ancient and Modern*, London, Whittaker, 1836, pp 299–300.
[29] L & M Directors, *Minutes*, 24 Sep, 19 Oct, 22 Oct 1940, 5 Apr, and 14 Apr 1841.

the Manchester, Bolton & Bury Railway, was carrying cotton via railway and canal around Manchester to Bolton for the same rate charged on cotton shipped only as far as Manchester. This bit of information did not help matters when the meetings got under way. The final opinion of the representatives of the companies[30] was that the L & M had only the right to complain of a lack of traffic in cotton. To remedy the situation the following agreement was drawn up and signed:

> That water companies made no discounts or allowances from rates of Freight alike charged by both Railway and Canals in re: following articles: Cotton, Dyewoods, Grains and Flour and Madders. That Warehouse Rent on Grain and Flour be charged both by Canal Carriers and Railway Company—after 3 months Free Storage. Canal Carriers charge additional 10d per ton on all goods on Flats going alongside ships. Scale of cartages to be arranged on basic charge of both Canals and Railways.[31]

This monopolistic stranglehold on freight traffic between Lancashire's two major cities was 'to commence immediately'. In a sense, the agreement turned out to be a mere truce, which lasted only about four months. The canals began carrying freight from Sheffield between Manchester and Liverpool at a reduction of 1s 8d (8½p) per ton. The railway issued a warning to the canals that if necessary they would reduce the rates since the agreement had been violated. Having waited another four months for a favourable reply, and again claiming that the L & M was not receiving the proportional amount of general traffic in freight which they had previously carried, especially in cotton, the directors took action against the canals.

> That it is expedient that the Railway Company be no longer parties to the arrangement as to rates with the Water Carriers; and the Treasurer is instructed to offer a discount of 15 per cent off the company's present charge of 10s for the conveyance of cotton; and to make such other reductions in the carriage of different articles as might appear to be expedient for the interests of the company.

This decision on the part of the railway led to another bout of direct competition with the navigation companies which took on the aspect of a price war. Charles Lawrence, Joseph Sandars, George Loch,

[30] The Duke's Navigation Company attended the meetings and entered into the agreement.
[31] L & M Committee Met With Old Quay & Duke's Deputations, *Minutes*, 26 Apr 1841.

William Rotheram and Thomas Sands were appointed as a committee 'to fix the Railway rates and charges, and generally to conduct the contest with the Canal Carriers'.[32] The committee immediately reduced charges on cotton, grain, flour, sugar, tallow, molasses, butter and eggs, and made further reductions on cartage charges both to senders and receivers. All freight sent down from Manchester to Liverpool was reduced by 8s (40p) per ton. Similar reductions were made by the canals, followed immediately by reduced rates on the railway. In April 1842, an emergency meeting between the L & M Traffic Committee and representatives of the canals brought the dispute to a quick but short-lived end.[33]

The directors were more than glad to see the contest come to an end, and they readily admitted there had been a resultant decrease in freight receipts. Also, the effects of the depression were being felt at the time,[34] and the directors suggested another meeting with the navigation companies in order to consider 'expedients that shall place the Traffic operations of the Three great Companies on a more satisfactory footing'. The overtures, although accepted, did not produce any worthwhile effects. The situation remained the same until September 1843, when the Old Quay Company announced a 50 per cent reduction on all freight between Liverpool and Manchester. The fight was on again, only this time the Old Quay Company told the L & M directors the canals would not charge anything for carrying freight during this new contest. After about two months the canal companies agreed to

[32] L & M Directors, *Minutes*, 14 Feb 1842.

[33] L & M Committee on Traffic in Conference with Canal Authorities, *Minutes*, 21 Apr 1842. The following arrangements were in effect from April 1842 to September 1843.

1 Down Goods: 11s per ton per Ry—10s per ton per water—additional charge of 10d for flats alongside ships.

2 Up Goods: Cotton, Grain & Flour, Madders, Dyewoods, Sugar, Tallow, be carried at equal rates. On all other articles canals at liberty to charge 5d below Railway.

3 Where flat sent into public docks at Liverpool to load up—extra 1s per ton—no cartage allowed at Liverpool to either canals or Railways.

4 Canal Authorities to make sure Subordinate carriers adhere strictly to the agreement.

5 6 Weeks notice in writing be given by any parties to other 2 parties, before relaxing or infringing upon these terms.

6 Through Traffic—Ry Co shall charge such rates as shall place the carrier by Ry, to and from places beyond Manchester, on equal terms with the carriers by water to and from Liverpool.

7 Wharfage or Warehouse rent be charged on following after they have remained 2 calendar months: Ale & Porter, Grain, Meal, Flour, Cotton, Madders, Shumach Dyewoods.

[34] *Directors' Reports*, 27 Jul 1842.

Page 83 Railway office Liverpool, and warehouses mouth of Wapping Tunnel

Page 84 Moorish arch, and taking water at Parkside

raise their freight rates again if the railway would do the same. With the knowledge that Lord Francis Egerton, MP, representing the Bridgewater Trustees, had contracted to buy the Old Quay Company, and feeling this would forestall any 'reckless contests' in the future, the railways agreed to bring their rates in line with the canals once again.[35] The disputes with the canals were virtually at an end. The canals insisted that the charge on cotton be reduced from 10s (50p) to 9s (45p) per ton, but other than this the rates were to be the same as those agreed to in 1842.[36]

In considering the income of the L & M, the struggles with the navigation companies indicate that the railway would have had a hard time financially if it had relied almost entirely on freight traffic, as the original estimates had anticipated. Without the passenger receipts, how well would the L & M have fared in its disputes with the canals? The answer to this question cannot be definite for obvious reasons, but it does seem that the L & M would in all probability have lost the struggle with the canals. No matter how far the canals went in their efforts to destroy the railway, the latter withstood the attacks financially because of the steady income on passengers. It was these same passenger receipts that enabled the railway to expand, compete favourably with canals and road transport and, most important of all, become a sound investment.

B.   The Liverpool & Manchester Railway as an Investment

The original investors in the railway project took upon themselves a very considerable financial responsibility since the entire area of railway finance was, for the most part, unexplored. In spite of this uncertainty the financiers of Liverpool and Manchester staked their wealth in the L & M and were richly rewarded for their daring. Laying the line across Chat Moss, building the Sankey Viaduct, digging the Lime Street Tunnel, and many other phases of construction, caused the directors many anxious moments, but in the long run they gained sizeable profits and, of course, became famous in financial circles.[37]

Early construction of the railway demonstrated that the directors' cost estimates had been too low, and the capital obtained through the original £100 shares would soon be spent. As a result they sought

[35] L & M Traffic Committee, *Minutes*, 26 Jan 1843; L & M Directors, *Minutes*, 2 Oct, 20 Nov, and 26 Dec 1843.

[36] L & M Carrying Committee, *Minutes*, 6 May 1844; L & M Directors, *Minutes*, 26 Dec, 30 Dec 1844.

[37] George S. Veitch, *The Struggle for the Liverpool and Manchester Railway*, Liverpool, 1930, p 67.

F

enabling powers from Parliament to increase the capital of the company through additional stock or through loans. Having obtained the necessary powers, the L & M proprietors authorised the directors to borrow £127,500 through bonds and mortgages in March 1830.[38] This did not prove sufficient to complete all the works, and further powers were obtained from Parliament to raise £159,375 in order to complete the line. Accordingly, in May 1831, 6,375 new £25 shares of stock were issued. They were first offered to company members; four £25 shares paid in full entitled the holder to one new share.[39] It was suggested that the new shares be included in the payment of the next dividend, but it was pointed out by legal authorities that the dividend could be paid only in proportion to the number of instalments paid by the time the dividend was declared. On 23 May 1831, when the first call of £10 was made on the new shares, not all who had originally indicated a desire to purchase them made the first payment. On 22 August 1831, when the second call of £8 was made, all who were in arrears on their payments forfeited their shares, with the result that many fractional parts of the new shares were available. The directors of the L & M decided to make whole shares of these fractional shares. In cases where fractional shareholders refused to give up their shares, those holding fractional parts were charged a premium of £4 per ¼ part of the new £25 shares. When a final call of £7 was made on the new shares in November, 1831, more fractional shares were forfeited and the above procedure was followed in disposing of them.

Continued financial success of the L & M was reflected in the great demand for shares in 1832. 'By 1832, the value of the shares had risen 100 per cent, and by 1836 almost 200 per cent above their original value'.[40] This enthusiasm for shares continued throughout the company's history. As will be seen below, there were those in England who attacked the L & M and its financial structure, claiming the railway had fooled the public into investing in a doubtful enterprise. It is quite possible that a few people could have been so duped by an evasive front put up by the L & M directors. But when one considers the demand for L & M shares, such a possibility seems unreal, and the success of the 'Grand Experiment' from a financial view is quite evident.

In spite of the favourable market for L & M shares in 1832, the railway experienced considerable expense and could not operate solely

[38] 10 George IV, *c.* xxxv, 14 May 1829.
[39] 1 William IV, *c.* ii, 22 Apr 1831.
[40] William T. Jackman, *The Development of Transportation in Modern England*, Cambridge University Press, 1916, II, p 529.

on its receipts. Accordingly, in the same year, the directors had to float a loan in order to complete plans for the Lime Street Tunnel project. An application was made to the Exchequer Loan Commissioners for £100,000 with the additional request that the Commissioners would postpone calling in capital already loaned the company. The Commissioner s reply was favourable:

> The amount unexpended of Old Capital £12,343, supposing that £5,800 repaid to Exchequer Loan Commissioners on 23 June last on account of the original loan of £100,000 was borrowed again under the powers of the Act of Parliament just obtained— Committee recommends this should be done, and of this sum £5,800 the committee recommended that £5,000 should be paid to Mr Gilbert Winter in part payment for Land at the Manchester station held in Chief Rent at 5 per cent per annum, to which part payment would give the company the option for another year, to redeem a further sum on account of the Principal to the extent of £15,000 at 5 per cent.

> A further instalment of £5,800 on Account of Principal, to be repaid to the Exchequer Loan Commissioners, on 23rd June next which Committee also recommended be borrowed—making loan now required £11,600 which Sum would constitute part of the Company's Capital, though standing in the name of the new Lenders instead of the Exchequer Loan Commissioners, whose claim on the Company would be diminished to the same extent.[41]

Thus, under this new arrangement with the Exchequer Loan Commissioners, the L & M directors were able to borrow £11,600 over and above the £100,000 loan requested, at a rate of interest which was not to exceed 4 per cent.

Further financial manoeuvrability was achieved by the L & M directors a few days later. This time, by Act of Parliament, the railway was empowered to borrow on mortgage or by bond £200,000 for the purpose of extending its facilities and setting up a branch railway. As soon as the securities for the first £200,000 were paid up, the directors could again borrow the same amount in the same manner.[42] A major

---

[41] L & M Directors, *Minutes*, 14 May 1832. The Loan Commissioners informed the L & M Directors that £5,800 on principal and £3,094 on interest would be due on 23 June 1833. The treasurer was ordered to borrow another £5,800 at 3½ per cent per year.—L & M Directors, *Minutes*, 3 Jun 1833.

[42] 2 William IV, *c*. xlvi, 23 May 1832. Becuase of the expansion of banking interests of the L & M, Moss & Company were commissioned to keep the accounts.— L & M Directors, *Minutes*, 3 Jun, 1 Jul 1833.

portion of this sum was used to begin the construction of the tunnel to Lime Street.

Extended operations and continued construction forced the L & M to negotiate a series of loans between 1833 and 1835. Wherever possible, the treasurer was authorised to borrow between £20,000 and £30,000 at a rate of interest not to exceed 4 per cent. The money thus acquired was to be used for the construction of the Lime Street Tunnel if needed. An additional £10,000 was ordered to be borrowed so as to pay off a bank debt and secure a better rate of interest. In 1835, the treasurer was given power to borrow any amount of money he might need from time to time. In no case was he to borrow the said money at more than 4 per cent interest.

A director, Mr Rathbone, suggested that the capital of the railway be increased by issuing one £50 share for each £100 share extant in 1835. This would increase the total capital to £12,000,000 in shares and £400,000 on loan. But the plan was not considered feasible at the time. Shortly afterwards, in March 1836, the proprietors suggested a plan be drawn up for the creation of new shares to redeem the mortgage debt of the company. This plan called for £50 shares to be paid by two calls per year over a period of three and a half years. The plan was approved and 7,986 new £50 shares were created. When paid up, they would remove £398,400 from the mortgage, leaving a debt of £29,100 which the directors and proprietors felt the company could readily carry. The new shares were offered to the company shareholders at one £50 share for every £100 share and one for every four £25 shares, and they were disposed of rapidly.[43]

General expansion continued to be characteristic of the L & M. With the running of Grand Junction trains over the line, some stations had to be enlarged, the shops expanded, staff added, and general operating expenses increased. As a result, the directors felt obliged to ask Parliament for permission to raise another £400,000. By the middle of 1837 the request was granted, allowing the L & M to 'raise by loan' £400,000 over and above the amount of money already granted in other Acts. If the railway borrowed the money from the Exchequer Loan Commissioners, the Commissioners' security was to have priority. Further, if the railway was able to pay off its securities, permission was granted to raise another £400,000. Finally, the company had the option of creating new shares to raise the money, but 'such new shares to be

[43] L & M Proprietors, *Minutes*, General Meetings, 23 Mar, 27 Jul 1836. Those proprietors who paid up their instalments on the £50 shares immediately were paid 4 per cent interest on the balance which they had with the company. L & M Directors, *Minutes*, 22 Aug 1836.

declared Personal Estate, and holders are declared to be owners and Proprietors of Stock in the said undertaking'.[44] In 1842, the Duke of Sutherland (formerly Marquis of Stafford) reportedly held 1,957 such shares.

Construction of an extension line to Hunts Bank increased the financial burdens of the L & M. Accordingly the proprietors gave permission to raise the necessary money to complete the Hunts Bank extension by mortgage or bond, but the amount borrowed was not to exceed the amounts stated in the various Acts. In order to keep a close check on all the borrowing going on at the time, the directors wanted a daily account of funds borrowed, and the seal of the company, without which it was impossible for anyone to take on financial obligations for the L & M, was given to the chairman and treasurer in joint keeping under two separate keys.

Another issue of shares was suggested in June 1844. During the discussion, the treasurer presented an interesting analysis of the financial condition of the company. The total share capital of the L & M was equal to 12,090 £40 shares.[45] One important consideration the directors had to make before recommending an issue of new shares was the condition of L & M shares on the stock market. The very day the new issue was discussed, a report published on L & M shares was quite encouraging: 'The transactions this week in Railway shares have been rather extensive, and generally at very steady prices—Liverpool and Manchester 223, the halves 109; and the quarters 54½'.[46] Consequently, the directors made the necessary suggestions for new shares to the proprietors at their next meeting. The latter voted to raise £483,600 through the creation of 12,090 £40 shares, in order to dispose of the L & M debt. The new shares were offered to shareholders in the ratio of one new £40 share to every £100 share held. All unclaimed shares remaining after 31 October 1844 were to be sold or otherwise appropriated at the option of the directors. Little difficulty was had in disposing of the new shares, and the market prices remained high— full shares 225, the halves 112 and 109, and the quarters 56 and 56½.[47]

[44] 7 William IV, c. xxvii, 5 May 1837. L & M shares still brought good prices on the share market. The reported price of a £100 share in 1838 was £320, 'the amount paid up is only £155 showing a profit to the original subscriber of £165'. *Mechanics' Magazine*, XXX (Nov 1838), 96. Directors Lawrence and Booth testified that if they had had more experience in running railways, the L & M would have been in a better financial condition.—Great Britain, Parliament, House of Commons, *First Report of the Select Committee on Railways*, 26 Apr 1839, 35.

[45] L & M Directors, *Minutes*, 24 Jun 1844.

[46] *The Liverpool Merchantile Gazette, and Myers' Weekly Advertiser*, 24 Jun 1844, p 3

[47] *Ibid.*, 29 Jul 1844, p 3.

In 1845, the L & M obtained still another Act empowering the company to raise £805,000 by the creation of new shares for the purpose of building a line to connect the M & L and L & M 'in Manchester Parish', and also to Altrincham 'in Chester County'. The new line was to be called the Manchester, South Junction and Altrincham Railway. Also, the company was empowered to borrow a sum of money equal to the amount of share capital extant in the L & M after 1845. However, the provisions of the Act were never put into effect by the L & M since it amalgamated with the Grand Junction Railway the following month and the powers were transferred to this company.[48]

When one considers the number of Acts granted the Liverpool & Manchester Railway between 1831 and 1845, for the purpose of raising money and for general expansion, the sound financial status of the railway becomes more and more evident. Here was a financial enterprise, even though it was for the most part experimental, that proved to be not only a sound investment but a profitable one. At first, the dividends were small. Once inexperience of operations was overcome, the dividends paid by the L & M were both steady and high.

The first dividend paid by the L & M was £2 per £100 share. This was paid out of railway income profits between opening day, 17 September 1830, and 31 December 1830. Naturally, the profits had been comparatively low due to a small volume of traffic on the railway. The lack of operational technique and locomotive power kept traffic to a minimum.[49] Upon hearing of the first L & M dividend, the secretary of the Exchequer Loan Commissioners reminded the directors that £9,300 was due the Commissioners the following June. The immediate reply was that payment would be made on time, and the promise was kept.[50]

The second dividend paid by the L & M increased considerably as is seen in the following resolution of the proprietors:

Dividend: to be paid on 5 October next: £4 10s per share of £100, and so in proportion of the Old Shares of £25 each, and at the rate of £4 10s per cent on the amount of the call of £10 paid prior to the 30th June last in respect of the New Shares of £25 each.

This dividend represented the near maximum profit placed on the L & M by Parliament. The next half year the directors suggested another dividend of £4 10s but the proprietors would approve of a dividend of only £4 per £100 share. The reason for this was:

[48] 8 & 9 Victoria, c. cxxiii, 21 Jul 1845.
[49] L & M Proprietors, *Minutes*, General Meeting, 28 Mar 1831.
[50] L & M Directors, *Minutes*, 4 Apr 1831.

The difference of 10s per share between this dividend and the preceding one was accounted for by the unfortunate calamity that has been so generall[y] injurious to trade and commerce here, the cholera morbus, preventing the extent of intercourse between Manchester, Liverpool and Ireland, that had previously existed.[51]

From this point on, L & M semi-annual dividends never again fell lower than £4 4s per £100 share. Even during the depression years 1837–8, the L & M continued to pay either £4 10s or £5 per £100 share every half year. A dividend of £5 per £100 share per half year was the maximum possible, and it was this dividend that was paid during depression years except in two instances.

Despite the fact that the L & M company was able to pay high dividends, the entire net profit was not always spent in dividends. For example, in January 1834, the directors appropriated 10 per cent of the net profit for a reserve fund which was to be 'applicable to future contingencies'. Surplus net profits were likewise used for a 'fund for the proceeding with Relaying of the Way with stronger rails'. In 1835, a total of £5,000 was set aside from the net profits to pay for the new rails.[52] These funds set up by the directors out of surplus profits constitute another indication that the L & M had made great financial strides since it opened to the public, and that the railway was proving to be a sound investment. The *Manchester Guardian* reported:

It may be worthy of remark that this is the first time that the dividend for the first half of a year has been entirely paid out of the receipts of that half-year, which is necessarily less productive than the second half. The expenses of Locomotive power are still heavy, amounting (including the purchase of three new engines) to £16,462. The cost of repairing engines amounts altogether to £7,594 13s 4d which is a reduction in the amount mentioned in former reports, especially when the increased amount of traffic is considered.[53]

Although the directors readily established the above-mentioned funds out of net profits, they were not of a mind to see the amount of

[51] *Manchester Guardian*, 28 Jul 1832, p 2.
[52] For a long time the L & M was desirous of having freight shipped over its line insured. Unable to understand its position as regards the 'Law and Average Clause' required by most insurance companies, it never signed an insurance contract. As a result, another fund was set up 'to make good losses arising from fire or any contingency'. The fund was to be increased gradually till it amounted to £20,000.— L & M Directors, *Minutes*, 12 May 1836.
[53] *Manchester Guardian*, 29 Aug 1835, p 3.

profits they could earn as a railway cut down. A Bill introduced into Parliament in 1836 would have had just that effect. The L & M, already limited to a 10 per cent dividend by its original Act, immediately attacked the proposed Bill and was not alone in its fight. Along with other railways, the L & M had additional support from the press. The railway position was pointedly expressed as follows:

> Many persons, for example, have recently given about three hundred pounds each for shares in the Liverpool and Manchester railway, in the reasonable expectation of receiving eventually something like five per cent for their money; and if the profits of the undertaking are to be hereafter limited to some smaller amount—say ten per cent on the original outlay, these parties will have great reason to complain of being hardly dealt with, especially so long as the shareholders in some canals are permitted to give forty, fifty or a hundred, or even three or four hundred per cent on their original outlay . . . if the limitation therefore is to apply to existing railways, it ought to include the existing canals and other public undertakings.[54]

In the summer of 1836, success crowned the efforts of the railways and press to defeat the Bill.

In the meantime, the idea of the right of original L & M share-holders to interest on their original shares was reopened. With little or no discussion, the proprietors unanimously approved the resolution to pay interest at the rate of '£5 per cent per annum' to the holders of the original £100 shares and £25 shares issued before the railway opened. The interest was to be paid on the period covered from the time of the original investment to the opening of the line.[55] No doubt this pronouncement established permanently the right of the original shareholders to interest. Nonetheless, all present at the meeting realised that the interest could not be paid during the fiscal year 1836. Depression was slowly but surely rearing its ugly head in England and already trade and travel had dropped to very low proportions through-out the country. Despite the recession, L & M dividends continued to be paid at a reasonable level, and for this the majority of shareholders were grateful; there was little or no objection to the interest on the original shares not being paid.

After paying a dividend of £5 per each £100 share on the net profits for the half year ending 30 June 1840, a surplus of £9,800 remained.

[54] *Ibid*, 21 May, 1836, p 3; 4 Jun 1836, p 3.
[55] L & M Proprietors, *Minutes*, General Meeting, 27 Jul 1836.

Although the directors did not unanimously favour a bonus at the time, they submitted the following report which the proprietors approved:

> Out of this balance the Directors recommend a First Instalment at the rate of £2 per Share, to be paid to the Proprietors of the 5,100 original £100 Shares, and 4s. per share to the holders of 5,100 old £25 Shares, being a portion of the interest to which these Shares are respectively entitled, and which it is enjoined by the Act of Parliament shall be paid at the rate of five per cent per annum out of any surplus balance, after dividing amongst the Proprietors at large, at the rate of £10 per annum on every £100 Shares.[56]

Accordingly, after June 1840, the L & M paid a 2 per cent bonus on the original shares. This bonus remained in effect until 1845, when the dividend for the half year ending 31 December 1844 dropped to £4 10s per £100 share. The directors had put aside a larger balance of the net profits in order to prepare 'for the contingencies of the following year; £900 for Statue of George Stephenson; and the desirability of a surplus during the Amalgamation proceedings.[57]

An interesting controversy developed within the L & M company on the question of Sunday travel. There were some proprietors who felt it was against their conscience to be connected with an organisation that provided Sunday train services. To receive any compensation from the net profits gained through Sunday travel would, they felt, be entirely wrong. Although the majority of the company's members voted that the trains be operated on the Lord's Day, they likewise agreed to respect the conscience of their colleagues. Therefore, a special fund was set up out of the dividends due on net profits from Sunday travel to those who would not accept the money. The fund as originally established had no specific purpose. Eventually, it went for charitable purposes. A rather severe winter in 1838 prompted the L & M Directors to grant £250 to the Liverpool District Provident Society, £100 to the Manchester District Provident Society, and £37 4s 2d (£37.21) to the Liverpool Strangers Friend Society. Other typical uses of the fund included a donation of £15 to the Reverend James Hornby for distribution to the poor of Lowton Township, £3 3s (£3.15) donated to the Manchester Eye Hospital, £10 given to the Manchester and

[56] *Directors' Reports*, 17 Jan 1841; *Herapath's Magazine* III, (Nov 1841), 995. In March, 1844, the L & M decided to pay the half-yearly dividends in warrants as most other railways did.—L & M Committee on Finance, *Minutes*, 18 Mar 1844.

[57] *Directors' Reports*, 29 Jan 1845.

Salford Dispensaries, and £50 to the Manchester Relief Fund. Whenever one of the above-mentioned dispositions was made, the directors were always sure to make it quite clear that the money came from a special fund in the company, and that they, as directors and guardians of the proprietors' interests, saw no possibility of replying favourably by donation to the many requests for aid which they received from time to time from religious and social organisations.

In conclusion we see then, that from the opening of the Liverpool and Manchester Railway to the time of its amalgamation with the Grand Junction Railway, the story of its finances is one of success; a success story which made its many investors quite happy. The original investors had taken upon themselves a grave responsibility and there were times when it seemed as though the railway project would collapse. Once in operation, inexperience often proved costly. Yet the L & M

TABLE I

Dividends Declared by L & M Proprietors at their General Meetings, 1832–45. — from Directors' Reports

Half-Year Ending	Dividend £100 Shares		
	£	s	d
31 Dec 1831	4	10	0 (£4.50)
30 Jun 1832	4	0	0
31 Dec 1832	4	4	0 (£4.20)
30 Jun 1833	4	4	0 (£4.20)
31 Dec 1833	4	10	0 (£4.50)
30 Jun 1834	4	10	0 (£4.50)
31 Dec 1834	4	10	0 (£4.50)
30 Jun 1835	4	10	0 (£4.50)
31 Dec 1835	5	0	0
30 Jun 1836	5	0	0
31 Dec 1836	5	0	0
30 Jun 1837	4	10	0 (£4.50)
31 Dec 1837	5	0	0
30 Jun 1838	4	10	0 (£4.50)
31 Dec 1838	5	0	0
30 Jun 1839	4	10	0 (£4.50)
31 Dec 1839	5	0	0
30 Jun 1840	5	0	0
31 Dec 1840	5	0	0
30 Jun 1841	5	0	0
31 Dec 1841	5	0	0
30 Jun 1842	5	0	0
31 Dec 1842	5	0	0
30 Jun 1843	5	0	0
31 Dec 1843	5	0	0
30 Jun 1844	5	0	0
31 Dec 1844	4	10	0 (£4.50)
30 Jun 1845	5	0	0

overcame these obstacles and proved to be a sound investment with a steady income. Much credit for this must go to the men who directed the company and its early, difficult stages. Despite the attacks of those who, for one reason or another, would have liked to have seen the destruction of the railway, the early projectors clung tenaciously to their belief that the railway would efficiently, economically and profitably help to solve transportation problems in Lancashire. That the L & M proved to be a sound investment became quite obvious after a few short years of efficient and successful operation and management.

C.   Early Attacks on the Finances of the Liverpool & Manchester Railway

The outcome of early operations on the L & M was of utmost importance to its investors and projectors. After many long years of construction and investment, the success or failure of operations would determine either the success or failure of the entire venture. It was during this time of expectant hope in the future results of the railway project that the opponents of the L & M became active in their criticisms. Public and personal attacks on the railway as an enterprise and the men who were running it forced the railway to reply to its critics and thus controversy arose.

First to attack the L & M extensively was Thomas Grahame, who openly questioned the financial structure of the company and accused the directors of mishandling the funds, covering up total amounts of expenditure, inaccuracies in stating their accounts, and paying dividends from capital account.

> The mistake which I have rectified, arises from the mixture, in the accounts of the sums received from the revenue, with the sums laid out in making and finishing the road and works; and has probably given rise to the statement that the railway company are in the regular habit of paying their dividends by borrowing money, or creating new stock; and certainly to persons not well acquainted with the state of the company's affairs, it is difficult to conceive how dividends of £33,000 and £35,000 and upwards, can be paid by parties who have only on hand £13,000 and £24,000, wherewith to pay these dividends, unless they borrow or create new stock.[58]

Grahame likewise attacked the accuracy of the early estimates of freight traffic on the L & M; in this he was correct and the L & M

[58] Thomas Grahame, *A Treatise on Internal Intercourse and Communication in, Civilised States and Particularly in Great Britain*, London, Longman, Rees, Orme, Brown, Green & Longman, 1834, pp 63–4.

directors readily admitted it. But, Grahame failed to point out that the estimates on passenger traffic were also wrong, and proved to be very favourable to the financial structure of the railway. He half-heartedly admitted the railway made a small profit, which he claimed was due to the fact that it was not taxed as the stage coaches were. Grahame professed to have no real argument with the railway, but he felt he had to prevent the public from being fooled by a false appearance of sound finance on the L & M. He was willing to admit that many of the directors' mistakes came from a lack of experience.

> In the case of the Liverpool Railway, the promoters and Directors having had little to guide them, except the calculations and theories of engineers, railways as general modes of conveyance being then unknown, can hardly be said to have exaggerated its benefits. All their statements were mere assumptions unproved by practice. There were no certain data, and without such, there cannot be said to be exaggeration.[59]

Attacking along the same lines as Grahame, R. Cort claimed that the L & M in 1833 did not have enough money available in any form to pay even 1 per cent interest. This the railway did not deny, since interest was not to be paid until £10 on each £100 share had been paid out of the net profits. Cort likewise claimed that the canals were beating the railways at a ratio of six to one, but failed to mention the basis for the ratio. Of the L & M freight operations he claimed that 'most of the freight in the waggon department [was] carried at at least 300% less than will pay one per cent nett profit'. He defended his statements by saying that it was almost impossible to prove anything against the railway since the directors kept two accounts. One was 'private', and the other Cort called 'public ordinary'. This type of 'deception' was used, Cort claims, to hide the fact that the dividends were being taken from the capital of the company and not from the net profits.[60]

[59] Grahame, *Treatise*, p 131.
[60] R. Cort, *Rail–Road Impositions Detected*, London, W. Lake, 1834, pp 44, 51, 52, 42. In 1832, an anonymous L & M critic published observations on the relative merits of canals and railways based, he claimed, on the L & M Committee Reports. He stated the railways could not carry bulk freight as cheaply as the canals, and thus they would not be able to make a profit on the freight business to the same extent as the canals did. This was nothing new, since the original projectors of the L & M realised they could never carry bulk at the profit gained by canals. The critic also said that if the L & M acted as carriers, the railway could not obtain the full amount of their tolls, since they would lose 4d. per passenger and 1¼d per ton on freight. The main point the anonymous critic seemed to be making was that the railways could not compete where the railway was parallel to canal or river navigations, mostly because of the cheapness with which freight could be carried on the

During the period when Grahame and Cort were criticising the L & M, there were others who favoured the railway and, in effect, denied the critics' allegations. Thomas Taylor, in his *History and Description of the Liverpool and Manchester Railway*, stated that during the first year and a half the traffic on the L & M indicated that the railway scheme 'was neither visionary or impracticable'. Also, the general public was satisfied with the new method of travel as compared to the canals and the stage coaches.[61] The Reverend Dionysius Lardner in his *Lectures on the Steam Engine*, noted that in spite of heavy operating expenses and inexperience, the railway had proved to be a sound investment by 1832.[62] *Mechanics' Magazine* carried the following open letter to Mr Cort:

> Every shilling of the company's capital—whether subscribed or borrowed, is a matter of no consequence—is shown to have been so employed, that to pay the dividends from any other source than 'profits' was literally impossible.

The writer continued by accusing Cort of merely repeating what Grahame had said, and pointed out that Cort actually quoted Grahame out of context.[63] Many others subscribed to the sentiments expressed by Henry Booth to Charles Lawrence in a letter dated 19 October 1838:

> It was my province to give effect to the deliberations and decisions of directors, who in former days, through evil and good report, without favour from the Legislature or encouragement from the public, while the risk was evident and the gain problematical, with intelligence, perseverance, and singleness of purpose pursued their

canals. He admitted that some good came from the railway, viz, that the price of freight between Liverpool and Manchester on the canals had been reduced by one-third.—A *Letter to a Friend Containing Observations on the Comparative Merits of Canals and Railways Occasioned by the Reports of the Committee of the Liverpool and Manchester Railway*, London, Longman, 1832, pp 12, 13, 16. The directors of the L & M vigorously denied that any dividends had been paid out of the capital account of the company. The total capital of the company, amounting to £1,024,375, was spent on the works, and the directors claimed each item was listed in the company books.—*Directors' Reports*, 23 Jan 1833. Another detailed refutation of the charges made by Cort and Grahame can be found in 'Great Western Railway Prospectus', *Railway Gazette*, LXI (November 1934), 850–3.

[61] Thomas Taylor, *A History and Description of the Liverpool and Manchester Railway*, Liverpool, 1832, p 60.

[62] Rev. Dionysius Lardner, *Lectures on the Steam Engine*, London, John Taylor, 1832, p 191.

[63] 'The Railway Calumniators', *Mechanics' Magazine*, XXII (January, 1835), 291–301, *passim*.

work till success crowned their labours, and multitudes were eager
to follow their example.[64]

Cort and Grahame accomplished at least one thing in their charges
against the L & M, and that was to leave uncertainty in the minds of
posterity as to whether or not their claims might have had some truth.
In 1952, a detailed and scholarly study of L & M finances was made by
Harold Pollins, and his findings refute those charges.

> An examination, however, of the figures of net profit earned and the
> amount paid out in dividends clears up the problem, for it can be
> seen that the railway made enough profit to pay its dividends.
> Up to December 1836, the Company earned £463,970 12s 6d
> (£463,970.62½) in net profit and paid out in dividends £442,504 7s 6d
> (£422,504.37½). . . . The increase in the capital of the company in the
> early 1830s was the legitimate and normal addition to physical
> equipment expected of an expanding public utility. The Company
> did not issue capital accounts but it is possible to use the various
> Acts of Parliament to reach this conclusion. . . . By 1837 some
> £1,224,275 had been raised, which had been authorized by the
> Company's acts up to 2 William IV, C. xlvi (£796,875 by shares and
> £427,500 by loans), plus 7,968 × £50 shares and 1,164 × £25 shares
> to pay off mortgage debts. The money authorised was probably
> spent on capital equipment . . . as the company was paying
> dividends from revenue. . . . The company, it must be admitted,
> did pay interest on shares, as did other companies, but paid them
> out of revenue . . . paying interest on shares was a method of
> ensuring that shareholders met calls.

Pollins concludes by stating that the L & M was not too worried about
the charges made against it nor with the adverse publicity. Such
complaints, he claims, were part of the atmosphere of suspicion that
surrounded the development of the railways in England. The opposition
to the L & M was more 'dramatic' but not an isolated case.[65] Dramatic

---

[64] Quoted in R. Smiles, *Memoir of Henry Booth.* pp 45–6. See also Nicholas Wood,
A Practical Treatise on Railroads, and Interior Communication in General &c, 3d ed,
London, Longman, Orme, Brown, Green & Longmans, 1839, p 582; Whishaw,
Railways, p 210; Henry G. Lewin, *Early British Railways: A Short History of Their
Origin and Development 1801–1844*, London, Locomotive Publishing, 1926, p 15.

[65] Harold Pollins, 'The Finances of the Liverpool and Manchester Railway', *The
Economic History Review*, V (January, 1952), 94–7, *passim*; see also Jackman, *The
Development of Transportation in Modern England*, II, pp 530–1. Samuel Smiles
wrote in the same positive vein as did Pollins about L & M finances: 'It is scarcely
necessary that we should speak at any length of the commercial results of the
Liverpool and Manchester Railway. Suffice it to say that its success was complete
and decisive'.—S. Smiles, *Life of George and Robert Stephenson*, pp 332–3.

or not, Pollins seems to forget that the attacks on the Liverpool & Manchester Railway did cause the company some concern as can be seen from the tone of the discussions on the matter. Also, the directors felt it necessary to answer the charges publicly and had their answer printed in circular form. Likewise the attacks on the L & M came at a time when public attention was focused on the railway with many waiting to see whether or not it would succeed or fail. At this period more than any other, the L & M needed the confidence of the public, and the bad publicity affected the railway unfavourably for at least a time. On the other hand, the fact that the L & M overcame financial and operational obstacles in spite of the criticism and a cooling of public opinion, proved in the long run the real worth of the railway as an investment and as a favourable means of transportation.

D.   The Financial Influence of the Liverpool & Manchester Railway

Aside from the general public, many vested interests watched the growth and progress of the Liverpool & Manchester Railway very closely. Prior to the opening of the L & M many different railway projects had been formulated but, for one reason or another, abandoned. Once the commercial success of the L & M was assured, these abandoned projects were revived and contributed to the 'minor railway mania' that swept England in 1836.[66] Of all the factors which contributed to the success of the L & M, perhaps the investors were most important, and Lancashire was not without a very shrewd group of men who were willing to take a chance on a railway investment. Clapham describes some of these astute businessmen as follows:

> Liverpool business men were particularly active in investment beyond their immediate area, which suggests not only that they had imagination but that the Liverpool and Manchester did pay better

[66] S. Smiles, *Life of George and Robert Stephenson*, p 340; Lewin, *Early Railways*, p 41. During the Parliamentary session of 1836 over fifty petitions for Bills requesting powers to construct railways were received. Parliament actually authorised the raising of £22,874,998 for railway purposes in 1836, and in the following year authorised £13,521,799 for the same purposes. In all the discussions in Parliament of the railway Bills, expansion of railways and speculations in railways, the name of the L & M was quite prominent. In London, the talk of the tremendous passenger traffic on the L & M led many promoters to believe that a 'good deal of business was to be had in the way of joy rides'.—Leland Hamilton Jenks, *The Migration of British Capital to 1875*, London, Alfred A. Knopf, 1938, p 82; O. S. Nock, *Engineers*, p 102; *Manchester Guardian*, 5 Mar 1836, p 3.

than it told. Stephenson was able to raise money at Liverpool for the Leicester and Swannington even before the L & M was open; and the group on whose money he drew, known in the early railway age as the Liverpool Party—Croppers, Rathbones, Horsfalls, Booths, Sandars—not only took an important share in creating the central link-lines of England between Mersey, Humber, Thames and Severn but, with Stephenson, had the long through routes before their minds from the first.[67]

It was these same Liverpool interests that invested heavily in the Grand Junction Railway. Since these Liverpool men were more than satisfied with their investment in the L & M, the Grand Junction project had little difficulty in gaining public support. As the *Guardian* put it:

> Little need be said of the merits of such an undertaking. The experiment and example daily exhibited to the public on the Liverpool and Manchester railway have proved, beyond all doubt whatsoever, the advantages and capabilities of the Railways. It is fortunate for those interested in the promotion of this branch of national improvement to have such a standard to refer to . . . that the public have derived infinitely greater advantages, there cannot be question.[68]

The construction of the Grand Junction was carried out in record time, and it was opened on schedule in 1837.

Once operational, the L & M and Grand Junction worked well together. Some men served as directors on both railways. This provided a 'beneficial combination which was advantageous to both; and it

[67] Clapham, *Railway Age*, p 387. Pendleton accused the Liverpool investors of acting as though they had struck gold. He compares the railway to a gold mine which yielded great profits, but ruined no one.—John Pendleton, *Our Railways: Their Origin, Development, Incident and Romance*, London, Cassell, 1894, p 51.

[68] *Manchester Guardian*, 20 Oct 1832, p 1. The following were listed as Grand Junction committee members:

John Moss, Chairman, Liverpool	Richard Harrison, Liverpool
Robertson Gladstone, Deputy Chairman, Liverpool	Joseph Hornby, Liverpool
	Daniel Ledsam, Birmingham
Charles Lawrence, Deputy Chairman, Liverpool	J. F. Ledsam, Birmingham
	Theodore Price,
Joseph Walker, Deputy Chairman, Birmingham	William Rotheram, Liverpool
	Joseph Sandars, Liverpool
James Bourne, Liverpool	Charles Shaw, Birmingham
John Cropper, Liverpool	Charles Tayleur, Liverpool
William Chance, Birmingham	John Turner, Birmingham
Hardman Earle, Liverpool	J. N. Walker, Liverpool
J. C. Ewart, Liverpool	(Engineers–Stephenson & Rastrick)
T. W. Gifford	

enabled them to settle their affairs with much more ease, expedition and cordiality'.[69]

Liverpool influence was demonstrated on many other railways in Britain. For example, when the proposal for going ahead with the Sheffield and Manchester Railway project came up for a vote among the shareholders, it was defeated, the majority of dissenting ballots having been cast by L & M subscribers and proprietors. Since the project would have competed with their interests, the L & M subscribers were unwilling to see a going concern faced with this competition.[70] Liverpool men were also prominent in the North Union Railway. At the time of its opening, Theodore Rathbone, Hardman Earle and William Taylor were serving as directors of that railway.[71] The projectors of the Manchester & Birmingham Extension Railway (Stone to Rugby) were well aware of the Liverpool influence from the very outset of their plan. Accordingly, the M & B attempted to avoid direct competition with the Grand Junction by inviting co-operation. When the latter demanded a controlling interest, the M & B reminded the GJ directors that Manchester people had interests also. Still, the Manchester & Birmingham company offered the Liverpool 'crowd' half of the number of directors. But the Liverpool party wanted more, and was reported to have said this was 'because they would become the monopolist of all the railways in this part of the Kingdom'.[72] Even the Midland Counties Railway was not free from the threat of the Liverpool interests. The new, self-styled railway king, George Hudson, who attempted to monopolise the Midland's railways, often found strong opposition from the Liverpool interests:

> For a few days after the fateful meeting, the Liverpool shareholders in the Midland met and formed themselves into a group which employed professional accountants to investigate his half-yearly balance sheets, and also launched a systematic campaign of letters to the Press, insinuating that Hudson was untrustworthy and his judgment unsound.[73]

[69] *Manchester Guardian*, 2 Feb 1839, p 3. Many were suspicious of the close relationships between the two Boards of Directors. In one instance the L & M directors were accused of favouring Grand Junction interests over L & M interests.— 'Liverpool and Manchester Railway', *The Railway Times*, IV (December, 1841), 1307.

[70] *Letter to a Friend*, pp 27–8.

[71] *Manchester Guardian*, 24 Oct 1838, p 2, quoting the *Liverpool Times*.

[72] *Manchester Guardian*, 8 May 1839, p. 4.

[73] Richard S. Lambert, *The Railway King, 1800-1871*, London, George Allen & Unwin, 1934, pp 185, 193–4.

G

The investing interests of Liverpool did not remain behind national boundaries. British influence felt on the continental railways could in many cases be traced to the success of the Liverpool & Manchester Railway, and the inveterate money interests of Liverpool who were willing to invest capital in a railway project on nearly every continent. George Stephenson, for many years chief engineer on the L & M, was hired by the Dutch government to draw up plans for a system of railways in that country.[74] The Paris & Rouen railway had an extraordinary amount of Liverpool capital invested in it. Although the English shareholders could not pass resolutions, meetings were held in Liverpool with representatives from France seeking both advice and support. John Moss presided at the meetings, and other Liverpool men who were directors of the Paris & Rouen, such as John Easthope, William Chaplin and Charles Lawrence, were generally very active in the meetings. Shortly after the Paris & Rouen company had been formed, half the capital had been contributed by British investors. Its entire projection, construction and operation reflected British and Liverpool influence.[75] In India, the Great Indian Peninsular Railway projected a line from Bombay to tap the great cotton-producing area of Nagpur. The Lancashire millowners pushed the cause through their lobbyists in London, and the eventual financial support for the branch line came from Bombay and Liverpool.[76] These were not the only cases of overseas investment, but they are the outstanding ones. Nor, did such investment come to an end in 1845.

Financially, then, the Liverpool & Manchester Railway proved successful. Its backers experienced a steady and reasonable income from just a short time after it opened until its amalgamation with the

[74] *Manchester Guardian*, 28 Apr 1832, p 3.

[75] *Manchester Guardian*, 29 Jul 1840, p 3, and 8 Nov 1843, p 5. Jenks says the following of British influence on the Paris & Rouen: 'It was the English Directors who named the engineer, Joseph Locke; and Locke named the contractors, William Mackenzie and Thomas Brassey. British "navvies" crossed the Channel to do the work. Iron and railway materials came from British shops or from shops in France manned by British operatives. English methods of construction were employed. . . . The Paris–Rouen railway was the first conspicuous effort of British construction enterprise abroad. . . . Not more than three or four hundred pounds had been employed at any one time in building the Paris–Rouen railway, and it was believed that the promoters had realised a profit of two millions. The promoters sold their Paris–Rouen shares at 100 per cent profit. By the end of 1846 it was thought that the English had made at least five million pounds upon their original investment in French railways'.—Jenks, *British Capital*, pp 142–3. In the seventh week of the second year of operations, the Paris & Rouen railway receipts on passengers increased £1,000, having carried 24,538 passengers in that week. The increase was compared to receipts for the same week in 1843.—*The Times* (London), 11 Sep 1844, p 3.

[76] Jenks, *British Capital*, p 210.

Grand Junction in 1845. Throughout, it had a fair amount of public confidence as was demonstrated through the value of its shares on the stock market, its ability to create new shares and dispose of them, and its success in floating loans through bond or mortgage. High operating costs, a lack of experience, and some adverse criticism gave the directors disconcerting moments. Yet, the bold venturesome spirit of the Liverpool and Manchester investors, along with their shrewd business sense and an unbounding willingness rapidly to absorb the intricacies of railway operation, saved the project from financial ruin, and in the long run made a major contribution to England's history.

CHAPTER V

Operations on the Liverpool & Manchester Railway

A. Freight Operations

Operational practice on the Liverpool & Manchester was developed in its early history on a trial-and-error basis. With the opening of the railway, operational procedure was based mostly on common sense. What did not work had to be changed immediately, and new methods introduced. These did not always solve the problems and a constant search for ever better operational methods was characteristic of the L & M.

During the first months of operations, the L & M made little effort to secure freight traffic, and the general carrying business was not operational until mid-December, 1830. Freight operations were carried out with great simplicity. To a considerable extent, the movement of freight traffic was determined by the volume of passenger traffic. This is not strange, since the greatest income of the railway came from the passenger department. But, in spite of this, the L & M endeavoured to move its freight trains as rapidly as possible so as to compete favourably with the other carriers. Should a passenger train appear behind a freight train, the latter was to be shunted off the main line and allow the passenger train to pass. An engineman could be dismissed for not doing so.[1] At the inclines, where freight trains were necessarily divided into several parts, wagons remaining at the bottom could be left on the line unless a passenger train approached, in which case they had to be pushed to the side. In an attempt to prevent passenger trains meeting freight trains on the main line too often, the directors forbade any freight train to leave Edge Hill less than a quarter of an hour before a passenger train was scheduled to leave the Lime Street station. The ideal situation was to have the freight train leave at least half an hour

---

[1] L & M Directors, *Minutes*, 29 Aug 1832. In 1833, the departure time of the morning freight train from Manchester was advanced one hour and was to carry only the most important freight. It was noted 'that on Mondays the Canals beat the Railways, by making their passage on Sundays'. The Sunday problem seemed to plague the L & M in every department.—L & M Directors, *Minutes*, 4 Apr 1833.

before the scheduled departure of the passenger train. In 1840, a major step in maintaining uniformity of operation was taken by the publication of a book of rules. The directives pertaining to freight trains as regards passenger trains were quite clear:

> ... that all enginemen having charge of Goods or Luggage Trains shall always exert themselves to keep out of the way of Coach Trains, by shunting if necessary, and, if doubtful of getting out of the way of a coach Train, shall direct the Gatemen and Platelayers to make a signal to Coach Trains that a Luggage Train is before them.[2]

At the inclines, the directives remained the same in spite of the presence of extra locomotives to assist the freight and other trains up. As long as the approaching train was a passenger train, the freight had to be shunted both at the top and at the bottom of the inclines. If a 'Ballast Train' had to stop on the main line, the engineman was to send the fireman back a distance of 400 yards to warn any approaching train and the fireman was to maintain this position until his train was ready to start.[3]

General safety in the operation of freight trains was the subject of a few other regulations issued in 1840. When freight trains approached a station where a passenger train was stopped to take on or discharge passengers, the freights were not allowed to proceed through the station. Along the entire line, policemen and gatemen were ordered to observe the freight train as it passed. If they noticed any dangerous overhang on the wagons they were to stop the train immediately and remedy the situation.[4]

There was little attempt to maintain a fixed schedule for freight as is done on the modern railway. The main principle of timetabling revolved around the departure time of the passenger trains. This might seem haphazard, but it must be kept in mind that the railway was not sure from day to day just how many freight trains would be required to carry the traffic. It is estimated that in 1842 there were between fifteen and twenty freight trains passing over the L & M in the course of any one day.[5] Besides the regularly scheduled passenger trains on the L & M,

[2] *Rules and Regulations To Be Observed By Enginemen, Guards, Policemen and others on the Liverpool and Manchester Railway*, December, 1840, p 6, hereinafter cited as L & M *Regulations*.

[3] L & M *Regulations*, pp 15–16, 19–20.

[4] L & M *Regulations*, pp 7, 24.

[5] J. H. Kennedy, 'Railways in England', *Magazine of Western History Illustrated*, X (July, 1889), 290. Between 1 July 1844 and 30 June 1845 the average amounts of

the Grand Junction ran six passenger trains on the line, and many private coal trains used it. With such heavy passenger and coal traffic, it was very difficult to have any type of a fixed freight schedule on such a short line. In the interests of general safety, the directors refused to allow Mr Hollinshead to run his own locomotive and coal wagons between Liverpool and Parkside. But they were willing to move his coal wagons for him for a very reasonable price.[6]

Another very serious problem in the operation of freight trains was the prevention of fire. When in use, the locomotives threw off sparks and small chunks of burning coke which would be carried back over the wagons, and in some instances set them on fire. From the outset, the directors realised that this would be a problem, and before the railway was opened George Stephenson was instructed to come up with some solution. Shortly after the opening, it was suggested that tarpaulins be used to cover the freight.[7] In general, the tarpaulins settled the problem, but from time to time fires did occur. In 1833, three wagons of cotton caught fire on Chat Moss, and considerable damage was done to the cotton and wagons. It was found in this case that ashes dropped along the way by the locomotive were propelled upward by the wheels of the various wagons, and thus caused the fire. To prevent this, ash boxes were added to each locomotive where possible; if this could not be done, then a wire screen was placed behind the tender in order to catch the cinders before they got to the wagons.[8] These improvements were not foolproof and another serious fire on a freight train took place the following year. Discovery of the fire by a company

freight carried on the L & M were as follows: cattle—8,500; sheep—18,000; pigs—108,123; 133,396 tons of coal; 216,237 tons of freight excluding minerals; and 652 carriages. In 1845, the L & M was the fourth largest carrier in tonnage and income. It is easily seen then, that fifteen to twenty freight trains would be required to carry this traffic.—Hyde Clarke, *Contributions To Railway Statistics in 1845*, London, John Weale, 1846, pp 8, 15, 16, 24, 25, 31.

[6] L & M Directors, *Minutes*, 29 Mar 1841. The L & M was very careful to see that all rolling stock of those individuals who were allowed to run their trains on the line was in good condition. In 1842, the company drew up a mark of approval which was required to be placed on all coal wagons used on the L & M. If the wagons did not pass inspection, they were to be taken off the line.—L & M Directors, *Minutes*, 19 Sep 1842.

[7] L & M Directors, *Minutes*, 27 Dec 1830. No mention is made of the material used on the first tarpaulins, but in 1836 Hardman Earle stated those then used were made of oil cloth.—*Select Committee Report on Locomotives in Narrow Streets*, p 77. The L & M required other carriers on the line to use tarpaulins also.—L & M Directors, *Minutes*, 15 Aug and 17 Oct 1831.

[8] L & M Directors, *Minutes*, 17 Jun 1833. Another cause of fire on railway wagons was misalignment of wheels, which caused the wheels to rub against the wagon box.—*Manchester Guardian*, 25 Jul 1835, p 3.

employee would have prevented much of the damage, but it was not noticed till a signal was given by a passerby. After this, the brakemen were ordered to ride on the last wagon of all freight trains so that in this way they would have a better chance of discovering the fire. It was realised that it would be very difficult to eliminate the danger altogether, but the damage could be limited by early detection.[9]

Although sparks from the locomotives caused much damage on the railway, there is little indication of damage caused to property off the line. Brush fires along the way were frequent, but these were on the railway's own property. In testifying before a Parliamentary committee, one of the L & M directors indicated that L & M locomotives never caused a fire off their own property. This testimony was directly contradicted at a later directors' meeting, and it is generally believed that, although slight, there was some damage caused in this way.[10]

Since many of the L & M freight warehouses were without windows, candles were used for light and this proved to be a great fire hazard. As a result, strict regulations covering the use of candles were issued. The Manchester warehouses, which were particularly mentioned as being in danger from careless use of candles, had extra protection in the form of a huge wrought-iron water tank built in one of the second-floor rooms, and a steam-operated fire engine. In an attempt to make the possibility of fire as remote as possible, the railway issued a regulation which forbade smoking on any of the trains or on any part of the L & M property. The penalty for violating this regulation was a £2 fine.[11]

Aside from the ordinary precautions against fire, under the circumstances the only other form of protection possible was insurance. It was not till 1840 that the L & M investigated the possibility of covering the entire line with fire insurance. Before that time, only one of the Manchester warehouses was covered for fire loss. What the railway wanted in 1840 was coverage for the goods in transit, as well as the goods stored in the warehouses. In all probability, the L & M was influenced to seek insurance by the Grand Junction Railway which was completely protected. For this purpose, the L & M directors set up negotiations with the Sun Insurance Company. For entire coverage, the insurance company wanted to charge 15 per cent of liability, provided the railway carried out certain stipulations such as providing a wire cap for the chimney on every locomotive, and building all ash grates so that no

[9] L & M Directors, *Minutes*, 2 Jun 1834.

[10] *Select Committee Report on Locomotives on Railways in Narrow Streets*, p 10; L & M Directors, *Minutes*, 4 Jul 1831 and 3 Jun 1833.

[11] Great Britain, Parliament, House of Commons, *First Report from the Select Committee on Railways Together with the Minutes of Evidence*, 26 Apr 1839, p 84.

hot coals would drop from the bottom of the locomotives. Being acquainted with the Grand Junction policy, the Directors felt the charge was too high. The insurance company then agreed to charge '10s 6d per cent', the same charged the Grand Junction company. Still, the railway thought the charge too much and the stipulation concerning ash boxes unacceptable, and the whole idea was dropped. At the same time, the L & M directors decided to set up a 'Reserve Fund' which would be kept solely for the purpose of paying any losses due to fire. There was no indication from what surplus source of income the fund was to come, and the tone of the *Minutes* suggested that the directors thought of the fund in terms of the future. Considering the circumstances under which the railway was operated, the amount of damage caused by fire was small. Most of the money paid in fire damages went to merchants whose goods were burned in transit.

B. *Passenger Operations*

Compared with freight, passenger operations on the L & M were more complex. Human cargo presented many more problems, and regulations for passengers were necessary from the very beginning of operations. The people who used the railway had been accustomed to riding on the outside of the stage coaches, and this habit carried over to the train. It became such a problem that the L & M had to incorporate a bylaw forbidding passengers to ride on the roofs of the coaches. Although this might seem odd in the twentieth century, the fact was that many who rode on the tops of L & M coaches were injured in falls from the trains, or were crushed against an arch or bridge along the way.[12] It is difficult to blame the people for their actions. They realised that they were travelling at a greater speed than they were used to, but it seems as though they did not comprehend the great danger involved, especially of stepping off a moving train. It was not uncommon at the beginning of railway operations for people to jump from a moving train just to retrieve a hat, or to save themselves time by not waiting until the train had arrived at their stop.

As early as 1831, smoking was prohibited in the first-class coaches. An L & M timetable, dated 20 February 1831, contained the following notice:

> . . . no smoking will be allowed in any of the first-class carriages, even with the general consent of the passengers present, as the

[12] L. T. C. Rolt, *Red for Danger: A History of Railway Accidents and Railway Safety Precautions*, London, Bodley Head, 1955, pp 16–17.

annoyance would be experienced in a still greater degree by those who may occupy the same coach on the succeeding journey.[13]

Apparently, smoking was not a problem on the second-class coaches, since at first they were completely open and smoking would have been nearly impossible due to the wind. Any desire to smoke in these coaches was probably thwarted by the steam and sparks with which the passengers were pelted while the train was in motion. By 1835, the directors ordered that notices be posted in all the 'closed coaches' prohibiting the smoking of cigars. These notices had little effect, and smoking became such a nuisance that the L & M drew up a bylaw prohibiting it in the coaches and L & M stations. The penalty was £2.[14]

The frequent stops made by the second-class trains along the line encouraged the sale of food and drink to the passengers by local tavern owners.[15] This became a nuisance to the railway, since some of the passengers indulged too heavily in liquor and sometimes became uncontrollable. Frequent fights broke out among the passengers which resulted in a general free-for-all. Eventually, all railway employees were forbidden to sell anything to passengers. But, the road houses near the line continued their brisk trade, and things came to such a state that trains were sometimes delayed due to the transactions among the passengers for food and drink. With this additional hazard to safety, the directors decided in 1837 to forbid anyone to sell anything to passengers. After this regulation was put into effect, little trouble was experienced in this matter, although the tavern and roadhouse owners constantly requested permission to sell their goods to passengers. Some tavern owners threatened the L & M with litigation, but their threats did not materialise. And passengers who felt they could not make the two-hour trip without refreshment carried their own food and drink with them, which the L & M did not forbid at any time.

As the volume of passenger traffic increased, many new steps had to be taken by the railway to handle the crowds efficiently and safely. The L & M was prepared in 1831 to carry 2,000 passengers a day but on many occasions was known to have carried upwards of 2,500[16]. In handling such large crowds, the greatest problem was to get the trains started at their scheduled time. With many passengers milling

[13] Charles E. Lee, *Passenger Class Distinctions*, London, Railway Gazette, 1946, p 36.

[14] In 1844, someone wrote a letter to the *Guardian* suggesting the railways provide a 'smoker's' coach.—*Manchester Guardian*, 9 Oct 1844, p 5.

[15] During the first few years of operations, many enginemen and firemen became intoxicated because of indulgence at the various stops.

[16] *Directors' Reports*, 28 Mar 1831; *Niles' Weekly Register*, 16 Jul 1831, p 340.

about the coaches, and the great numbers that usually came to say goodbye, the L & M porters experienced great difficulty in making their directions to board the train heard. Therefore, a large bell was installed at the Liverpool and Manchester stations. The bell was rung five minutes before the train was to depart. A smaller hand bell was rung for several minutes warning the people that it was time to board the train. When the railway depended on omnibuses to bring passengers to the stations at Edge Hill or Manchester, the trains would have to wait if these buses were late. To encourage the bus drivers to be on time, the company published a regulation requiring all omnibuses to be at the station at least ten minutes before train time. With the opening of the Lime Street station, Liverpool, many passengers came directly to the station, and frequently many were late and attempted to run for the train. To stop such a dangerous practice, a gate was constructed across the platforms, and the gate was closed at the exact time the train was to depart. Once closed, no one was allowed to get on to the platform or train.[17]

Passenger class distinction was maintained on the L & M throughout its history. First-class passengers had a choice of enclosed coaches with either four or six seats. The latter were less expensive. Usually, the first-class trains stopped only at Newton. Second-class trains were at first completely open, but after 1833 were covered with flat roofs. In 1839, the North Union Railway requested permission to book their second-class passengers on the L & M first-class trains. After an investigation by the committee on North Union arrangements, the directors decided that such a practice would be out of order and might possibly hinder their own first-class passenger traffic.[18] It was not until 1840 that the use of third-class coaches on the L & M was considered. At the same time, it was suggested that the second-class coaches have windows installed, and be completely closed in. In order to save time and expense, new second-class coaches were to be built, and the Blue Coaches, which had been used for the second-class traffic, were set aside as third-class coaches. It was very strongly made known that the coaches

[17] L & M Directors, *Minutes*, 29 Aug 1832 and 6 Feb 1833; *Manchester Guardian*, 6 Aug 1836, p 1. In 1838, the crowds at the Lime Street Station became so big that the railway had to appoint a second superintendent to handle the traffic.—L & M Directors, *Minutes*, 25 Jun 1838.

[18] In 1836, the L & M started a 'mixed' or 'merchants' train which consisted of first- and second-class coaches. It left each end of the line at seven in the evening and stopped only at Newton. In 1841, a mixed train was run at two in the afternoon from each end. In 1844, the evening mixed train stopped at Huyton Gate, Rainhill, St Helens Junction, Newton, Parkside, Kenyon Junction, Bury Lane and Patricroft.— L & M Directors, *Minutes*, 4 Jul 1836, 16 Aug 1841, and 15 May 1843.

were at all times to continue to be operated as three separate and distinct classes. The first third-class L & M train began a regular schedule on 1 October 1844, and it ran once a day each way between Liverpool and Manchester. These trains were so well used that in April 1845 arrangements had to be made for the third-class trains to go between Liverpool and Manchester twice a day each way. No new equipment was needed for this additional train since the same coaches and locomotives were used.[19]

At times the L & M extended its services for the benefit of special groups by making extra stops. As a result of several letters from farmers on Chat Moss, the railway built stations at Flow Moss and Lamb's Cottage and said it would stop as many passenger trains there as were required for the 'convenience of the public'. In some cases, the company went so far as to cater for individual families.[20]

Some safety regulations were developed as the L & M grew with experience. The coach doors facing the opposite rails were ordered to be locked. This would prevent passengers from getting off the wrong side, and stepping into the path of trains on the other line. In order to allow for safer entrance and exit from the coaches, footboards were placed along the entire length of the coach. Formerly, three separate steps were used and much time was consumed while the passengers got on and off. This new type of step was much safer.

The tunnel which led to the Lime Street station was the scene of some accidents due to the trains coming down too fast and not having enough braking power. To prevent further accidents, another brakeman was added to all coach trains as they went down the tunnel. Also, all trains that entered the tunnel were to have brakes on at least half the coaches.[21]

The railway ticket came into use on the L & M shortly after the line was opened. During the first months, the passenger had to go through a very complicated process to obtain a seat on a railway coach. Passengers were required to make application twenty-four hours before train time, giving their name, address, place of birth, age, occupation, and reason for travelling. They then had to travel on the train named on the ticket. If the train did not reach its destination before night, the passenger had to pay for his own lodging. Finally, the company did not hold itself responsible for luggage that got wet

[19] L & M Directors, *Minutes*, 18 Apr, 9 Sep 1844, 3 Apr 1845.

[20] The Directors approved 'with great pleasure' stopping a first-class train at Patricroft for Lord and Lady Francis Egerton 'where they would be met by their barge'.

[21] L & M Directors, *Minutes*, 1838–42 *passim*.

while being carried on the roof. Although these regulations are attributed to the L & M, it seems strange that any mention of lodging should be made, since the L & M was only thirty-one miles long.[22] Nonetheless, with the tremendous number of passengers who wanted transport over the L & M, the company was forced to find a better method of handling the booking arrangements. It was the introduction of a ticket system that saved the railway much time, and enabled them to maintain tight schedules and carry such large numbers. The first tickets on the L & M were made of oblong slips of paper and were divided in half by a perforated line. Several entries were made on the tickets. They were the name of the company, the name of the passenger, his destination, the date of issue and the time of departure of the train. When filling out the ticket, the 'booking agent'[23] had to write everything except the name of the company on the counterfoil. Tickets used on the L & M were white, and those used on the branch lines were different colours. Heavy black lines of different lengths were drawn on the back of the tickets in order to indicate the destination of the passenger to the illiterate ticket takers.[24] Besides granting the privilege of travelling on the L & M coaches, the ticket admitted the passenger to the outer waiting rooms of the stations, next to the train platforms. No one else was allowed there and hence the necessity of a large bell to remind the passengers of the nearing time of departure. If a passenger had already purchased a ticket, and then missed the train, he could claim half the fare paid, as long as he presented his ticket within forty-eight hours.[25]

A variety of commutation tickets was eventually introduced on the L & M. In 1842, Mr William Owen of Liverpool, who used the L & M trains six times a week, asked for a reduction in fare if he should purchase his ticket for the entire year. A one-third reduction on his fare between Liverpool and Rainhill was granted if he would pay six months' fare in advance. This was the first multiple trip ticket sold on

[22] 'Yes Conditions are Better Than 100 years Ago', *Railway Age*, LXXIX (September, 1930), 591.

[23] The 'booking agent' kept a diagram book with the numbers of coaches and seat numbers and a corresponding number for each ticket sold, along with the destination of the holder. Before printed tickets were used, this was the only information the ticket takers had.—L & M Directors, *Minutes*, 25 Apr 1831.

[24] Marshall, *One Hundred Years*, p 24; Boulton, *Railways of Britain*, pp 341–2; 'The Queen's Reign: Railway Progress, 1837–1897', *Railway News Supplement* (May, 1897), ii. Veitch contradicts the majority of sources and states that passengers on the L & M had a choice of seat once they paid for the ticket. Because of the weight of all the other evidence this does not seem likely.—Veitch, *Struggle for the L & M*, p 67. After having boarded the train, some passengers would go beyond the station for which they had purchased a ticket. Anyone who was caught was fined £5.—L & M Directors, *Minutes*, 6 May 1833. [25] Marshall, *Centenary History*, p 69.

the L & M. In 1843, annual tickets were sold to the proprietors of the L & M for £60 each, which was to be paid in advance. The ticket could be used at any time during the year and was not transferable. If the proprietors wanted to use the second-class coaches the charge would be proportionate. In 1844, the return or day ticket was introduced on the L & M. The ticket for a round-trip between Liverpool and Manchester cost 12s (60p), the regular first-class fare being 6s 6d (32½p) each way. Second-class passengers could take advantage of the same type of ticket in proportion to second-class fares. The holder could not sell or give his ticket away. This became a very popular ticket among the merchants of Manchester and Liverpool whose business required them to make the round-trip each day. They were eventually sold for trips between the intermediate stations at a proportionate charge. The annual tickets were soon given gratis to a few influential individuals; then the privilege of purchasing them was extended to company employees for 50 guineas. Each member of the employee's family could use this ticket as long as his or her name was on it. In 1845, annual tickets were sold to the general public for £40, for the trip between Liverpool and Manchester. The ticket entitled the holder to travel on the regular trains any day, at any time, for the entire year, but it could not be lent to another person.[26]

In 1831, the L & M made it very clear to its employees that no one connected with the railway was to ride on the trains without charge unless he be on company business. Even in such a case, the individual was to book passage as all the other passengers were required to do. In 1833, the directors made reference to a 'Director's Ticket' which the proprietors who had been directors of the company would be allowed to keep. The ticket provided free access to the railway, the stations and all the property of the railway, but did not provide for free rides on the trains. Resident agents of the branch railways were given permission to travel free over the L & M line while they were on their way to or coming from the branch lines. However, only one free pass was alloted to each of the branch companies.[27] After a time, the company became more lenient. The wives of policemen and gatemen employed by the

26 L & M Directors, *Minutes*, 5 Dec 1842, 13 Nov 1843, 22 Apr, 1 Jul, 11 Nov, 18 Nov, 23 Dec 1844, and 27 Jan 1845; *Directors' Reports*, 24 Jul 1844; *The Liverpool Merchantile Gazette*, 21 Oct 1844, p 4. There is no description available of the annual tickets. Since it was the general practice to collect tickets before passengers boarded the trains, the annual tickets were undoubtedly kept in possession of the owner.—Whishaw, *Railways*, p 205; L & M Directors, *Minutes*, 19 Mar 1838 and 27 Dec 1841.

27 Since ballasting along the L & M took place in daylight, the supervisors could go from one part of the line to another on passenger trains free of charge.—L & M

L & M were allowed to ride to Liverpool or Manchester free of charge once a week. A seemingly illogical rule was set up for law officers: policemen who worked for the towns along the way were allowed to ride the passenger trains without charge when they were 'chasing thieves'. They had to show an identification pass from the superintendent of police indicating that he authorised the trip. If the policeman was successful in catching the thief, the L & M expected to be paid regular fare; if unsuccessful, the company did not demand payment. In 1839, the L & M agreed to allow S. Welsby, a doctor, to ride free of charge at all times. He was the surgeon for a benefit club to which a number of the L & M employees belonged, and he agreed to look after any L & M men injured in accidents. This service would be his payment for the free passage along the line.[28]

Perhaps one of the most intricate problems in general passenger operations on the L & M was timetabling. Since the railway was an experiment, the directors had no idea of the amount of passenger traffic they would handle. Weather conditions, seasonal travel, the opening of branch lines, running powers granted to other railways, and a fluctuating economy all affected L & M schedules. As stated above, freight traffic was secondary, and since any extra freight could be sent over the line at night, strict freight schedules were not set up. But, where regularly scheduled trains would bring passengers to the stations, a very efficient system was needed.

Many people used the L & M to make stage coach connections for the nearby seacoast towns, and as a result passenger traffic usually increased in the summer.[29] To handle the extra passengers expected in 1831, the railway advertised an extra second-class train to leave Manchester every morning at 6.00 am and return from Liverpool at 6.30 pm the same evening. Since the newspapers proved to be the best means for announcing changes in schedule, the L & M used them for this purpose as a matter of policy. Summertime also meant the beginning of the horse races at Newton on the L & M main line. To handle the race crowds, the railway provided extra trains which 'were to return

Directors, *Minutes*, 17 Oct 1831. The 'free tickets' on the L & M consisted of a round ivory disc. In the centre the words 'Liverpool and Manchester Railway' were printed in black. The ivory disc was used as a ticket on other English railways, but it was never used on the L & M for regular passengers.—Dolfus, *Histoire*, p 63.

[28] L & M Directors, *Minutes*, 15 Oct 1835, 30 May 1836, 26 Oct 1839.

[29] Passenger totals quoted to Parliament demonstrate this trend: 1838: 5 Jun–2 Jul, 59,044 passengers; 3 Jul–6 Aug, 74,796 passengers; 7 Aug–3 Sep, 67,171 passengers; 6 Nov–3 Dec, 39,766 passengers; 4 Dec–7 Jan, 51,863.—Great Britain, Parliament, House of Commons, *Second Report of the Select Committee on Railways*, 1839, p 394.

immediately after the races'.[30] In 1836, the company established a twelve-train timetable for the summer months, stating that once the summer travel had slackened the regular ten trains would be run each day. Departures were timed so that the first-class trains would remain the same, since their times were so well known. Trains left both Liverpool and Manchester at the following times:

6.00 am (summer)	2.00 pm (First class)
7.00 am (First class)	3.00 pm
7.15 am	4.00 pm (summer)
9.00 am	5.00 pm (First class)
10.00 am (First class)	5.30 pm
12.00 m	7.00 pm

The winter season also found the directors being petitioned by various groups of merchants who used the trains each weekday. In these cases, whenever possible, the L & M readily agreed to a change in times to provide the desired service.[31] By 1836, the general timetable detailed above took reasonable care of all requests for regular transport both in summer and winter.

On special occasions the railway was expected to provide extra service for the public. These special trains posed no difficulty and there is no evidence that any of the extra trains run on the L & M was ever involved in an accident which resulted from poor timetabling. However, these trains were never run without the express permission of the directors. In some instances, instead of actually putting an extra train on the line, the regular schedules were altered.[32]

Due to an increase in passenger traffic, and anticipating a still further increase with the opening of the North Union Railway, the L & M published a new timetable in 1839, announcing eleven trains a day each way between Liverpool and Manchester.

Depart Liverpool		Depart Manchester	
7.00 am	2.00 pm	7.00 am	2.00 pm
7.15 am	2.30 pm	7.30 am	2.45 pm
8.45 am	4.45 pm	9.00 am	5.00 pm
10.00 am	5.50 pm	10.00 am	5.30 pm
11.00 am	7.00 pm	11.15 am	7.00 pm
11.45 am		11.45 am	[33]

[30] *Manchester Guardian*, 30 Jul 1831, p 1; L & M Directors, *Minutes*, 13 Jun 1832.

[31] L & M Directors, *Minutes*, 1832–43, *passim*; *Manchester Guardian*, 16 Jul 1836, p 3. Enginemen who maintained their schedules were given a bonus.

[32] Extra trains were run for the Conservative Club, troops required during an election, excursions during Whitsuntide Week at reduced fares, the Liverpool Assizes, and excursions to the steamer *Great Britain*.—L & M Directors, *Minutes*, 1835–45, *passim*. In 1836, the L & M added an extra first-class train which left each end of the line at 9.00 am. The first-class train regularly scheduled to leave at 10.00 am would not leave till 11.00 am.—L & M Directors, *Minutes*, 10 Nov 1836.

[33] *Directors' Reports*, 24 Jul 1839.

In an attempt to provide accommodation for the North Union traffic, the directors ordered the 9.00 am and the 5.00 pm trains to pass Newton without stopping, but the people in the neighbourhood of Newton complained so bitterly that they had to alter their decision. If anybody appeared for the two trains involved, then they had to stop. This did not satisfy the people, and continued pressure was put on the company until it finally agreed to allow the trains to stop as originally scheduled. In November 1839, the two morning trains which left Liverpool at 7.00 am and 7.15 am, and those leaving Manchester at 7.00 am and 7.30 am, were to be replaced by one second-class train which would start at 7.00 am from each end of the line. This arrangement still did not solve the problem of too few passengers on the early morning trains, and the second-class train which was to leave Manchester at 7.00 am was timed for 7.30 am. In 1844, when the L & M inaugurated its third-class trains for the first time, the timetable was not altered. The third-class trains started from Manchester at 6.30 am and from Liverpool at 6.30 pm.

In granting running powers to other railways, the company did not give up the right of determining the over-all timetable for the line. When the Grand Junction began to run its trains along the L & M, it had to conform with the L & M times. If any outside company wanted to make any changes in its schedules originally agreed to, the L & M directors had to approve.[34] In general, the L & M was liberal in its policy of making exceptions for the various companies. It readily conveyed passengers of other lines, changed its agreements with the other lines, allowed special coaches to be attached to its own trains even though these belonged to another railway, and sometimes changed the times of its trains to make better connections with trains running on other lines. Where it proved feasible, the L & M gave way to trains from other lines. In one case, the L & M and Grand Junction trains left Lime Street as one unit, and the Grand Junction section was even allowed to go first, 'since it was a mail train'. In order to enable the London & Birmingham and Grand Junction through trains between Liverpool and London to maintain their schedules, the L & M delayed its evening trains to allow the through trains to start. Such courtesy paid off in the long run, since the company received a larger income from the running powers granted when the railways holding these powers had

---

[34] The L & M usually worked on the principle of not allowing any passenger train to follow another along the same line by less than one-half hour. This policy was maintained for the most part, except in cases where slow trains followed express trains.—L & M Directors, *Minutes*, 17 Sep 1838.

Page 117 Lime Street Station—interior

Lime Street Station—exterior

Edge Hill Station

Page 118 Bridge over Water Street, Manchester, and Irwell Bridge

an increase of traffic. When the people saw that the through trains were granted special right-of-way privileges, they were assured of a faster, on-time journey, and thus used the railway rather than other means of transportation.

Sunday traffic on the L & M was very light. Only one train was run in the morning from each end of the line, and two in the evening from each end. A company bylaw forbade running any trains along the line during the time of church services. This was generally conceived to be between the hours of 9.00 am and 1.00 pm. But the bylaw extended this ban on rail travel up to four in the afternoon. When the Grand Junction line proposed to change its Sunday timetable in 1839, the bylaw was called into question. Legal counsel was sought by the directors and opposite opinions were given. Sir William Follett, one-time Attorney General, felt the bylaw was legal as regards the L & M and its equipment, but that it did not apply to others using the line. Sir William Wightman, member of the Bar, stated that if the bylaw was posted when the agreement was made with the Grand Junction to use the L & M line, then the Grand Junction company was bound by the bylaw. The result was the directors decided that the bylaw should remain and the Grand Junction company was 'earnestly requested' to change their timetable as soon as possible.[35] This was not very strong language and it appeared as though the L & M was going to leave the matter up to the conscience of the Grand Junction. On the L & M, Sunday travel never developed to a very great extent, and in 1842 the company had to reduce its Sunday trains because of the light traffic.[36]

Whenever the L & M published timetables, there was never any indication as to what time the trains would arrive at their destination. When the people wished to board the trains at the intermediate stations, they would have to estimate the time, and in most cases allow themselves at least ten minutes before the calculated time of arrival. Being an experimental railway, it was difficult at first for the L & M directors to estimate the correct time of arrival. There were many causes for delay, some necessary and others which the directors could have readily prevented.[37] Despite the company's attempt to guarantee the best type

[35] In 1837, Mr Lawrence and Mr Moss requested the Postmaster General to run his mail trains so as not to break the company bylaw covering Sunday travel.— L & M Directors, *Minutes*, 31 Jul 1837.

[36] L & M Directors, *Minutes*, 1 Dec 1842.

[37] One L & M engineman who drove locomotives for two years speaks of duels with bulls, people hitching horses and wagons across tracks, pigs getting stuck between rails, and waiting for 'important people', all of which caused delays.— Edward Entwhistle, 'How I Ran The First Railroad Train', *New York American*, (Magazine Section), 21 Jul 1907, pp 1–2.

of service through its utilisation of improvements in locomotives and other rolling stock, the L & M would under no circumstances guarantee the arrival of its trains at any particular time. In this, the railway was similar to twentieth-century railways which, although they print arrival times, do not guarantee them.

C. Accidents

From the day the L & M was opened, accidents were not infrequent on the line. Since little experience had been had in the operation of locomotives pulling several coaches or wagons, many factors which readily led to accidents were at first given scant attention. Such an increase of speed as was used on the railway was an entirely new concept in travel. Those in charge of the trains did not realise what could possibly happen to their trains and the passengers should the train jump the track, go over an embankment, run into another train or come against buffers without the application of brakes. Again, the L & M had to learn from experience. In this phase of railway operation, the learning came as a slow and hard process due to the variety of circumstances under which the accidents would occur and, more especially, due to the predominance of the human element involved in the operation of the railway. But the L & M proved a very willing student and was quick to remedy any and all situations which would provide for the safer operation of the line.[38]

Of all the causes of accidents on the L & M, weather conditions were responsible for the least number. The people in charge of the trains had already experienced the effects of the weather peculiar to the Lancashire area, and probably knew of several bad accidents on the rivers and roads caused by weather conditions. Hence, it was not difficult to apply a sense of caution in operating the railway. But the weather did cause some few accidents. A very serious accident took place at Rainhill in 1832 due to fog. Several people were killed when one train rammed a stationary train. As a result of the accident, the directors passed the following resolution:

> In future, in fog or thick weather, when a train stops to pick up or drop passengers, the Gateman or Policeman of the station im-

---

[38] In 1831, the L & M decided to keep a record of all accidents involving personal injury to passengers or employees, along with the particulars of the accidents. This same practice is used today on nearly all railways.—S. M. Philip, 'British Railways Eighty Years Ago', *The Railway Library 1911*, 3rd Series, Chicago, Gunthrop-Warren Printing, 1912, p 15.

mediately run 300 yds behind the Train, or so far as may be necessary to warn any coming Engine.

Where the train had to stop along the line other than at a station, if no platelayers or other staff were available, the fireman was to run back 300 yards to warn the approaching trains. Only two other accidents occurred on the L & M due to weather. In each instance there was no loss of life.

There were many attempts on the part of deranged or disgruntled persons to cause accidents on the railway. In 1831, the directors received a report stating that many mile posts and sleepers had been put across the rails at Sutton. These would have been sufficient to throw the locomotives off the rails if they had not been discovered in time. The directors immediately ordered that a public notice of a £10 reward be posted for the 'discovery and conviction in the present case and in any future case'.[39] In 1834, a special directors' meeting was held to discuss an accident and a near-accident due to objects being put on the line. A first-class train being pulled by *Meteor* was thrown off the tracks after hitting a platelayer's 'laurie' or pushcart, which it was discovered had been put on the line intentionally. Fortunately, there was little damage to the locomotive and coaches or injury to passengers. On the Sandy Main Embankment, a train had been jolted by a sleeper placed across the line. To prevent any future accidents the directors had an 'iron guard or stay' put on all locomotives in front of the wheels, with the idea of throwing aside anything put on the tracks.[40] In another instance, *Lightning*, pulling the 7.00 am train from Manchester, ran into a laurie. Some damage was done to the locomotive and there was a half-hour delay. The directors held Mr Cummings, who was in charge of maintenance of the way, responsible since he had not locked the lauries up so that 'drunken or ill-disposed persons' could get at them. In 1839, a twentieth-century youthful pastime cropped up on the L & M. Two boys were caught throwing stones at a passenger train on the Sutton incline. It turned out the boys were children of company employees, who were told to correct the boys and that any future incidents would not be treated so lightly. In an attempt to stop people who were trying to cause accidents, the L & M, through the Postmaster

---

[39] Bricks and iron chairs had been placed on the rails near Wavertree Lane, and the directors then considered the possibility of hiring more policemen.—L & M Directors, *Minutes*, 8 Aug and 31 Oct 1831.

[40] A few days later stone blocks were put on the rails at nearly the same place where *Meteor* had gone off the line. The Directors offered £100 for the discovery of the offender in either case.

General, asked for legislation which would protect the railways. On 10 August 1840, *An Act for Regulating Railways* was given royal assent and contained this provision:

> Anyone obstructing Railways in any way so as to endanger safety of persons conveyed thereon shall be guilty of misdemeanour— on conviction be imprisoned with or without hard labour not exceeding two years.[41]

The L & M continued to offer rewards for conviction of persons who put obstacles on the line, since the above punishment could not be effective unless the guilty party were caught, identified and convicted.

Many fatalities and personal injuries suffered by passengers and employees on the L & M were due to their own carelessness. In most instances the injured or deceased failed to obey simple company regulations. The *Manchester Guardian* reported the first 'serious injury' on the L & M on 19 March 1831. A man had stepped from a train before it came to a stop, and it was obvious that the railway was not at fault'[42] One time after a train had made a stop at the Bury Lane Tavern, a drunken man fell from one of the Blue Coaches and was killed. On another occasion, in 1833, passengers, whose train was delayed by a freight train stalled on the line, got out of their coaches and walked up and down the other line. The steam from the stalled engine enveloped the area and the people did not notice a coal train coming up the line and three were killed. After this, signs were posted in all coaches warning passengers not to get out at any places other than stations. In Olive Mount cutting, a train came from behind and struck a man who was balancing himself on a rail. Near Bury Lane a passenger was killed when he jumped from the Blue Coaches in order to save himself a short walk. At Newton Junction a boy was killed when he ran across the tracks after waiting for a freight train to pass. He did not notice a train coming up the other line. Another boy trespassing on the railway was struck and killed by a train between Patricroft and Eccles. Another boy, only three years old, was killed by a train after having

[41] 3 & 4 Victoria, *c.* xcvii, 10 Aug 1840; Henry Tuck, *The Railway Shareholders' Manual; or Practical Guide to the Railways of Great Britain, Completed, in Progress, and Projected, Forming an Entire Railway Synopsis, Indispensible to all Interested in Railway Locomotion*, London, Effingham Wilson, 1845, viii; L & M Directors, *Minutes*, 3 Dec 1840.

[42] *Manchester Guardian*, 19 Mar 1831, p 2. 'From the first opening of the Railway in September to the end of that year, more than 70,000 persons passed by it for various distances, between Liverpool and Manchester, without personal injury to a single individual except one person, who while mounting the roof of one of the carriages had his leg severely bruised'.—'The Manchester and Liverpool Rail-Road', *The Penny Magazine*, II (April, 1833), 167.

wandered on to the tracks. In most of these instances, little or no blame could be placed either on the directors or on the mechanical devices used on the railway.

Several employees of the railway lost their lives in doing imprudent things while on the line. One fireman was killed when he fell under a train; he had been trying to unhook two locomotives which were in motion. This was strictly against regulations. In Wapping Tunnel a brakesman was run over while attempting to disengage the rope mechanisms from the wagons at the top of the tunnel. As a result, a regulation was passed forbidding brakesmen to do this while a train was in motion. A luggage porter was killed when a train moved up the Lime Street Tunnel. He had not finished packing the luggage when it was time for the train to start, and instead of waiting for him to finish, the train moved up the tunnel and he was killed while getting off. It had been the custom for the porters to remain on top if not finished, but now that was forbidden. At Edge Hill a coach porter was killed trying to hold back two horse wagons while the one in front of him was being pulled into a siding. At the Broad Green cattle sidings, a fireman passing from wagon to wagon while the train was in motion had his arm crushed and later died. Although there was evidence of carelessness on the part of the company employees involved in accidents, it was likewise obvious that the railway, in consideration of the safety of its employees, should have been more cautious and not have allowed certain dangerous conditions to exist.

Before the beginning of the 'Railway Age' in Britain, many dire predictions were made about the number of accidents with consequent loss of life that this new method of transport would cause. However, these predictions were wrong. Mechanical failure as a cause of accidents on the L & M was comparatively small, although one such failure which caused some accidents was broken axles. *Etna* jumped the tracks on the Brosely embankment because of a broken axle. *Fury's* 'cranked axle' broke and sent the locomotive and two coaches over an embankment, but the passengers were not hurt. Near Bury Lane, an axle on *Patentee* broke and the engine and coaches went down a slope. Although the coaches were badly damaged, the passengers suffered little injury. Because of the frequency of this type of accident, the *Manchester Guardian* carried an article suggesting that the railway put a few empty wagons next to the locomotives and then attach the coaches. This would prevent the coaches from leaving the tracks if the locomotive went off.[43]

[43] L & M Directors, *Minutes*, 5 Sep, 7 Dec 1831, 18 Apr 1836; *Manchester Guardian*, 23 Apr 1836, p 3.

In one instance, the axle of a first-class coach broke, but the only result was a very rough ride and a few scared passengers. A freight train travelling at a very high speed was derailed when one of the wagon axles broke. Many of the wagons were demolished, and the engineman was fined for going too fast.

Several accidents were caused by wheels breaking. The most serious accident of this type involved *Orion*, which was thrown off the tracks and went over a slope. Fortunately there were no injuries. Other accidents due to broken wheels were only minor.[44]

On two occasions the breaking of the tunnel ropes caused accidents; no personal injury resulted in either case. A brakesman was killed when *Manchester* 'got away' on the Sutton incline. The engineman blamed the wet tracks for his lack of control of the locomotive. Since *Manchester* had no reverse power, the only means of retarding early locomotives, he was unable to bring any braking power on the engine. Poor brakes caused only one other accident on the L & M. A Grand Junction train ran into the rear of a stalled L & M passenger train, injuring several passengers. The Grand Junction engineman admitted that his brakes did not work.[45] On two occasions, trains got away in the Wapping Tunnel due to their extreme length and great weight. The brakesmen could not control them and they ran wild. As a result, the directors ordered that no more than twenty wagons should ever enter the tunnel at one time.

Before the opening of the railway, when the critics were loudest, the pet-theme was the possibility of explosions on the locomotives. Only two serious explosions took place on the L & M during fifteen years of uninterrupted operations. In 1837, *Liver* burst its water chamber between the two fireboxes; the engineman was severely scalded and the fireman had his thigh broken. In 1838, *Patentee's* outer casing burst, killing both engineman and fireman.[46]

The most frequent cause of accidents on the L & M was carelessness

[44] L & M Directors, *Minutes*, 1836–9, *passim*.

[45] L & M Directors, *Minutes*, 4 Mar 1833 and 26 Nov 1838. The Grand Junction directors readily admitted they were at fault, agreed to pay the damages, and promised the L & M directors they would take all the necessary means to see that such an accident did not happen again.—*Manchester Guardian*, 1 Dec 1838, p 3.

[46] L & M Directors, *Minutes*, 16 Jan 1837 and 19 Nov 1839. After the explosion on *Patentee*, all L & M locomotives were inspected to see whether or not the 'staying of the Fire Box above the Fire Door and of the Boiler End next the Chimney were strong. The *Patentee* blew up when it was pulling forty-one wagons. It was felt there was enough water in the boiler, and the tubes did not burst. The explosion then was blamed on the great strain due to the heavy load. It probably would not have happened if the regulation about splitting trains on the inclines had been observed.— *The Times* (London), 15 Nov 1838, p 6.

on the part of employees. In general, there seemed to be a lack of a sense of responsibility, along with little or no safety consciousness. This careless attitude is emphasised by the number of times enginemen, firemen and other railway employees were found intoxicated while on duty. It was the company's policy to dismiss any man found drunk while on duty, but even this practice did not seem to deter the many who worked on the line in such a condition.[47]

The enginemen working on the L & M were strictly forbidden to push coaches or wagons ahead of the locomotives. On three occasions serious accidents involving personal injury and damage occurred on the line when enginemen failed to heed the regulation. All were severely reprimanded.[48] Sleeping while on duty, which sometimes had serious consequences, was a common occurrence on the L & M. One policeman left a point open while he slept and several wagons ran off the tracks. The man was fined £3. A train arrived at Manchester station with only one man on the engine and this man was asleep. The station porter had to jump on the train and bring it to a halt. Another passenger train went down the Lime Street Tunnel without brakes because the guard was asleep. No passengers were injured, but the sleepy guard was taken before a magistrate and given two months' imprisonment with hard labour.[49] In several cases, employees left things along the line, and passenger and freight trains crashed into them. One Simon Fenwick, who left wagons on the Sutton Incline, was fined £5. A policeman at the Manchester station did not inform a passenger train that coal wagons were on the line. The train was going faster than it should have been and crashed into the wagons. There were no injuries and the two men involved were reprimanded, but kept in the company's service since it was their first accident.[50] Three serious accidents took place as a result of points being left the wrong way. *Mars*, pulling the Blue Coaches, jumped the track after hitting an open point. Two ladies were seriously injured. At St Helens Junction, *Star* was thrown on the opposite line and collided with *Caledonia*. The engineman was killed and a mechanic had his foot crushed. Both engines were severely damaged. All this was due to a point 'left wrong placed'. *Goliath* was

---

[47] L & M Directors, *Minutes*, 3 Dec and 10 Dec 1832.

[48] L & M Directors, *Minutes*, 18 Nov 1833, 11 Jul 1836, and 19 Jun 1837.

[49] L & M Directors, *Minutes*, 8 Mar, 15 Nov, 27 Dec, 30 Dec 1841. On two other instances when passenger trains went down the Lime Street Tunnel without brakesmen due to confusion, spring buffers in the station saved the coaches from damage and the passengers were only shaken.—L & M Directors, *Minutes*, 18 Jun 1838 and 3 Mar 1845.

[50] L & M Directors, *Minutes*, 1832–40, *passim*.

also involved in a head-on collision due to an open point. In all three instances, the men responsible were discharged from the company's service, and one was held for the magistrate.[51]

Carelessness among the enginemen took a variety of forms. Sometimes through pride or stubborness, the enginemen would refuse to give way at junctions, or where lines crossed the main line directly. One person was killed, and many injured when a Grand Junction train crashed into an L & M train at Kenyon Junction. It was found that the Grand Junction engineman had not kept a proper lookout on the line. However, it must be remembered that the engineman and fireman had no protection and were frequently blinded by the sparks and steam of their own locomotive. Two men in charge of *Vulcan* were discharged in 1838 for not keeping a good lookout and, as a result, running into a first-class train. On another occasion, *Goliath* came on the line from a siding as a Grand Junction passenger train was approaching. It hit the train and damaged several coaches. The fireman and engineman were held responsible and were discharged. On the Whiston Incline, a thirty-two-wagon freight train ran back down the line when the connecting chain broke. The runaway train hit an approaching Bolton train and many wagons on both trains were destroyed. The engineman of the L & M train, who had disobeyed the regulation requiring an assistant locomotive behind all freights on inclines, was discharged. In 1840, one David Fletcher took *Buffalo* down the wrong line and nearly caused a head-on collision. He was discharged and a warrant was sworn out for his arrest.[52]

The public was well aware of the accidents on the L & M as on the other railways of the country. In 1838, the *Manchester Guardian*, which was usually favourable to the L & M, suggested that more severe measures be taken against employees who were 'trifling with the lives of the public'. Discharge from the company was not enough. In *The Times* for 31 October 1840, there were six letters to the editor demanding that certain stringent steps be taken for better railway safety. Railway accidents, usually written up in minute detail in newspapers, were frequently exaggerated. In one instance, the *Manchester Chronicle* printed a completely untrue story of a fatal accident at Parkside. The *Manchester Guardian* came to the rescue of the L & M and refuted the account.[53]

[51] L & M Directors, *Minutes*, 18 Oct 1832, 2 Mar 1835, 31 May 1841.

[52] L & M Directors, *Minutes*, 1837–43, *passim*; *The Times* (London), 12 Sep 1837, p 6; *Manchester Guardian*, 13 Sep 1837, p 2.

[53] *Manchester Guardian*, 10 Feb 1838, p 3, and 27 Jul 1842, p 3; *The Times* (London), 31 Oct 1840, p 5.

Taken together, the accidents on the L & M seem considerable. However, it must be kept in mind that the number of accidents over a fifteen-year period for a railway that had had no operating experience on which to base its policy, was comparatively small. After ten years of operations, the L & M had a record year for safety. In the year ending 1 September 1840, there were only eighteen minor accidents, and three fatalities. These latter were due to the carelessness of the individuals involved, and the railway was directly responsible for only two injured people.[54] Considering the risks involved, the newness of the operations, and the lack of co-operation on the part of passengers, bystanders and some employees, the L & M safety record was reasonably good.

D. *Liability*

Accidents on the railway raised a very serious legal question. Was the L & M responsible for personal injury and loss of life sustained by passengers while they were being carried by the railway? The question was never definitely answered until after the L & M had amalgamated with the Grand Junction. Between 1831 and 1845, the L & M tried to follow a definite policy, but the directors were never quite sure just what their liability was. They constantly sought legal advice, but never received a firm answer. The railway then decided to weigh each case on its own merits and usually settled damages out of court. Some cases, however, where the injured party was not satisfied, were taken into court. Such was the case of Newton versus Liverpool & Manchester Railway in 1837. Newton was injured when his omnibus ran against a railway gate, which the plaintiff argued should not have been erected across the road but across the railway. Newton won the case and the L & M had to pay him £50.[55] When the question of liability for personal injury was finally settled the railways lost out:

> Compensation for accidents in which personal injury is sustained is recoverable by one process: an Act, 9th and 10th Victoria, Cap. 93, being an Act for compensating the families of persons killed by accidents, commonly called Lord Campbell's Act, provides a special means of empowering juries to give verdicts compelling railway companies to pay sums of money to the representatives of persons killed by railway accidents.

[54] *Reports Relative to Railways*, p 129; L & M Proprietors, *Minutes*, Annual General Meeting, 27 Jan 1841; *Herapath's Magazine*, II (September, 1840), 694.
[55] *The Times* (London), 14 Apr 1837, p 7.

Naturally, Lord Campbell's Act produced many fakes who brought cases against the railways and in some instances were given large sums of money.[56]

On occasions when personal luggage was lost on a train, the L & M doubted its liability. Once when a man claimed he lost a bag worth £136, the directors agreed to make a 'donation' of £50. This indicated their unwillingness to admit that they were in any way responsible for lost or stolen luggage. At no time did the L & M admit liability in cases where passengers lost money which had been hidden in luggage or parcels. Insurance was available for those who wished to carry large amounts of money on the trains, but its use was optional. Those who did not use it could not ask the company for repayment if their money was lost while they were in the coaches. In all such cases, the L & M steadfastly refused to pay compensation.

Goods shipped by freight were sometimes sent to the wrong place and were lost by the L & M freight offices. In such cases the company agreed to pay for the material.[57] An indefinite policy was adopted as regards cotton shipped on the line. In 1832, the company informally agreed to assume risk in case of fire from the time the cotton was received by the railway in Liverpool until it was put in the company warehouse at Manchester. On 22 July 1835, a large shipment of cotton was burned while on the line. The directors then sought legal counsel as to whether or not the comapny would be liable. Mr Charles Compton said that, according to the Carriers Act, the company was not liable. But the merchants protested, stating that no notice had been posted at the railway's warehouses or receiving houses. When this new information was submitted to legal counsel, it was decided that the company was liable on goods belonging to Clay, Son & Co, since this was the specific case tried. The directors decided to pay claims to all parties, but this was not an indication that they conceded liability in all cases in the future. Pritt, Clay & Swift, legal counsel to the L & M, then suggested that the company draw up notices as to their liability for all goods shipped, and circulate them to all their prospective customers. The notices were drawn up with legal advice, and the railway made itself liable only on freight that could not be readily hauled away from the railway. To offset any loss, the company's warehouses at each end of the line were insured for £20,000.[58]

[56] R. Smiles, *Memoir of Henry Booth*, pp 71–6 *passim*.
[57] L & M Directors, *Minutes*, Aug 1831.
[58] Great Britain, Parliament, House of Commons, *First Report of Select Committee on Railways*, p 37; Great Britain, Parliament, House of Commons, *Second Report of Select Committee on Railways*, p 224.

Some other general claims made against the railways were settled as individual cases. One party claimed compensation for glass mirrors which were broken while being transported on the line. Pritt & Co told the directors they were not responsible for such breakage. The company was requested to carry gold on several occasions. The directors would not take responsibility for shipping it, but would allow anyone to ship gold on the passenger trains, provided the shipper sent a clerk along. On the first sixty pounds of gold there would be no charge other than the regular fare for the clerk. In other cases the directors categorically refused to pay for a cow that was killed after it wandered on to the tracks, and for a horse that died of a cold due to the 'imperfect condition of the carriage'.

Where accidents on the line involved trains from another company, a special principle was followed as is seen in the agreement with the Grand Junction Company:

Where an accident arises from various causes implicating both companies, or where evidence is not explicit, the damage should be considered the result of accident merely, each company bearing its own particular loss.[59]

To carry this principle into effect, a commission was set up each time such an accident occurred. Representatives from both companies tried to reach an agreement. If this was not possible, the matter was then referred to a court-appointed referee.

E. Development of Safety Consciousness

From the beginning of operations, the L & M was careful to regulate the speed of the trains, especially the passenger trains. During the first year of operations, passenger trains ran at an average of about 17 mph, and were never to go over 20 mph. All trains were required to slow down when crossing public roads, running over high embankments, and approaching places where the locomotives took on more water.[60] In 1831, at the suggestion of George Stephenson, the directors ordered that the first-class trains were not to make the trip between Liverpool and Manchester in less than two hours, and the second-class trains in less than two and one-half hours. The following year, because of improvements to the permanent way, Stephenson suggested that the

[59] L & M Sub-Committee on Liabilities, *Minutes*, 19 Apr 1838; L & M Directors, *Minutes*, 23 Apr 1838 and 21 Nov 1842.
[60] S. Smiles, *Life of George and Robert Stephenson*, viii; L & M Directors, *Minutes*, meetings of 20 Sep and 18 Oct 1830.

time for the first-class trains be cut down to one and one-half hours, and the second-class trains to two hours. If the road was wet, the enginemen were to take more time if they found it necessary.[61] Simon Fenwick, engineman, drove *Vulcan* over the entire line in one hour and eight minutes in December 1832. When he was called before the directors, Fenwick offered as an excuse a strong west wind. Nonetheless, he was reprimanded. Several other cases of early arrivals were reported and the enginemen were warned that disobedience would bring dismissal from the company. In an attempt to put an end to the practice of trains arriving early, the enginemen were ordered not to leave Newton Station until one hour after they had departed from Liverpool or Manchester. In 1834, the time for the first-class trains was cut to one hour and twenty minutes, although it was not unusual for such trains to make the journey in one hour and ten minutes. But enginemen who did this were warned that they would be fined if they did not adhere to the schedule.[62] In 1837, the time for the trip was shortened to one hour and fifteen minutes in the summer months for the first-class trains. It remained one hour and a half during the winter months.[63]

Regulations established in 1840 stated that locomotives were not to go over 25 mph down the inclines and, in going down the Whiston Incline, they were not to increase speed until they reached Huyton Quarry.[64] Trains passing from the L & M to the Grand Junction line were to slow down to 15 mph. The running times established in 1840 remained in effect until 1845. The speeds allowed were not the maximum possible with the L & M equipment at the time[65], but in view of braking problems, it was felt that they were the safest speeds, and they were certainly fast enough for the competition the railways had at the time.

There was little difficulty in regulating the speed of the freight trains. Usually, the loads were so heavy that the trains could do little other than operate at a safe speed. The official time prescribed for all such

[61] At the December meeting, George Stephenson suggested that all bridges should have check rails, or a second set of rails laid within and parallel to the regular rails.

[62] L & M Directors, *Minutes*, 15 May 1834, 9 Feb 1835. One train was reported as having made the trip in one hour and four minutes, including a stop at Newton.— *Manchester Guardian*, 28 Nov 1835, p 2.

[63] L & M Directors, *Minutes*, 9 Oct 1837; L & M *Regulations*, 1840, p 13. The time for the trains to run between London and Liverpool was reduced in 1838 to eleven hours.—*Manchester Guardian*, 26 Sep 1838, p 2, quoting the *Liverpool Times*.

[64] L & M *Regulations*, 1840, pp 17, 25.

[65] *Panther*, pulling a special train, made the trip in forty minutes.—*Manchester Guardian*, 28 Sep 1842, p 2. In 1841, however, George Stephenson suggested that railways should not run their trains faster than 40 mph.—'George Stephenson and the Board of Trade', *The Railway Gazette*, LXXXIX (December, 1948), 744.

trains was two hours and twenty-five minutes between the Liverpool and Manchester freight depots.[66] There were instances of freight trains being run at unsafe speeds, especially when descending the inclines. Frequently, enginemen would attempt to make time on these and the resultant strict regulations for inclines are easily understandable.

The development of a safe system of signals was the one thing wanting in most of the early nineteenth-century railways. Considering the kinds of traffic on the L & M, its early signal system was crude and ineffective. For a few years the signals consisted only of directions given by men along the line with different coloured flags. The difficulty for the engineman was to ascertain the colour and position of the flag as he approached the signalman. The steam, sparks and wind blowing in his face did not help him make a correct interpretation, and thick weather often caused him to miss the signals altogether. Policemen at the stations along the line were also an integral part of the early signal system. If a policeman stood erect with his arms outstretched, that signified a clear line. If he stood at ease, there was something wrong ahead and the engineman was to slow down and use caution. When passengers were waiting at a station, the policeman hoisted a red flag. At night, a swinging lamp was used. Also, the last passenger coach carried a blue light and a red light. When the train was moving the red signal was displayed, and when stopped the blue.[67] This was the extent of the early signal system.

In 1833, first attempts to improve the system were made by erecting flag poles at junctions and crossings. When there was another train on the line, or if some accident had taken place, a flag was hoisted on the pole by the policeman and this would warn an approaching train to stop. In heavy weather these poles and flags were not too effective.[68] The L & M directors, after having studied the printed regulations of the London & Birmingham Railway in 1838, inaugurated several improvements in their signal system. Day and night signals were placed at the points along the line. All locomotives were required to carry a bull's eye lamp[69] at night and, to distinguish the Grand Junction locomotives from those of the L & M, the Grand Junction used two bulls' eye

[66] *Reports Relative to Railways*, p 101.
[67] S. Smiles, *Life of George and Robert Stephenson*, p 333; *Panoramic Exhibition*, 1835, pp 11–12.
[68] L & M Directors, *Minutes*, 27 Feb 1833 and 5 Jul 1838.
[69] The bull's eye lamp was a large lantern-shaped gas lamp with two openings covered with a thick circular lens through which the light was focused. One lens was white, the other red.

lamps.[70] Although the locomotives had whistles before 1839, it was not till after a boy had been killed at Rainhill, while running across the tracks from behind a stopped train, that enginemen approaching a station where a train had stopped were ordered to blow their whistles and slow down.[71]

In 1840, the L & M drew up and had printed regulations for its signal system, which were complete and practical in every way. When locomotives came to public roads they were to give one long whistle when 200 yards away. When enginemen wanted to signal guards or brakesmen to put on the brakes, they would sound the whistle in short quick succession. At night, a white light if stationary meant all was well; if it was waved up and down, it was a signal to stop; if waved sideways, it meant proceed cautiously. During the day the red flag meant stop. A blue flag indicated that a second-class train should stop for passengers or luggage. A black flag indicated the line was under repair and the train was to pass slowly. Finally, a flag or lamp of any colour which was 'violently waved' was always a signal to stop. All tenders were to carry a swivel lamp, one side of which was red and the other white. It was to be changed according to the direction the locomotive was travelling. A set of intricate directions was made for handling the traffic at Newton Junction, both by day and night. The Grand Junction Company readily agreed to the new signals, and bound itself to have its employees observe them. Many other practices inaugurated at this time are still in use on some railways today.[72]

The new signal system was complemented by the regulations drawn up in 1840 for the employees of the company. Blue lights were to be displayed at stations which had passengers waiting for trains. If no passengers were there, then a white light was used. Locomotives were never to be left on the line without someone to take care of the proper signals. All enginemen were required to stop when signalled to do so, whether or not they understood the reason. Every train was to have a red bull's eye reflector on the last coach or wagon, and the guards of the coach trains and brakesmen of freight trains were to make sure that the reflector was changed if any part of the train was detached or

[70] L & M Directors, *Minutes*, 11 Oct, 24 Oct 1838, and 28 Mar 1839. The editor of the *Manchester Guardian* suggested using a type of signal that could be heard. He felt every locomotive should have a bell which would be rung constantly during foggy weather. He said the steam whistle would be better, but it depended on the will of the engine-man, whereas the bell could be rung by the motion of the locomotive.—*Manchester Guardian*, 28 Nov 1838, p 2, and 7 Dec 1838, p 3.
[71] L & M Directors, *Minutes*, 4 Feb 1839.
[72] L & M Railway Co., *Code of Signals To Be Observed on the Liverpool and Manchester Line*, 1840, *passim*, hereinafter cited as L & M *Code Signals*.

augmented. Gatemen were to light the gate lamps at dusk, and have an extra lamp lit for emergency use. In general practice, all employees were warned to be more careful during foggy or thick weather. When trains approached a station, they were to do so with caution, and enginemen were to use the whistle frequently. The practice of running back 400 yards to warn approaching trains of a stalled train was reinforced. Bells were placed at all gatehouses and police stations. When any train approached the bell was rung by the policeman or gateman in charge to give warning to the engineman. It is doubtful whether these bells could be heard by the enginemen and firemen above the noise of the locomotive but, since they served to warn road travellers and pedestrians of the coming train, the bells were kept and always rung.[73]

There were many favourable comments on the L & M *Regulations* as to their thoroughness and effectiveness. But the editor of the *Guardian* stated that some modification was desirable. He felt the red light or the red flag should always be used as a warning against danger.[74] Although red is commonly used today as a danger signal, there is no indication that the L & M ever reverted to the red signal as a sign of danger. There were some parts of the rules for operation that were less than satisfactory. Newton Junction was still the scene of numerous accidents. It was the busiest and most complicated point on the line, and it took time for the new regulations to become effective.[75]

From the company's point of view there were several desirable regulations developed for general good order and safety along the line. In 1833, a policy was adopted of sending a locomotive from each end of the line after the 2.00 pm coach train to clear away any goods dropped and to remove all coal wagons that might get in the way of the evening trains. Handbills were printed and posted on the line warning all people to stay off the railway, and all gatemen and policemen were to stop coming on to the line without evident need. If they failed in this duty they 'would incur the serious displeasure of the Directors'.[76]

[73] L & M *Regulations*, 1840, pp. 5–6, 8, 14–15, 20–1, 23–4, 30. The practice of using blue lights was copied from the Royal Post Office Packets. Mr Edward Woods, with the help of the Eastern Counties Railway, experimented with the blue lights and found them the most effective.—L & M Directors, *Minutes*, 16 Nov, 30 Nov and 7 Dec 1840.   [74] *Manchester Guardian*, 2 Jan 1841, p 4.

[75] Newton Junction was the location of the L & M main line, two curved branches of the Grand Junction, a line connecting with Turner and Evans' Colliery, another line leading to the chemical works of Muspratt & Co, and two roads 200 yards apart.—*The Times* (London), 24 Dec 1841, p 6.

[76] The L & M also posted notices prohibiting people from crossing the Irwell bridge. Further, in 1840, the Board of Trade told the L & M it was responsible for preventing accidents to people not connected with the railway by keeping them from trespassing on the line.—L & M Directors, *Minutes*, 16 Dec 1839, 21 Sep 1840.

Operation of the locomotives was more minutely regulated by the new code of rules drawn up in 1840. Locomotives were never to run on the wrong line, and the engineman and fireman were always to keep a good lookout. If an accident forced a locomotive to go down the wrong line, a man had to be sent ahead with a light and wave it up and down. At the same time, the whistle was to be blown constantly and the locomotive had to go off the wrong line at the nearest points. When locomotives moved in the same direction along the line they were required to keep 600 yards apart, and 900 yards apart on inclines. The trailing locomotive was responsible for maintaining the distance. No engineman was allowed to stop his train in such a way so that part of it would block a public road. For every such offence there was a 10s (50p) fine. Locomotives were only to push coaches or wagons from behind in case of an accident on the line, and then the train was to be pushed only as far as the first siding. If the tracks were obscured by steam or smoke, the trains had to stop and make sure the way was clear before proceeding. Locomotives which were rostered to help trains up the inclines were always to push from behind. They could go only to the top of the incline, and if any policeman, gateman or other employee saw this regulation broken, he was to report it to the directors immediately.[77] Many of these regulations reflect the reaction of the directors to the various types of accident which had been reported to them. As protectors of the proprietors' interests, they were obliged to seek out the safest, most efficient and economical operation of the railway. Thus, these general regulations served both the interests of the railway and the public.

The respect with which the L & M regulations were held at the time is demonstrated by the events of a general railway conference held early in the winter of 1840. Representatives of the Birmingham & Gloucester, Chester & Birkenhead, London & Croydon, Birmingham & Derby Junction, Newcastle & Carlisle, Great Western, Manchester & Leeds, Grand Junction, and the London & Birmingtham Railway organised the meeting, the purpose of which was to draw up general safety regulations. At the suggestion of the London & Birmingham directors, the L & M was asked to prepare a draft of regulations which was to be sent to all the other companies. On 19 January 1841, Charles

[77] L & M *Regulations*, pp 3, 4, 5, 6–7, 8, 9, 18–19; L & M Directors, *Minutes*, 6 Jul 1840. The L & M would allow no steam locomotive to be operated on the line unless a regular engineman was in charge. All other locomotives not authorised to run on the line had to be taken as freight behind an L & M locomotive.—*Rules and Regulations To Be Observed By Enginemen, Guards, Policemen and Others on the Liverpool & Manchester Railway*, 1841, p 23.

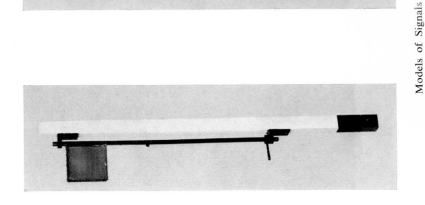

Models of Signals

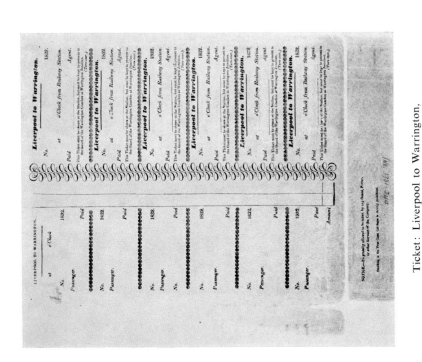

Ticket: Liverpool to Warrington,
c 1832

Page 135

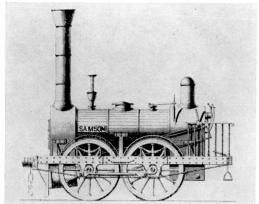

Page 136 'Phoenix', 'Liverpool', 'Samson', and 'Manchester'

Lawrence and Henry Booth went to a second meeting at Birmingham well prepared with printed copies of the L & M rules and regulations as well as copies of the L & M *Code of Signals*. Many of the L & M regulations were adopted without change, and utilised by various members of the conference.[78] This spoke well for the over-all safety rules in effect on the L & M. In just a little over ten years, the 'Grand British Experimental Railway' had produced a set of workable, operational regulations, which became the basis for the development of British railway theory and practice.[79]

F. Policy Towards Employees

One of the most serious problems facing the L & M directors immediately before the public opening of the line was that of obtaining experienced men to operate the locomotives. Because of his past experiences, George Stephenson was asked to recruit the necessary men. His knowledge of locomotives prompted Stephenson to seek men who were known to be steady, sober, have common sense, and a little practical experience in handling the steam locomotive. Unfortunately, there were few such men in the Lancashire area. Stephenson made contacts in the north around Newcastle, and it was from this area that many of the first firemen and enginemen on the L & M came.[80] As time

[78] L & M Directors, *Minutes*, 16 Nov, 30 Nov, 14 Dec, 21 Dec 1840, and 4 Jan 1841; *Manchester Guardian*, 2 Jan 1841, p 4. An interesting note is found in *The Times* which indicates the effect of the L & M regulations. 'Those who were most conversant with the management of railways stated their conviction that by far the greater part of the accidents which had occurred were referable to the neglect and disobedience of orders on the part of railway servants. . . . It must be to an improved state of discipline and more responsibility on the part of men employed on railways that the exemption of accidents must be looked for'. *The Times* (London), 22 Jan 1841, p 4. Another paper pointed out that 'During the same year [1840] 1,052,000 passengers were conveyed upon the Liverpool and Manchester Railway with but one accident—and that one the case of a passenger who recklessly jumped out of a second-class train, whilst it was going at full speed, to save himself a few miles walk'.—*Manchester Guardian*, 6 Feb 1841, p 2.

[79] Great Britain, Parliament, House of Commons, *Report from the Select Committee on Railways appointed to consider whether it is desirable for the Public Safety to vest a Discretionary Power of issuing Regulations for the Prevention of Accidents upon Railways, in the Board of Trade; and if so, under what Conditions and Limitations; Together with the Minutes of Evidence Taken Before Them*, 27 May 1841, pp 74, 94.

[80] S. Smiles, *Life of George and Robert Stephenson*, p 336. In 1832, the directors stated that about sixty enginemen employed by the L & M were from Durham and Northumberland Counties.—*Liverpool and Manchester Railway: Answer of the Directors To an Article in the Edinburgh Review, For October 1832*, Liverpool, Wales and Baines, 1832, pp 7–8.

I

passed, the experience gained by them served to provide a sufficient supply of enginemen and firemen. In 1834, no engineman or fireman could be hired without first being approved by the L & M sub-committee. It was expected that when a man was taken on as fireman, he would eventually be advanced to engineman. Experience in the company's fitters' shops would better qualify a man for either position. When vacancies occurred, the directors felt they should be filled with men from the company repair shops. An additional requirement for new enginemen was the signing of an agreement to give the railway three months' notice before resigning. The contract was to be accompanied with a deposit of £10 as a security for good conduct.[81] With the coming of many new railways in the Lancashire area and in other parts of England, enginemen were frequently taken away from the L & M with promises of higher wages, and this contract was an attempt to put a halt to such a practice.

Few regulations were in existence on the L & M covering coach porters, luggage porters, policemen, gatemen and other workmen. They were taken on if they were able to do the job, and were just as readily dismissed. In 1838, coach porters were told to wear a uniform, which was to include a badge with a number for identification. The outdoor porters were to wear a distinctive badge, and they were to remain in the goods yards and not interfere with other departments of the railway. After making a special study of the situation, a list of regulations was drawn up for the yard porters.[82]

The employment of any man after 1839 was to be in the nature of a nomination. In order, each director would have the right to select a person to fill a vacancy in the company. The individual was to have all the necessary qualities, the most important of which was that he be

[81] L & M Directors, *Minutes*, 13 Nov 1834. In 1840, all newly hired enginemen had to have the printed rules and regulations read to them at least once.—L & M Directors, *Minutes*, meeting of 7 Dec 1840.

[82] L & M Directors, *Minutes*, 12 Feb 1838, 18 Feb, 4 Jul, 21 Oct 1839. Yard porters were to be given two new suits of clothing each year in April and October, and 1s per week was to be deducted from their pay over a period of six months to pay for the clothing. The head superintendent at Manchester, Liverpool and Newton was to wear a distinct uniform. The company supplied the first uniform, and after that the employee supplied it. The superintendent was to call the roll of porters from time to time to see that all were present. It was the duty of the superintendent to see that the numbering of seats in the coaches be done correctly. He was also to inspect hackney coaches entering the yards, allowing only those with a licence to enter, provided they were clean and their drivers had a respectable appearance.— L & M Sub-Committee on Yard Porters & Hackney Coaches, *Minutes*, meeting of 21 Oct 1839. The uniform of the coach porter consisted of a drab or olive jacket, moleskin trousers and a cap.—L & M Committee on Coach Porters, *Minutes*, meeting of 4 Nov 1839.

less than forty years old if applying for the position of a coach porter. Porters in the Lime Street station were given the opportunity of advancing themselves according to seniority. If a vacancy occurred in a higher position, the men in Lime Street would have first choice before anyone else was taken on to fill the vacancy. Other than this, there was little advancement in any of the departments of the railway. The only hope an employee had of advancing was to a higher scale of wages which, for all classes of porters, was rare. When a man grew old or became too ill to fill the original position he held with the railway, the directors then arranged for employment suitable to his age and condition and were sure to see to it that his wages were adjusted accordingly, usually downward.

One of the most controversial points in employer–employee relations on the L & M was the wages of enginemen. They were not paid a weekly wage, but 1s 6d (7½p) each trip. They were paid only for the trips they were booked to make, and were not compensated if they had to make any extra trips. This rate was reduced in 1833 to 1s 3d (6p) per trip, and the firemen's wages were reduced at the same time from 1s (5p) to 10d. If an engineman and fireman were employed on Sunday, they were to be paid 4s (20p) and 3s (15p) respectively for the entire day. Those enginemen who drove the locomotives on the inclines were to receive the same wage as the other enginemen, which was calculated at five trips a day. As a result of the reduction, the enginemen protested. They admitted they could not find better wages elsewhere, and the directors refused to change the wages. A complaint was also made about being constantly assigned to the inclines, since the work was harder and the hours longer. In order to remedy this situation, the directors ordered the enginemen to take turns on the inclines.[83] In studying the wage problem, the sub-committee noticed that the firemen received about 15s (75p) per week as compared to £2 for the enginemen. They felt the difference was too great, and recommended to the directors a reduction in the enginemen's wages and 'perhaps to raise in some degree the Firemen's wages'. The directors approved, and all the enginemen were given three months' notice that their wages would be reduced. Under the new scale, enginemen on passenger trains would receive 1s (5p) per trip and firemen 8d; on freight trains, enginemen were allowed 1s 3d (6p) per trip and firemen 10d. On Sundays all enginemen would get 5s (25p) and firemen 2s 6d (12½p) for the day. For extra wagons picked up, enginemen would get 1d and firemen ½d per wagon. Naturally, the

[83] The complaints of the firemen about the reduction in wages prompted the directors to hire boys to take their places.—L & M Directors, *Minutes*, 2, 22 May 1833.

enginemen did not receive this news with great enthusiasm, and they immediately informed the directors that they intended to quit the service of the railway in a body if the reduction was carried out. The threat was considered by the sub-committee, which found no reason to alter its position, and the treasurer was requested to write to each engineman indicating that he had ten days to change his mind about leaving the company. If the enginemen persisted after ten days their decision would be 'irrevocable' and the directors would hire men elsewhere. On 29 October 1835, the enginemen came to the sub-committee in a body and further protested about the reduction. They mentioned such things as long hours, and the destruction of their clothing, as points that should be reconsidered by the directors. Their appeals fell on deaf ears, and on 8 February 1836 all the enginemen stayed off the job. The railway then took legal action against those who had signed an agreement with the railway not to quit without giving proper notice. The absence of the enginemen at first caused many delays, but men from Mr Melling's shops were hired to run the locomotives and operations were soon back to normal. There was little indication of public sympathy for the enginemen in their strike.

> The engineers on the railway still remain out, but their places are now well supplied, and some three or four of them who left their work contrary to agreement have been sent to study practical mechanics on the rotatory engine at Kirkdale House of Correction, commonly called the tread-mill.[84]

The severity of the measures taken against the enginemen in this case caused the L & M a considerable increase in expenditure for a short time. Many accidents resulted from having 'green' men on the locomotives. Yet, in the minds of the directors, the severe measures more than paid off. It was better to their way of thinking to suffer a financial setback than to give in to the desires of the enginemen.

> The Directors have taken care that their present enginemen should all enter into agreements of service, and they have every reason to believe that the strict measures adopted in this first display of insubordination will tend powerfully to secure discipline and good conduct hereafter.[85]

Here was laissez-faire capitalism in action. It was a question of the enginemen working for the company at company-granted wages and liking it, or not working at all. Eventually the directors had to admit

[84] *Manchester Guardian*, 13 Feb 1836, p 3, quoting the *Liverpool Times*.
[85] *Directors' Reports*, 27 Jul 1836, p 2; *The Times* (London), 29 Jul 1836, p 3.

that they did not have the authority by law to make enginemen sign a promise to give a month's notice before leaving. Even with this admission, the L & M continued to insist that all who applied for the position of enginemen sign the agreement.[86]

In 1839, the enginemen asked for an increase in their salary when they worked the incline planes. Extra time on duty was required at the inclines, because of Grand Junction luggage trains which were assisted at night. A rise was granted, and those enginemen working 'bank engines' were to get 7s (35p) a day for their periodic two-week shift. The firemen were to receive 4s 4d (21½p) a day for the same fourteen-day period. Also, firemen and enginemen in charge of the 7.30 pm train would receive an extra 4d and 6d respectively over and above the ordinary wages for passenger trains.[87] Salaries of the enginemen and firemen then remained as indicated for 1835, except as just mentioned. In 1842, the sub-committee discussed the possibility of reducing wages of all employees because of the general depression of the time. This was never done due to the fact that, before a decision was made, there was a general revival in railway traffic.[88]

Early in its history, the L & M tried to regulate the wages and salaries of the majority of its employees on a scale proportionate to the traffic or net profit of the company. The plan proved to be effective only in the freight and permanent-way departments.[89]

Labourers who were taken on to do general outdoor tasks requiring little or no skill usually averaged about £1 to 23s (£1.15) per week. There were exceptions to the rule and some might receive increases due to longer hours, increase in traffic, or need for special clothing to carry out their duty. Many of the ordinary labourers who worked in the shops received the same level of salary. The following is a list of typical salaries on the L & M:

	s	d		
platelayers	3	6	(17½p)	per day
head parcel porter	18s (90p) to 21		(£1.05)	per week
weighing machine man	21		(£1.05)	per week
gateman—Manchester end	17	6	(87½p)	per week
cokemen—Crown Street	18s (90p) to 21		(£1.05)	per week
firemen—stationary engine, Edge Hill	21		(£1.05)	per week
brakemen—'luggage trains'	21		(£1.05)	per week
policemen	21		(£1.05)	per week
fitters in engine department	4	6	(22½p)	per day[90]

[86] Great Britain, Parliament, House of Commons, *First Report of the Select Committee on Railways*, 26 Apr 1839, p 38.

[87] L & M Directors, *Minutes*, 5, 15 Aug 1839.

[88] The directors intended to make a 10 per cent reduction on all wages at the time.

[89] L & M Directors, *Minutes*, 7, 21 May 1832; *Directors' Reports*, 26 Jul 1832.

[90] L & M Directors, *Minutes*, 1831–5, *Passim*, Whishaw, *Railways*, p, 197.

The clerks in the coach offices were usually paid a stipulated sum for the year. In 1830, Mr Ellwood, head clerk at the Liverpool Coach Office, Dale Street, received £200 per year. The head bookkeeper for the company was paid £150 per year. Clerks in the company's general offices received between £100 and £130 per year. From time to time the clerks' salaries were raised, due to the fact that they incurred many risks and liabilities in handling the money of the company. As the traffic increased, assistants were needed in the coach offices, and boys were hired at 5s (25p) per week. One of the highest salaried clerks in the company's employ was Mr Beausire, who after six years with the L & M was earning a salary of £210 per year. He was head bookkeeper in the company's general office.[91]

Henry Booth, treasurer of the L & M, was the highest paid employee of the company. His salary up until 1834 had been £750, when it was raised to £1,000 per year. Four years later the salary was again increased until it totalled £1,500. His duties were many and his responsibilities more. Booth had been a faithful servant of the L & M from its very inception, and continued his zealous and efficient service even after the L & M amalgamated with the Grand Junction.[92] Other men in the company who held positions of responsibility were paid accordingly.

For example, the superintendent of the Manchester Coach Office received '£2 20s' per week, the superintendent of the Crown Street coal yard 26s (£1.30) per week, the superintendent of the Edge Hill freight station £2 per week, and the foreman of the coach builders £3 10s (£3.50) per week. Mr George Scott, who was hired as sub-engineer, was paid £80 his first year, £90 the second year, and £100 for the third year. Mr John Dewrance, who had charge of the locomotive shops, received £250 during his first year of service, and £300 for the second. Finally, the foreman of the Crown Street yard received £130 per year.[93]

In 1841, the railway decided to apprentice several boys in the various company shops. The first two years they would receive 3s (15p) per week; for the third year 4s (20p) per week, and then a yearly increase of 2s (10p) per week until the seventh year. It was also suggested that one boy should be apprenticed as a mechanical engineer, and learn fitting, turning, pattern making and drawing. But this latter plan did not work out. After 1841, the only way an individual could get employment in the L & M shops was to apprentice himself to the company.[94]

[91] L & M Directors, *Minutes*, 1803–9, *passim*.
[92] L & M Proprietors, *Minutes*, Special General Meeting, 23 Jan 1834 and 25 Jul 1838.
[93] L & M Directors, *Minutes*, 1836–41, *passim*.
[94] L & M Directors, *Minutes*, 28 Jun, 1, 5 Jul, 6 Sep 1841.

The L & M held the right to dismiss employees at any time it felt the need arose. In 1832, due to a decrease in passenger traffic, the directors decided to dispense with five enginemen. George Stephenson wanted one of the enginemen, and the remaining four could stay with the company if they chose to do so. If they did, nine firemen instead of five would be dismissed. The nine firemen were to be given about ten days' notice of their discharge, and there was no indication that they would receive any bonus considering the circumstances of their dismissal. At the same time, twenty policemen received notice that their services were no longer needed by the railway. But the L & M paid them two weeks' wages before they let them go. In 1833, an economy move on the part of the company brought about the dismissal of several employees. Mr Allcard was told to discharge six of his platelayers, and Mr Dixon was to dispense with ten. All engine fitters were warned that many would be redundant in the near future and they should be on the 'lookout for new situations'. In 1839, Mr Melling, head of the locomotive shops, and his two assistants Grays and Tyfe, were told that after three months their services would no longer be needed. The cause was given as 'changes in the Locomotive Department'.[95] There were frequent dismissals for misconduct on the part of employees. The directors did not hesitate to dismiss those men who were found drunk while on duty, and it was a rare case when one was rehired. This policy of the company was reinforced by an Act of Parliament passed in 1840, making it legal for any officer or agent of the railway to detain any employee who was found drunk or violating the rules and regulations. The offender could be brought before a Justice of the Peace immediately and without warrant. The main purpose of this Act was to protect the safety and welfare of the public, and it indirectly protected the interests of the railways.[96]

From time to time the employees of the L & M were rewarded with premiums and bonuses. Good conduct, care of the equipment, an increase in traffic, personal services rendered to the company, long and faithful service, and a record free of accidents, were the many reasons given by the railway for the granting of the bonus.[97] In one instance the

[95] L & M Directors, *Minutes*, 23 Dec 1839.

[96] L & M Directors, *Minutes*, 20 Dec 1830 and 11 Apr 1831; 3 & 4 Victoria, *c.* xcvii, 10 Aug 1840; *Manchester Guardian*, 14 Oct 1840, p 3. Frequently coach porters would take money from passengers for little 'extra' services performed, or the guards would not charge passengers full fare. Both actions caused discharge from the company.— L & M Directors, *Minutes*, 29 Jul and 16 Sep 1839.

[97] L & M Directors, *Minutes*, 1833–42, *passim*. In 1843, the L & M set up a circulatory library and reading room for the employees. The directors had to approve of the books and periodicals used there.—L & M Directors, *Minutes*, 7 Aug 1843.

bonus, granted because of an increase in traffic with consequent longer working hours, became an integral part of the wages. At Wapping station the men were content to forgo the bonus and work shorter hours. In each individual case a man was given his choice.[98]

The directors of the L & M were interested in having their employees save some of their earnings for unforeseeable contingencies. A plan for an annuity fund was circulated by the directors in 1831. But there was never any indication as to whether the employees accepted the plan as a group. The original policy of the L & M was to give some financial aid where employees were sick or injured. A wheel and axle examiner who was confined with an injury was given 5s (25p) per week while out of work since he had been with the company for six years. The medical expenses for two brakesmen and one workman, seriously injured while at work, were paid by the company. When a man was injured on the line, a notice was sent to the treasurer when 'surgical treatment' was necessary. It was then up to the treasurer to decide how long the treatment would continue at the expense of the railway. This usually meant that when the railway decided to stop paying the doctor's bills the injured man was 'recovered'.[99] This policy on the part of the L & M continued up till 1837, when Hardman Earle proposed that in the future the railway would not pay half wages to men who were injured on the line. Instead, Earle felt the employees should be advised to join a Benefit Society, and the directors agreed not to take on anyone in the future who was not a member of such an organisation.[100] In 1841, a survey found that 883 employees out of a total of 1,180 belonged to 'Benefit Clubs'. Only a very small proportion of the men in these organisations were employed at the Manchester station and at this time they were warned of the advisability of getting into such a group 'as the Directors consider themselves absolved from any obligation to assist men under accidents or sickness who refuse to join some Benefit Society'.[101] After this announcement, no payments were made by the

[98] The porters at Wapping had to work from 6.00 am till 10.00 pm and sometimes till 11.00 pm or 12.00 midnight. They made between 19s and 20s per week, 3s of which was in the form of a bonus. It would take between thirty to 130 extra men to shorten the hours. The men were willing to give up the bonus for the shorter hours. When the final settlement was made, the L & M 'liberally' gave up its portion of the bonus, allowing the men to receive 19s per week and an extra 1s 6d bonus. The new hours were from 6.00 am to 9.30 pm, or 8.30 am to 11.00 pm.—L & M Directors, *Minutes*, 27 Jun and 5 Sep 1844.

[99] L & M Directors, *Minutes*, 1831–34, *passim*.

[100] As late as 1840, the directors made some exceptions to Earle's proposal. A labourer asked for 10s (50p) per week for the fifteen weeks he was laid up, and it was granted.—L & M Directors, *Minutes*, 4 Jun 1840.

[101] L & M Directors, *Minutes*, 14 Jun 1841.

L & M to employees injured on the line. Even in cases where employees were killed on duty, the railway did not hold itself liable to the survivors. When petitioned for assistance in such cases, the directors would let the treasurer consider the merits of the case, and he usually made a contribution from the benevolent fund.[102]

Successful operations on the L & M were a good indication that in all phases of railway practice, the 'Grand British Experimental Railway' provided gratifying and successful results. A sound investment, an excellent permanent way, and the best to be had in rolling stock, could alone never have produced a railway. One thing more was needed to complete the organisation. Freight and passenger operations carried out safely, swiftly and economically were necessary to prove to Britain and the world that the L & M was truly a success. No other method than trial and error could be used, and yet everything depended on the successful outcome of this last phase of the experiment. It is to the credit of the directors, their engineers and their employees that the goal could have been accomplished with relatively little 'error' when one considers the many 'unknowns' the railway had to meet. The operational success of the L & M was hailed throughout the world. It was not a success that came all at once, but one that resulted from a long and difficult series of experiements carried out with courageous self-confidence. We need not look to the L & M alone for evidence of its success. The influence of the Liverpool & Manchester Railway was felt all over England, the Continent, America, and even as far as India. The L & M directors received many requests to testify on behalf of proposed railways before Parliament, and the members of Parliament did not hesitate to call on the L & M for experienced men to assist their various investigations concerning railways. A constant stream of mail reached the directors requesting information on such things as experiments with locomotives, rails, coaches, wagons and communications. Many railways sent observers to the L & M to learn about railway techniques used, so that they could stay clear of the many pitfalls the L & M had been unable to avoid through lack of information. Finally, many newspapers, periodicals, journals and other literary works of the time testify to the great influence of the L & M on the development of the railway, and the great debt of gratitude many railways owed to the Liverpool & Manchester.[103]

[102] L & M Directors, *Minutes*, 5 Dec 1832. Another attempt to found a savings organisation was made in 1841. However, it never got off the ground.—L & M Directors, *Minutes*, 26 Apr 1841.

[103] The following railways sought information, aid or testimony from the L & M: Sheffield & Manchester, Edinburgh & Glasgow, North Union, Wigan, Hull & Selby,

London & Birmingham, Grand Junction, London & Greenwich, Manchester & Cheshire, Brighton, Glasgow, Paisley & Greenock, Midland Counties, Newcastle & Carlisle, Sheffield & Rotherham, Birmingham & Gloucester, Lancaster & Preston, Preston & Wyre, Blackwall, Manchester & Leeds, Dublin & Kingstown, Baltimore & Ohio, Leipsig & Dresden, Paris & Rouen.—L & M Directors, *Minutes*, 1831–45, *passim*. Visits were received from and information given to the following groups or important personages: King of the Netherlands, Turkish Ambassador, a group of German engineers, The French Consul, Council of the British Association of Science, and the Railway Society of London.—L & M Directors, *Minutes*, meetings of 2 Mar 1834, 16 Feb 1835, 25 Apr 1836, 9 Oct, 14 Aug 1837, and 15 Jul 1839. Testimony of the great contributions and influence of the L & M on other railways is found in the following: Cecil John Allen, *Railways of Britain*, London, Thomas Nelson and Sons, 1958, p 13; C. H. Ellis, *Four Main Lines*, London, George Allen and Unwin, 1950, p 125; 'The Centenary of the Liverpool and Manchester Railway', *The Engineering Journal*, XIII (September, 1930), 564; Jackman, *Transportation in Modern England*, II, p 548; Lambert, *Railway King*, p 28; Lardner, *Lectures on the Steam-Engine*, pp 198–9; Edward T. McDermott, *History of the Great Western Railway*, 2 vols, London, Great Western Railway Company, 1927, I, 3; *Manchester Guardian*, 28 May 1831, p 2; 7 Jul 1832, p 1; 5 Jan 1833, p 3; 8 Jun 1837, p 3; 14 May 1842, p 2; 1 Feb 1845, p 6; Marshall, *Centenary History*, vi; 'A Chapter in Transport History: Centenary of Liverpool-Manchester Railway', *Modern Transport*, XXII (January, 1930), 8; 'Liverpool-Manchester Centenary', *Modern Transport*, XXIII (August, 1930), 1; 'Foundations of the Railway System', *Modern Transport*, XXIII (September, 1930), 2; 'Liverpool and Manchester Railway', *Museum*, (December, 1830), 499; A. Notre, *Description of the Railroad from Liverpool to Manchester, Together With a History of Railroads, and Matters Connected Therewith*, Trans. J. C. Stocker, Boston, Hilliard, Gray, 1833, p 7; Andrew C. O'Dell, *Railways and Geography*, London, Hutchinson's University Library, 1956, pp 149–50; Pangborn, *World's Railways*, p 60; de Pambour, *Treatise*, vi; 'Railways', *The People's Magazine*, I (October, 1833), 127; *The Pioneer Period of European Railroads: A Tribute to Thomas W. Streeter*, Boston, Baker Library, Harvard Graduate School of Business Administration, p 5; Sherrington, *One Hundred Years*, p 36; R. Smiles, *Memoir of Henry Booth*, p 49; James S. Walker, *An Accurate Description of the Liverpool and Manchester Rail-Way, The Tunnel, The Bridges and other Works throughout the Line; with a Sketch which it presents Interesting to the Traveller or Tourist*, Paterson, N. J., D. Burnett, 1830, title page; Whishaw, *Railways*, pp 186–7; Wood, *Treatise*, x-xi.

CHAPTER VI

Growth of the System and Amalgamation

A. Branch Lines

When the Liverpool & Manchester was in its projection stage, there were various other lines under consideration seeking to serve the Lancashire area. Eventually, several of these made a connection with the L & M. Some had an agreement for running powers, others to pay tolls for freight and passengers carried on the L & M. In one case, the St Helens Railway merely crossed the L & M, and had no official agreements with the company. One advantage for branch lines having a connection with the L & M was direct access to Liverpool and Manchester. Since the branch railway could provide direct service to the two largest cities in Lancashire, there was a general increase in traffic on these railways. Hence, when contracts were drawn up between the L & M and the branch railways, the L & M was in a better position to bargain since it controlled the flow of rail traffic between Liverpool and Manchester. And the L & M was, for the most part, interested in making favourable arrangements with the branch lines, since this meant an increase in traffic with a resultant increase in income.

The Bolton & Leigh Railway, opened in June 1831, was one of the first connecting railways to the L & M. It was $7\frac{3}{4}$ miles long and ran between the Manchester, Bolton & Bury Canal, at Bolton, and the Leeds & Liverpool Canal at Leigh. Although the Bolton & Leigh did not originally intend to have a connection with the L & M, the link was made when the Bolton & Leigh took over the operations of the Kenyon & Leigh Junction Railway. The latter was only $2\frac{1}{2}$ miles long and had as its specific purpose the connection of the L & M and the Bolton & Leigh. Once the Kenyon & Leigh Junction and Bolton & Leigh were operational, merchants and passengers using the L & M had direct rail connections with Bolton, and from Bolton it was easy to reach Bury via the Manchester, Bolton & Bury Canal.[1]

The Bolton & Leigh and the Kenyon & Leigh Junction companies

---

[1] Lewin, *Early Railways*, p 24; *Directors' Reports*, 28 Mar 1831.

contracted with John Hargreaves of Bolton to provide locomotives and rolling stock and operate both railways. Thus, the L & M dealt directly with Hargreaves in drawing up the necessary arrangements for running powers, tolls, rates, and other necessary agreements for these branch lines. The L & M insisted that Hargreaves provide all the necessary locomotives for his line as soon as possible. Until he could do this, the L & M would provide locomotives to the extent that they were needed on its own line. For all coal carried between Manchester and Kenyon, Hargreaves would pay the L & M 1s (5p) per ton. The charge on each passenger to Manchester would be 1s 3d (6p) and from Manchester the charge would be 1s (5p). Hargreaves could not charge any passenger between Manchester, Leigh or Kenyon less than 2s 6d (12½p) inside and 2s (10p) outside. This latter regulation would assure the L & M that its passenger traffic between Manchester and Kenyon would encounter no competition.[2] The Leeds & Liverpool Canal represented a major competition for freight, so Hargreaves asked the L & M to relieve him of his obligations so that he could effectively compete with the canal. To do this, the L & M estimated average tolls for the months of February, March and April 1832. Hargreaves then signed a three-month contract in which he agreed to pay the average tolls as calculated by the L & M. In effect, Hargreaves had to pay much less than had been agreed to in the original arrangements, but the L & M expected Hargreaves and the Bolton & Leigh to make proportionate reductions in order to meet the canal competition.[3] Since a new agreement seemed desirable on the passenger side, the L & M agreed to book passengers for the Bolton & Leigh and carry them to Kenyon Junction, where they would then change to a Bolton & Leigh train. Passengers coming from Bolton would be picked up by the L & M Blue Coaches and taken to Manchester. The charges for passengers would still be 2s 6d (12½p) first class and 2s (10p) second class. Instead of an individual tax on each passenger, the L & M would receive two-thirds of the gross receipts, while the Bolton & Leigh would take one-third.

The continued competition of the Leeds & Liverpool Canal caused both the Bolton & Leigh Railway and Hargreaves to complain to the L & M of their financial difficulties. The L & M, to protect its own

[2] L & M Directors, *Minutes*, 12 May and 26 Dec 1831. The L & M supplied the Bolton & Leigh with coke and also sold them one of its locomotives.—L & M Directors, *Minutes*, 3 Oct 1831 and 2 Jan 1832.

[3] L & M Directors, *Minutes*, 7 May 1832. In its anxiety to keep the Bolton & Leigh operational, the L & M dropped the charge of 2s (10p) per trip for the use of the L & M assistant locomotives.—L & M Directors, *Minutes*, meeting of 21 May 1832.

interests, warned the canal company that if it continued to carry freight to Leigh at half the authorised rate, the L & M would take steps to interfere with the rates on the canal between Wigan and Liverpool. At the same time, the L & M reduced the contract price with the Bolton & Leigh to £1,000 for as long as the canal competition continued.[4] Hargreaves was still not satisfied, and he made known his intentions of giving up his contract to operate the Bolton & Leigh. In order to remedy the situation, the L & M set up a special committee which decided to reduce the charges made on Hargreaves by the freight department.[5] Nevertheless the situation continued to be grave, and it was decided that either the Bolton & Leigh or Hargreaves should pay the Leeds & Liverpool Canal Company £1,800 per year. In this way the canal would agree to charge the authorised rates and relieve competition with the Bolton & Leigh. Shortly after this acceptable arrangement was made, traffic increased on the Bolton & Leigh to the extent that the L & M felt it necessary to raise the rates charged on the Bolton traffic passing over the L & M.[6] Conditions remained about the same until 1842, when Hargreaves petitioned the L & M to reduce its rates. He felt that competition was again hurting him, and he also wanted relief from the fine which was payable to the Leeds & Liverpool Canal when he did not ship fifty tons of freight on the canal each day. The committee on Bolton traffic refused to recommend the reduction in spite of Hargreaves's threat to give up operations on the Bolton & Leigh. As usual, Hargreaves did not carry out his threat. In 1844, the L & M proprietors gave the directors permission to make arrangements with the Bolton & Leigh for the consolidation of interests. This consolidation eventually took place when both companies amalgamated with the Grand Junction.[7]

In 1831, the Warrington & Newton Railway was opened between the

[4] L & M Directors, *Minutes*, 19 Nov 1832.

[5] L & M Directors, *Minutes*, 2 Jun and 4 Aug 1834. In December 1832, Hargreaves made one of his many threats not to renew his lease on the Bolton & Leigh. The L & M directors suggested that the Bolton & Leigh purchase Hargreaves's rolling stock and run the line itself; the L & M would charge only £2,000 on freight passing over its line. Once he saw how easily he could be replaced, Hargreaves did not let his lease run out.—L & M Directors, *Minutes*, 24 Dec 1832. In order to give Hargreaves a better position in the competition with the canal, the L & M allowed him to carry freight to Chorley, Burnley and other places along the canal via Wigan instead of going through Leigh. For this privilege Hargreaves was charged £100 per month as long as his freight totals did not double.—L & M Directors, *Minutes*, 6 Oct 1834.

[6] L & M Directors, *Minutes*, 3 Aug and 21 Sep 1835; L & M Committee on Bolton Traffic, *Minutes*, 17 Jul 1837. Tolls on freight between Liverpool and Bolton were raised from 1s 6d (7½p) to 2s (10p) per ton, and from 1s (5p) to 1s 3d (6p) per ton between Manchester and Bolton.

[7] L & M Proprietors, *Minutes*, Special General Meeting, 24 Jul 1844.

towns of Warrington and Newton Le Willows, where the line connected with the L & M. The total length of the W & N was 4½ miles, and from the outset it received enthusiastic backing from the L & M. The directors agreed to provide the necessary locomotives and wagons for the W & N until that railway could get its own. For each passenger carried by the L & M to Liverpool or Manchester from Newton, the L & M was to receive 1s 6d (7½p). The charge for the intermediate stations was to be not less than 1s (5p), except when passengers were taken only between Newton Junction and Kenyon Junction, in which case the toll would be 6d. If the Warrington company desired, it was allowed to attach one of its coaches to a second-class L & M train, provided it paid 2s 6d (12½p) for each second-class passenger, and 3s (15p) for each first-class passenger. On the freight side, the L & M agreed to provide locomotives between Newton Junction and Manchester, take care of the delivery and collection of freight, and manage operations at Manchester, all for a charge of 4s 2d (21p) per ton. Freight shipped to Liverpool under the same conditions was charged at 5s (25p) per ton. The freight wagons and tarpaulins were to be supplied by the Warrington company. However, with both freight and passengers, L & M tolls proved to be excessive for the W & N since anticipated traffic volume was not realised. As a result, the L & M agreed to reduce the tolls.

One of the innovations on the L & M as a result of its connection with the Warrington & Newton was the transporting of a few London stages each day between Liverpool and Warrington. People would board the stage in Liverpool after it had been fixed to a flat wagon. Having arrived by train in Warrington, the stage would then go over the regular turnpikes to London.[8] This practice was stopped in 1837 when the Warrington & Newton Railway, having been absorbed by the Grand Junction, formed a part of that main line which in turn provided direct rail service between London and Liverpool via Birmingham.

Another offshoot from the Liverpool & Manchester Railway was the Wigan Branch Railway which ran to the town of Wigan, leaving the L & M main line at Parkside. It had a branch of its own, called the Springs Branch, three miles long and serving nearby collieries. The main line was seven miles long. It is interesting to note that the Act providing for the construction of the Wigan Branch Railway required the line to be built under the direction of L & M engineers. This was an early indication of the close association the two companies were to have throughout the Wigan company's short history.[9]

[8] L & M Directors, *Minutes*, 28 May 1832.   [9] George IV, *c.* lvi, 29 May 1830.

The Wigan Branch was ready for operations in June 1832, but the Wigan company was not ready or able to operate it. Hence, in July 1832, Theodore Rathbone, William Blaine and James Chapman, representing the Wigan company, asked the L & M directors to operate the line in their own way and on their own terms for a few months. In this way the Wigan company would be able to determine a reasonable rate of rent for the line. The L & M directors agreed and operations were begun on this basis. For three months, the L & M supplied locomotives and coaches to run between Wigan and Parkside and L & M porters were likewise used. At the Wigan end of the line, the Wigan company provided clerks, porters and other needed workmen. The passenger fare between Liverpool and Manchester and Wigan was 5s (25p) first class and 3s 6d (17½p) second class. The L & M kept all receipts it made on its own line and received one-half the gross receipts collected at Wigan. The L & M also provided locomotives for the freight traffic along with the necessary wagons. The toll on freight carried between either Liverpool or Manchester and Wigan was 5s (25p) per ton. The directors felt that, as the arrangements stood in August 1832, they would be 'inadequately' compensated, unless the Wigan Branch created increased traffic on the L & M.[10] On 23 January 1833, the directors reported that the Wigan Branch Railway had failed to bring the desired traffic increase. Yet, six months later, they reported a considerable rise in passenger receipts, freight traffic, and parcel business because of the Wigan Branch.[11] In 1834, the Wigan Branch and the Preston & Wigan Railway consolidated under the title of the North Union Railway,[12] and this brought additional traffic to the L & M as will be seen below.

The St Helens & Runcorn Gap Railway, one of the largest colliery lines, extended from St Helens to the River Mersey, seven miles distant. Although its main line crossed the L & M main line by viaduct, the two railways were joined by spurs. Freight was carried via these spurs to St Helens at a charge of 4s 6d (22½p) per ton. In 1834, the L & M allowed one of its 'closed coaches to run along the St Helens line for the accommodation of Southport passengers to and from Manchester'.

[10] The L & M contracted with Hargreaves to manage the Wigan Branch freight operations, charging him 3s (15p) per ton. He gave this up in 1835, and a Mr John Hargreaves offered to manage Wigan freight traffic using L & M locomotives on the Wigan line, and using his own wagons, the charge being 2s 6d (12½p) per ton. L & M Directors, *Minutes*, 8 Oct 1832, 12 Oct, and 21 Dec 1835.

[11] *Directors' Reports*, 23 Jan and 24 Jul 1833.

[12] *Directors' Reports*, 23 Jul 1834; Marshall, *Centenary History*, p. 118.

It was up to the St Helens Company to keep the coach in repair.[13] In 1844, the St Helens Canal and Railway,[14] formerly the St Helens & Runcorn Gap Railway, proposed to build a line directly from St Helens through the Rainford coalfield and then to Southport via Bickerstaff and Ormskirk, but nothing came of this.[15]

Many of the colliery owners in the area served by the Liverpool & Manchester Railway asked the permission of the company to make a rail connection from their collieries in order to facilitate the transport of their coal. In general, the L & M was agreeable to most proposals for such connections. Lines were laid to Mr Willis's collieries at Halsnead and Whiston. Since these branches would bring more traffic on to the L & M, the owners of the collieries charged the company a toll on any of their coal it carried. Also, special concessions had to be made to those people whose property was crossed by these rail links.[16]

The L & M had plans for many more extensions and branch lines and was a very active participant in the 'railway mania' of the middle 1840s. In May 1845, the L & M petitioned Parliament for powers to 'extend and enlarge the said Railway and to make certain Branch Railways'. Two months later the L & M received the powers requested. These included permission to build a branch railway and tunnel from Edge Hill to Smithdown Lane in West Derby. Another branch was to be built from Patricroft to the Manchester, Bury & Rossendale Railway, making a junction with that railway and passing through Barton-upon-Irwell, Worsley, Winton, Monton, Little Houghton, Swinton, Pendlebury and Clifton. A third branch was to run between Newton and Parkside on the main line of the L & M and terminate in a junction with

[13] L & M Directors, *Minutes*, 19 Nov 1832, 15 Sep 1834; Marshall, *Centenary History*, p 116–17.

[14] After merging with the Sankey Brook Navigation Company, the St Helens & Runcorn Gap Railway was known as the St Helens Canal and Railway.

[15] L & M Directors, *Minutes*, 2 Sep, 16 Sep, and 19 Sep 1844 (special meeting). Special arrangements were made with other Lancashire railways and individuals. The L & M arranged to sell through tickets from Manchester and Liverpool to Lancaster via the Lancaster & Preston Railway. Mr Blundell, a coal dealer, was permitted to run his own locomotive between Parkside and Liverpool at the regular Parliamentary toll. In 1845, the Bury & Rossendale Railway was granted the use of Victoria Station, Manchester. The charge was 2d, 1½d, and 1d respectively on first, second and third-class passengers.—L & M Directors, *Minutes*, 20 May 1841, 10 Jan 1842, 19 May, 2 Jun 1845.

[16] L & M Directors, *Minutes*, 15 Nov 1830, 17 Oct 1831, 22 Oct 1832, and 8 Apr 1833; Marshall, *Centenary History*, pp 116–17. Mr Willis and his partner, John Ashton Case, received 1½d on every ton of coal belonging to them carried along the line. In order to compensate Mr Unsworth for crossing his property, the L & M had to give him £300 per year and carry his coal from Huyton Hey Colliery to Liverpool free of charge.—L & M Directors, *Minutes*, 31 Dec 1832 and 19 Aug 1833.

the North Union Railway at Lowton. Still another branch was proposed to start at a junction with the St Helens Canal and Railway's line near St Helens station and terminate in Rainford Township, passing through Prescot, Windle, Sutton, Parr and Rainford.[17] But before these lines were put under construction, the L & M was amalgamated with the Grand Junction. The L & M's contribution to the 'railway mania' demonstrates that this was a very active company with great plans for the future. In this case amalgamation was not a matter of giving way to others who had more energetic notions of railway operations. It was strictly a good business deal. Again, the L & M directors evidenced sound judgement in their position as protectors of the proprietors' investments.

B. Junction Lines

More extensive and complicated operations and agreements were shared by the L & M with the Grand Junction and the North Union Railways. Both of these actually ran their equipment over the main line of the L & M. As early as 1833, four years before the Grand Junction became operational, arrangements were being drawn up for the proposed railway to run both freight and passenger trains over the L & M to Manchester and Liverpool. The basis of all these agreements was the principle of mutual advantage.[18] The preliminary arrangements had been negotiated by the L & M directors without the counsel of the proprietors. When workable agreements had been completed, the directors called a special meeting of the proprietors in July 1834 to get their approval; this was obtained with little difficulty.[19]

The Warrington & Newton having been absorbed by the Grand Junction company in 1835, the latter proposed that the L & M operate the W & N line for two years, starting in 1835, and pay the Grand Junction £3,000 per year. Considering the amount of traffic on the W & N and the terms laid down by the Grand Junction, the L & M directors refused to take on the responsibility. Arrangements were then made to lease the line to Mr George Stubbs until the GJR became operational. Eventually, the Grand Junction Company operated the W & N, and on learning of this the L & M directors informed the Grand Junction directors that they would hold them responsible for all accounts due from the W & N to the L & M. In reality, then, the first

[17] 8 & 9 Victoria, c, cxxiii, 21 Jul 1845; L & M Proprietors, *Minutes*, Special General Meeting, 20 May 1845; L & M Directors, *Minutes*, 6 Jan, 23 Jan, 3 Mar, and 24 Mar 1845.
[18] L & M Directors, *Minutes*, 19 Aug and 25 Nov 1833.
[19] L & M Proprietors, *Minutes*, Special General Meeting, 23 Jul 1834.

link of the main line of the Grand Junction Railway was opened six years before the major portion of the line between Warrington and Birmingham was completed.

Because of the level terrain, and other natural conditions conducive to railway construction, the Grand Junction line was completed in record time and at a comparatively low cost per mile. The construction engineer in this project was Joseph Locke, who had served under George Stephenson during the construction of the Liverpool & Manchester. From the outset of the construction, the Grand Junction anticipated an early opening. As early as 1835, the company had coaches and wagons built; it was officially opened on 4 Jul 1837.

The increase in traffic created by the opening of the Grand Junction called for new porters, police and luggagemen. It was agreed that these men should, for the most part, be employed by the L & M; and the L & M would in turn charge the Grand Junction for the extra expenditure.[20] As regards the freight traffic, the Grand Junction was to use its own locomotives for freight carried between Liverpool, Manchester and Warrington. Out of the charge of 6s (30p) per ton on freight, two-thirds was to go to the L & M, 2s (10p) being the toll and 11¾d the charge for porters and clerks. Six months later, the L & M decided to operate the GJ freight departments at Manchester and Liverpool independently. Clerks, porters, trucks, and cranes for loading, receiving, and dispatching the Grand Junction freight would be provided at a charge of 18d (7½p) per ton. Additional charges were made for books and stationery. Finally, if Grand Junction equipment was damaged by fire or because of the negligence of L & M employees, the former could not hold the latter responsible for any losses.[21] In 1839, the part of the

[20] L & M Directors, *Minutes*, 24 Jun 1837. The advantages of the mutual arrangements entered into by both companies is indicated in a statement issued by a committee appointed to examine the quarterly report of the Grand Junction: '. . . It appears clear that by a joint working under one management the expenditures under these heads will be considerably less than if each company were to provide their own separate Establishment of Porters, Gatemen etc. what appears to your committee, therefore, the correct principle, . . . to be adopted in the future, is to ascertain by comparison of the work done, and service performed, what would be the cost to each company on a separate and independent system of working'.—L & M Directors, *Minutes*, meeting of 16 Oct 1837; Great Britain, Parliament, House of Commons, *Second Report of Select Committee on Railways*, 9 Aug 1839, ix.

[21] L & M Directors, *Minutes*, 24 Jun, 11 Dec 1837. In 1838, the Grand Junction told the L & M it would carry freight between Liverpool, Manchester and Birmingham beginning on 1 Feb 1838. L & M Directors, *Minutes*, 15 Jan 1838. At one time, the Grand Junction proposed to build a branch line to join the L & M near Huyton via Fiddler's Ferry, but eventually dropped the idea. L & M Proprietors, *Minutes*, Annual General Meeting, 24 Jan 1838; L & M Directors, *Minutes*, 29 Jan, 23 Apr 1839; L & M Sub-Committee, *Minutes*, 1 Feb 1838.

agreement which covered the handling of Grand Junction freight at both ends of the L & M was modified. The new charge for porters and agents was 1s 9d (9p) per ton instead of 18d (7½p).[22]

Although an agreement was reached for charges on Grand Junction passengers travelling over the L & M line, there is no indication as to the specific parts of the contract. The L & M required the Grand Junction to submit a weekly statement as to the number of passengers and parcels carried over its line. When reporting the first return on passengers received from the Grand Junction, the L & M directors were not too enthusiastic. From 4 July 1837 to 31 December 1837, the Grand Junction paid the L & M £7,539 in tolls on passengers, but the directors reminded the proprietors:

> This sum however must not be considered as clear accession of income. The Warrington Passenger Traffic previously belonged to the Company, and in a more profitable form than at present; and the Directors apprehend that a pretty large class of Travellers, especially those from Ireland, Scotland and Foreign parts, who formerly proceeded by the Railway to Manchester and then Southward, now take their places in the Grand Junction Trains, direct to Birmingham or London.[23]

Even though the situation as stated by the directors was true, there was no evidence of any attempt on their part to remedy it. One gets the impression that the overall income from the Grand Junction was satisfactory.

Where two separate companies were working so close together, there was bound to be many suggestions, counter-suggestions, complaints, adjusting of agreements, and disagreements. In 1840, the Grand Junction company asked for a new locomotive shed. The L & M refused, pointing out that the heavy expenditure already made on similar buildings would require a higher return from the Grand Junction than 6 per cent. The turntables in the Grand Junction locomotive shed were too weak for the locomotives, and the company requested new ones. The L & M agreed to get these on the understanding that they would be its own property. Permission was given to the Grand Junction to run an extra train from both ends of the line during the Grand

[22] L & M Directors, *Minutes*, 2 Sep 1839. Other carriers using the Grand Junction and L & M lines for freight between Liverpool, Manchester and London were charged 2s 3d (11p) per ton.—L & M Sub-Committee, *Minutes*, 7 Nov 1938.

[23] L & M Directors, *Minutes*, 23 Oct 1837; *Directors' Reports*, 24 Jan 1838; *Manchester Guardian*, 11 Jul 1838, p 3. In case of emergency, both companies agreed to borrow locomotives at a charge of 5s (25p) per mile. This was to include the crew's wages, fuel, water, and ordinary wear and tear.

Music Festival in Birmingham. When the L & M laid heavier rails at Edge Hill, the Grand Junction was ordered to pay 6 per cent for their use since the L & M had paid the original cost.[24] A rather involved argument developed over the rental of buildings. The Grand Junction wanted to be released of its obligations to rent all the warehouses, sheds and other parts of L & M premises agreed to in the original contract. Legal counsel for the L & M stated the Grand Junction did not have the power to do so. However, in the face of continued Grand Junction pressure, the L & M finally agreed to allow the company to sublet the buildings as long as the tenants were approved by the L & M. Even though this proved unsatisfactory to the Grand Junction, the L & M remained firm and refused to allow the company to stop paying rent on all buildings originally contracted for.[25] These typical instances of the dealings between the two companies until their eventual amalgamation in 1845 are noteworthy in so far as many L & M directors were also GJR shareholders. No doubt the situation likewise reflected the powerful influence the Duke of Sutherland exercised in L & M affairs.

The second of the junction lines, the North Union Railway, was formed when the Wigan Branch Railway and the Preston & Wigan Railway amalgamated in 1834. The directors of the North Union Company wanted to develop these two branch lines into a major railway to serve northern Lancashire. It would be to their advantage to make a junction with the Liverpool & Manchester and run their trains directly to either Liverpool or Manchester. With this in mind, the North Union company contacted the L & M directors in 1837, and the latter were more than anxious to enter into reciprocal arrangements. Immediately, the L & M set up a committee on rates and tolls for the North Union line. Its first recommendation was that an arrangement similar to that made with the Grand Junction should be entered into with the North Union.[26] This was not going to be as easy as it sounded. It was first suggested that between Preston, Liverpool and Manchester the railway would be worked jointly; each company was to provide locomotives and a certain number of passenger coaches. In return, the L & M would receive 2s 6d (12½p) for each first-class passenger, and 2s (10p) for each second-class passenger carried. Each company was to be responsible for repairs to coaches, accidents on its own line, and the government tax on passengers. Both companies would keep passenger

[24] L & M Directors, *Minutes*, 2 Mar 1840, 4 May, 14 Sep, 29 Mar 1841.
[25] L & M Directors, *Minutes*, 3 Jan, 21 Jan, 7 Feb 1842, 23 Jan, and 1 May 1843.
[26] L & M Committee on Rates & Tolls for North Union Line, *Minutes*, 8 Aug 1837; L & M Directors, *Minutes*, 14 Aug and 21 Aug 1837.

and parcel money collected at their stations. It was later agreed that the North Union company would keep all fares received at Newton and Parkside Junctions. One of the biggest stumbling blocks to the negotiations was the length of time the agreement was to last. The L & M did not like the idea of a temporary agreement; it wanted it to be for three or four years. In 1838, the same year the junction with the North Union at Parkside was ready for operations, the L & M proprietors gave their permission to the directors to enter into final agreements with the North Union.[27] In spite of this, the North Union and L & M directors remained apart on a final decision. On 25 March 1839, both groups indicated their willingness to compromise, but this was not forthcoming until 23 November 1840. The agreement was essentially the same as mentioned above, and the new contract was to run for four years.

Because of the increase of traffic at Parkside due to the new junction line, the L & M was forced to construct a new station slightly east of the original one. It was agreed that the three companies using the station would pay for it. The L & M was to pay one-quarter, and the remaining three-quarters was shared equally by the North Union and Grand Junction railways.[28]

In 1843, the opening of the Bolton & Preston Railway threatened the traffic on the North Union. The latter tried to reach an agreement with the Bolton & Preston, but it would not listen. The Lancaster & Preston had already agreed to run its passenger trains over the Bolton & Preston to Manchester instead of using the North Union and L & M via Parkside as had been the case since 1840. Henry Booth, treasurer of the L & M, was told to complain to the Lancaster & Preston of its partiality towards the Bolton & Preston, but his complaints were of no avail. The L & M then decided, in conjunction with the North Union, to run special trains from Preston to Manchester via Parkside, stopping only at Wigan. Each company would run the train on its own line, and the receipts would be equally divided.[29] This arrangement did

[27] L & M required the North Union to pay the complete cost, £1,713 4s (£1,713.20), of the new junction at Parkside.—L & M Directors, *Minutes*, 11 Jun 1838. The newspapers described the terms of agreement as being very liberal—*Manchester Guardian*, 28 Oct 1837, p 2, quoting *Gore's Liverpool Advertiser*.

[28] L & M Directors, *Minutes*, 3 Jun 1938 and 3 Aug 1840. The L & M charged the NU £2 per year for land at Parkside on which the latter built its coach sheds.

[29] L & M Sub-Committee and North Union Directors, *Minutes*, 12 Jun 1843; L & M Bolton & Preston Opposition Committee, *Minutes*, 22 Jun 1843. The members of the North Union Board were Theodore Rathbone, Mr Wistanley, Dr Reynolds, Mr Calrow, Hardman Earle, Mr Hornby, Mr Swainson, Mr R Earle, and Mr Chapman.

not last long since in 1844, when the North Union contract with the
L & M expired, the former united with the Bolton & Preston. It
retained the title of North Union, but its trains thereafter used the
direct line to Manchester rather than that via Parkside. Nonetheless,
the incident shows that the L & M directors were willing to back their
junction lines to the hilt, and again indicates their ever-ready attitude to
fight for traffic they felt was rightfully theirs.

The Manchester, Bolton & Bury Railway wanted to establish a
junction with the L & M, and opened negotiations for this purpose in
1835. Before the negotiations got under way, however, the L & M made
it clear that, should an agreement be reached, the MB & B would have
to pay for the building of the junction. Two plans submitted for a
junction were unacceptable to both parties, and the MB & B then
suggested that a short connecting line between the Manchester stations
of the two companies be built, to which the L & M directors agreed.
In 1839, Parliamentary powers to construct the line were obtained, and
the enabling Act stated that the connecting line was to be considered
'as Parcel' of the L & M.[30] It was not until 1844 that agreements
involving rates and tolls were made between the L & M and the
MB & B. It was a simple arrangement which gave the L & M two-
fifths of the passenger traffic receipts and one-half of the freight traffic
income.[31]

C. Extensions

On several occasions the L & M directors attempted to extend the
main line. These extensions were for the most part comparatively short,
and were generally a matter of convenience; this was especially true at
the Liverpool end of the line. Since the railway extended only as far as
Edge Hill, with the tunnel to Wapping, the movement of passengers
and freight from the more populated areas of Liverpool proved inconvenient. Less than a year after the L & M was opened, the directors
were exploring ways to extend the line further into the city of Liverpool.
Plans and sections of a line from Edge Hill to Dean Street were drawn
up and submitted by George Stephenson. Since the directors could not
come to any immediate agreement on the design, they were put aside in
favour of plans to build a tunnel that would carry the railway to the
North Docks, Liverpool. This tunnel would have been included in the

[30] 2 Victoria, c. xli, 14 Jun 1839.
[31] L & M Committee to Secure 2/5 Passenger Traffic and ½ Toll on Merchandise
Passing between Preston & Manchester, Minutes, 2 Jan 1844; L & M Directors,
Minutes, 8 Jan 1844.

same petition to Parliament for the Lime Street tunnel, had Stephenson had sufficient time to draw up the plans. The tunnel to the North Docks became a reality in 1849, four years after the L & M amalgamated with the GJ. In fact, the first L & M extension was the tunnel to Lime Street, Liverpool. The Act, giving the L & M power to build the tunnel, stated definitely that it could be used only for passengers traffic; and this restriction was rigidly observed.

The L & M directors were extremely anxious to get permission to build a line from Wapping to the dock areas in Liverpool. Its main purpose was to carry coal directly to ship-side. After much discussion, it was felt that a line to either the Princes Dock or Clarence Dock would be the most desirable, so a petition was sent to the Liverpool Dock Committee asking permission to build a branch along the docks from Wapping to Clarence Dock. The petition, drawn up in 1833, was also sent to the Common Council, and the Commissioners of Sewers of the town of Liverpool. Receiving little encouragement, the L & M directors informed the town authorities they would build the line at their own expense under the following conditions:

> . . . that if it should appear to be a work of undoubted utility and such as might be advantageously used by the public at large, the Railway Company would surrender it to the proper authorities, at first cost for the use of the public . . . if it proved an inconvenience the Railway Company would remove it.[32]

In spite of this manœuvre, opposition continued. The Liverpool Select Finance Committee resolved that no one had the power to give permission to lay a railway along the docks, and the Common Council agreed.[33] A surprising about-face took place in 1835, when the Dock Committee allowed the L & M to carry through a plan to build a line from Wapping station to the timber wharfs at Brunswick Dock. This extension afforded the convenience of loading on to the trains at ship-side, using the dock cranes, and then hauling the timber directly to Manchester. Using old thirty-five-pound rails, the line was begun in July 1836. During the heavy season in the timber trade, construction was suspended and it was not completed until early 1837. The following year, the L & M was given permission to use the railway already built along the east side of Queens Dock. This power was granted 'till some practical inconvenience' would result. Four years later, the railway had to be removed and the section repaired by the L & M since it was felt

[32] L & M Directors, *Minutes*, 23 Sep, 7 Oct 1833, and 14 Apr 1844; L & M North & South Communication Committee, *Minutes*, 16 Sep 1833.
[33] L & M Directors, *Minutes*, 7 Jul 1834.

the railway was occupying too much space and thus causing a public inconvenience.[34]

The most controversial project during L & M history centred around the Hunts Bank extension line. The lack of a rail connection between the L & M station at Liverpool Road, Manchester, and the Manchester & Leeds Station at Oldham Road, constituted the only missing link in rail communication across England from the Mersey to the Humber.[35] At first, it appeared that both the L & M and the Manchester & Leeds were anxious to complete the lines. The distance that would have to be covered by both was less than a mile, and the connection was to be made at Hunts Bank, where the Manchester & Leeds had agreed to build a new station to handle the traffic. The first suggestions for such a link were made as early as 1830,[36] although the Manchester & Leeds was not opened until 1836. In 1838, the M & L started negotiations with the L & M. At first the L & M was amenable to the M & L's plan to connect the two railways in Salford. Since it was suggested that the L & M use a portion of the Manchester, Bolton & Bury in making the link, the directors first approached that company. The MB & B balked at the cost, stating that it had no funds. Negotiations continued through 1839; and after many proposals, counterproposals, threats, cajolings and even an ultimatum, the MB & B and the L & M reached a favourable agreement as to running powers, rates and tolls.[37]

However, it was at this point that the L & M began to advance reasons as to why the Hunts Bank Junction project should not be carried through. Such things as the possibility of making a junction with the Manchester & Leeds and the Manchester & Birmingham in the eastern section of Manchester, the amount of traffic between Liverpool and Leeds and Liverpool and Rochdale not being as great as the directors of the Manchester & Leeds had stated, danger to safe operations, and high tolls on the MB & B, were the excuses offered.[38] These delays did not please the M & L, which publicly condemned the L & M for it hesitancy. The only reaction of the L & M was in agreeing to keep up an 'amicable correspondence' with the M & L as to the possi-

---

[34] *Directors' Reports*, 22 Jul 1835; L & M Directors, *Minutes*, 1835–41 *passim*.
[35] Lewin, *Early Railways*, p 67.
[36] L & M Directors, *Minutes*, 1 Nov and 15 Nov 1830.
[37] L & M Directors, *Minutes*, 1838–9, *passim*.
[38] L & M Directors, *Minutes*, 19 Aug, 16 Dec 1839, 13 Jan, and 2 Mar 1840; Joint Committees on Leeds Junction, *Minutes*, 16 Dec 1839; *Directors' Reports*, 29 Jan 1840. Lewin suggests that the L & M had made agreements with certain canals which would be injured if the proposed junction went through; this would explain L & M reluctance in the matter.—Lewin, *Early Railways*, p 122.

bility of a junction in the future.[39] In 1841, the M & L having completed its section of the proposed extensions, made an arrangement that the L & M should book passengers straight through between Liverpool and Leeds via Manchester. Omnibuses were used to carry them from the L & M Station at Liverpool Street to the M & L Station at Hunts Bank.[40]

The traffic situation between Manchester and Leeds did not improve, and the L & M saw no reason for considering the junction. On 17 January 1842, the directors decided to inform the M & L that they had completely abandoned the idea of a junction line to Hunts Bank. But, two things helped change their minds. A group of L & M stockholders, agitated by Captain Laws, manager of the M & L, who seems to have become an L & M director in order to develop opposition to the company's policy on the Hunts Bank question, swung into action. Also, the Manchester & Birmingham informed the L & M that it had agreed to make a junction with the M & L at Hunts Bank by means of a tunnel. Accordingly, a special meeting of the proprietors was called for 15 March 1842 to discuss the situation. The proprietors favoured a south line through Manchester connecting all three railways if possible, to the advantage of each. In any case, the directors were told to negotiate for some sort of junction line, and the arrangements were to be such that the MB & B would be included in a favourable agreement.[41]

The L & M presented the idea of a south line to the M & L and the MB & B, which both refused to consider. The negotiations swung back to the original plan for a junction at Hunts Bank. The M & L, in return for co-operation on the part of the L & M directors, promised to get them a more favourable agreement with the MB & B. At the same time, the M & L warned the L & M that if it continued to balk, the M & L had already made plans to make a junction with the 'Northern Railway Company' and the Manchester, Bolton & Bury in Salford.[42] In spite of this threat, and the mandate of the proprietors to settle the question, some of the directors continued to delay negotia-

[39] *Manchester Guardian*, 16 Mar 1840, p 3, and 21 Sep 1840, p 3; L & M Directors, *Minutes*, 2 Nov 1840.

[40] L & M Directors, *Minutes*, 1 Mar, 5 Apr, and 7 Jun 1841.

[41] *Directors Reports*, 27 Jul 1841; L & M Directors, *Minutes*, of 17 Jan, 21 Jan and 24 Jan 1842; L & M Proprietors, *Minutes*, Special General Meeting, 15 Mar 1842. In a letter to Charles Lawrence, H. Houldsworth, the M & L chairman, stated that the M & L had nothing to do with the circular published by Captain Laws on Hunts Bank, in which he accused the L & M directors of favouring the Grand Junction interests.—Letter from H. Houldsworth to Charles Lawrence, 29 Jan 1842.

[42] L & M Proprietors, *Minutes*, Special General Meeting, 20 Apr 1842; L & M Directors, *Minutes*, 7 Mar and 24 Mar 1842. The 'Northern Railway Company' is probably a reference to the Bolton & Preston Railway.

tions. They appealed to the proprietors and were told to drop their opposition and proceed as quickly as possible with the extension.[43] With this admonition, the directors went into action. The idea of running over a portion of the MB & B was dropped, and agreements with the MB & B were ended. Several new contracts for the purchase of land were quickly signed. In the meantime, in Parliament a new Bill for the L & M junction with the M & L went ahead rapidly, the customary standing orders having been disposed with. The Act was given royal assent on 30 July 1842 and it gave the L & M power to build a junction line from Ordsal Lane to the Manchester & Leeds Railway at Hunts Bank.[44] Contracts for the use of the Hunts Bank station were in progress by 26 September 1842. Still, the public was growing impatient and the *Manchester Guardian* accused the L & M directors of wasting too much time. The *Manchester Courier* suggested that they were delaying active operations until still further powers were obtained from Parliament. When the M & L put this to the L & M Board, it was vehemently denied by the directors. And, by 21 December 1842, the L & M was the object of more favourable publicity:

> We understand, that the directors of the Liverpool and Manchester Railway Company have made a contract for their cast-iron bridge; and in about a fortnight they expect to contract for the erection of their great viaduct through Salford. . . . We are assured that the whole of the work is to be proceeded with as expeditiously as is consistent with substantial and economical operation.[45]

On 4 May 1844, the Hunts Bank extension was finally opened although the M & L section had opened on 1 January. This was probably the most controversial mile of railway on the L & M system and caused nearly as much concern as did the Chat Moss section during the original construction of the main line. The actual importance of the mile link is stressed in a *Guardian* article reporting the opening of the line: 'There is now therefore, one continuous line of railway communication across the country from Hull to Liverpool, and the Irish Channel is thus brought into close neighbourhood with the German Ocean.'[46]

With the opening of the Hunts Bank extension, the L & M system

[43] L & M Directors, *Minutes*, 4 Apr, 14 Apr, 22 Apr, and 27 Apr 1842. The *Guardian* carried an article stressing the great importance of this Hunts Bank Junction to the entire country. *Manchester Guardian*, 28 May 1842, p 2.

[44] L & M Directors, *Minutes*, 6 Jun 1842; 5 & 6 Victoria, *c*. cviii, 30 Jul 1842.

[45] *Manchester Guardian*, 12 Oct 1842, p 2, and 21 Dec 1842, p 2; L & M Directors, *Minutes*, 19 Dec 1842.

[46] *Manchester Guardian*, 8 May 1844, p 4; Lewin, *Early Railways*, pp 177–8.

was complete. Although there were other proposed extensions, branches, and junctions for which Parliamentary notices had been published, no actual construction of new line took place on the L & M after 1844.

D. Liverpool & Manchester Opposition to Potential Competitive Railways

During the early struggle to get Parliamentary powers to construct the L & M, its directors made many indignant statements as to the monopolistic tendencies of the canal interests which were opposed to the railway. Having failed in their first attempt to push through an Act for the construction of the line, the L & M directors used all the invective at their command against the laissez-faire economic system which protected canal owners. Yet, the L & M was hardly in operation before the very same directors began to employ the same devices, tactics, and public campaigns which had been used against them. This was perhaps additional evidence of canal interests at work within L & M management. The directors wanted to stop the projection of railways they felt would compete with the L & M, and the very things for which they condemned the canal interests within the decade, they were guilty of themselves.

As early as 1831, the directors were watching the progress of a Bill in Parliament, which would give the Manchester, Bolton & Bury Canal & Railway powers to construct a line between Clifton and Liverpool. As the Bill progressed, and the directors became more uneasy, the company hired Charles Vignoles to act for the L & M in opposition to the North Line, as the new railway was called. The Bill was not passed in the session of 1833, and it came up again the following year. Charles Lawrence, Robert Benson, Edward Wilson, John Cropper and Theodore Rathbone were appointed as a committee to take all the necessary steps to prevent the passage of the Bill. The committee compiled data as to the cost and necessity of the proposed line and inserted an abstract of its report in the newspapers. Its brief against the North Line was printed in circular form, and discreetly distributed by the sub-committee.[47] L & M opposition to the Bill was successful, and its denial by Parliament was reported as follows:

> The Bill for this project [North Line], which had been before Parliament for about a fortnight was finally thrown out on Monday

[47] The sub-committee at this time consisted of Charles Lawrence, John Cropper, Robert Benson, Hardman Earle, Joseph Hornby, and Theodore Rathbone. The title of the brief was *Case of the Liverpool & Manchester Railway Against the projected North Line.*—L & M Directors, *Minutes*, 7 Apr 1834 and 2 Feb 1835.

the 30th ult. .... It is understood that the projectors of this North Line made a proposal of compromise to the Liverpool and Manchester, to allow that company a period of fourteen years from opening of their line before the new company should be allowed to carry between Liverpool and Manchester. . . . The projectors of this branch forgot they had no such power to make such a compromise.[48]

From the outset, the projectors of the North Line did not have a chance. Expected opposition from the L & M was ever present, but the public opinion against the line caused more pressure. Even had the conditions been better, there was still much doubt in the public mind as to the utility of the railway when investment and inconvenience of construction were considered. Using the same public opinion which opposed the projectors of the L & M, the directors were able to stave off unwanted competition and protect their investment.

A line of railway between Bolton and the North Union Railway was projected in 1836. As soon as the L & M directors learned of this, they opposed it. They immediately contacted the General Committee on Railways, composed of representatives of the L & M, the Grand Junction and the North Union Railway, which had been set up at the suggestion of the L & M directors for the express purpose of creating combined opposition against railways calculated to be 'uncalled for and competing Lines'.[49] The decision of the committee was that the expenses of the opposition should be shared by its three component railways. The L & M share would be one-quarter of the total; the others would each pay three-eighths. George Loch, with the aid of legal counsel in the person of Mr Swift, was sent to London to carry out the opposition. They were instructed to try and make an agreement with the Bolton & Preston company to form a junction with the North Union Railway instead of building an independent line between Bolton

[48] L & M Directors, *Minutes*, 21 Feb 1831, 11 Nov 1833, 1 Dec 1834, 19 Jan 1835, 2 Feb, 21 Feb, and 6 Apr 1835; *Manchester Guardian*, 4 Apr 1835, p 3. There were rumours in 1836 that another railway to run in the vicinity of Liverpool and Manchester was about to be formed. The *Liverpool Times* attacked the idea and gave reasons why it should not be approved. 'In the first place there is not the slightest necessity of a new line. The fares on the present railway are very reasonable; the speed of travelling is very great; the management is excellent; the conduct of persons employed by the company is civil and obliging; and there is the greatest readiness to rectify anything that may be amiss. . . . It is absurd to ask for liberty to drive off the road a company which has expended upwards of a million in money in trying an experiemnt of the greatest public importance which has not yet received any sufficient remuneration'.—*Manchester Guardian*, 25 Jun 1836, p 3, quoting the *Liverpool Times*.
[49] L & M Directors, *Minutes*, 4 Nov 1836.

and Preston. At first the B & P was willing to compromise, but the L & M balked at the terms and, as a result, lost the battle.[50] The Bolton & Preston received Parliamentary powers and was opened on 20 June 1843, forming a junction with the NU at Euxton instead of an independent line to Preston.

Several other lines were actively opposed by the L & M. In 1837, the L & M and Grand Junction shared the cost of opposing the Chester & Birkenhead Railway. The interests of the Grand Junction were at stake since the C & B would shorten the distance between Liverpool and London, although its passengers would have to cross the Mersey by ferry. Their opposition failed, and the Grand Junction resorted to a boycott of the C & B. The L & M warned the projectors of a proposed Bolton to Wigan and Liverpool line that it would oppose their undertaking, especially the section leading from Wigan to the north end of Liverpool. On the other hand, the L & M would not oppose a line built to the coal districts west and south-west of Wigan, connecting at an 'agreed on' place with the L & M main line. Arrangements were made by the L & M to oppose the following railways in 1845—Chester & Preston Brook, South Junction & Altrincham, and Liverpool, Ormskirk & Preston.[51] However, after 1841 L & M opposition to railway projects was not too effective since the company had run into some opposition of its own. The Railway Department of the Board of Trade, established by Lord Seymour's Act, took a determined stand against the L & M petitions on the ground that what the company was trying to do was to set up a monopoly which would be detrimental to the private interests connected with the projected railways and to the general welfare of the public in Lancashire.[52]

[50] L & M Directors, *Minutes*, 5 Sep, 5 Dec 1836, 24 Apr, and 1 May 1837.

[51] L & M Directors, *Minutes*, 1837–45, *passim*; *Directors' Reports*, 5 Dec 1844.

[52] The following is an indication of the attitude of the Board of Trade: 'If the projects of the Liverpool & Manchester Railway Company were fully sufficient to satisfy the district, the reasons which induced us to recommend the projection of the old-established companies in other cases, must have operated equally in their favour; but protection in this case could only be regarded as establishing an injurious monopoly. The towns in that district have increased in population and commerce to an extent which justifies them in objecting to be served by branches of Railways only. The Liverpool & Manchester Railway has for its first object the Liverpool and Manchester traffic, to which that of adjacent towns must necessarily be subservient. ... The branches therefore must be, in comparison ill served, and this inconvenience attaches to every town so supplied. Hence the large manufacturing towns of Wigan, Bury and Bolton, on the one hand, claim to have a railway for themselves into Liverpool, and, on the other hand, Manchester, Stockport and other places, desire to have access to Birkenhead as an additional outlet for their manufactured goods, and an inlet for the raw material which they work up'.—*Report of the Railway Department of the Board of Trade on Schemes for Extending Railway Communication in Lancashire and adjoining Districts*, 1845, p 363.

E. Amalgamation

The first trickle of agitation for amalgamation[53] on the part of the Liverpool & Manchester Railway appeared in 1843. *The Railway Times* carried an open letter to the shareholders of the L & M suggesting that the company amalgamate with the Manchester & Leeds and the Hull & Selby. The same publication carried another letter on the same topic the following month. In this case the writer asked why the L & M receipts were steadily declining[54] while the receipts of other railways were increasing. His answer to his own question was that if the L & M wanted to survive all the new competitive projects it would have to amalgamate. A third writer claimed that Lord Francis Egerton, owner of the Old Quay Company, had great influence on the L & M directors, and that it was this influence which prevented the company from amalgamating with the Manchester & Leeds. He pointed out that Egerton would not want a through system of railways because it would be too much competition for his canal interests.[55] Although this was the opinion of one unidentified individual, it is necessary to point out that his judgements were false since the L & M directors' actions a few months later proved the statements wrong.

On 19 February 1844, the L & M directors studied a suggestion made by Dr Brandreth that the Bolton & Leigh Railway and the L & M be united into one company. Accordingly, they passed a resolution to accept Dr Brandreth's suggestion as far as their powers as directors allowed.[56] The first discussions which were eventually to lead to amalgamation with the Grand Junction Railway took place on 26 August 1844. The chairman, Lawrence, stated that it would be in the best interests of the L & M and the Grand Junction to consolidate their

[53] For a technical and detailed explanation of amalgamation, see William Edward Simnett, *Railway Amalgamation in Great Britain*, London, The Railway Gazette, 1923, p 3.

[54] There had been a decline in L & M receipts in 1843 when compared to receipts for 1841 and 1842. A nominal increase was had in the first half of 1844, and by the first half of 1845 they had increased considerably.—See Appendix A.

[55] 'Liverpool and Manchester Railway', *The Railway Times*, VI (December, 1843), 1833; 'Liverpool & Manchester Railway', *The Railway Times*, VII (January, 1844), 11; 'Liverpool & Manchester and Manchester & Leeds Railways', *The Railway Times*, VII (January, 1844), 54.

[56] On 30 Sep 1844, the L & M directors instructed Mr Clay, legal counsel, to secure the necessary Parliamentary powers for an amalgamation of the L & M with the Bolton & Leigh. Mr Clay was also to retain Mr Talbot as parliamentary agent for the company's interests in the next session of Parliament. This request for power to amalgamate was later dropped in favour of another Bill including the Grand Junction and the North Union Railways.

position because of the various rival projects, some of which were already in operation, and others which had been proposed and approved. This statement received the unanimous approval of the Board, and a committee was appointed to meet with the Grand Junction directors to make the preliminary arrangements for an amalgamation. At first, the GJ directors were in favour of shortening the distance between Liverpool and Birmingham, and proposed a joint proprietorship for the line. The L & M committee objected to the difficulties which would be involved in making agreeable terms for such a line, and the Grand Junction countered with the proposal of a joint committee or a working union.[57] The L & M called a special Board meeting to consider the suggestion and eventually rejected it. In its place, the L & M directors strongly stated that the interests of the two companies would best be served by an amalgamation. From this point on, the two companies worked hand-in-hand with this end in view.

In the meantime, negotiations were under way with the North Union Railway to consolidate its interests with the L & M. At first, the North Union suggested that the L & M take a lease on its line in perpetuity. This the L & M directors rejected immediately. When the directors of both companies met, they then agreed on amalgamation and with very little difficulty the preliminary arrangements were made. For every £100 share of stock in the L & M, £100 of North Union stock 'A' would be considered £75; and £100 of North Union stock 'B' would be considered £45. It was first agreed that the L & M Board would be the Board of Management of the amalgamated company, but the arrangement was changed to include six directors from each company. This arrangement prevailed until an Act of amalgamation was obtained. The terms as stated to the L & M proprietors were that each £100 of consolidated North Union stock would be considered equivalent to £64 7s 6d (£64.37½). The agreement was approved immediately by the proprietors.[58]

The discussions involving amalgamation with the Grand Junction did not go as well at first. A joint committee carried on the negotiations,

[57] 'A *working union* is for all practical purposes an amalgamation, the companies retaining a separate formal identity and separate capital, and managing the joint property by a committee composed of directors of both companies'.—Simnett, *Amalgamation*, p 3.

[58] L & M Directors, *Minutes*, 2 Nov and 4 Nov 1844; L & M Proprietors, *Minutes*, Special General Meeting, 10 Dec 1844. In December 1844, the North Union suggested that instead of having a committee of six from each company, the North Union Board would manage the lines until the Act of amalgamation was procured. The L & M indicated its disapproval by not replying.—L & M Directors, *Minutes*, 23 Dec 1844.

but there were points of difference. The L & M directors suggested
selling a portion of the line to the Grand Junction, specifically, from
Huyton Quarry to Liverpool, including the tunnel and stations. Newton Junction was not considered since, at this time, the GJ was again
planning a direct line from the south avoiding Warrington and the
Sutton and Whiston inclines. In fact, the L & M was not going to sell
outright, but merely confer equal ownership on the Grand Junction for
a suitable price. Another L & M suggestion was that the companies
should operate independently of each other, with the details of such
an arrangement being worked out by a joint committee. This would
have meant little return for either company. Being of a mind not to
amalgamate at the time, the Grand Junction asked the L & M to name
a price for its line. The L & M was not prepared to do this and asked
the Grand Junction to name its price. The Grand Junction reply was
an unexpected one; it was now willing to discuss amalgamation, and
the L & M appointed another committee to meet with the GJ directors
immediately. By 18 November 1844, detailed arrangements had been
drawn up and presented to the L & M directors, who in turn approved
them. The next step was to publish notice of a general meeting of the
proprietors to solicit their approval.[59] Before the meeting, the directors
prepared a special *Report* which was sent to all L & M shareholders.
The *Report* was a part of a 'softening-up' process, and for the most
part advised the proprietors on the advantages of amalgamation and
why they should support it. 'Combined capital may easily accomplish
what individual resources would have hesitated to undertake; whilst
the interest of the associated companies will be best served by affording
the amplest accommodation to the trade and commerce of the port'.[60]
With little hesitancy, the proprietors gave the amalgamation project
their unanimous support:

Resolution: Unanimously That the additional agreement of the
Directors for the Amalgamation of this Company with its projected
Branches and Engagements (including the Bolton & Leigh and

[59] 'All parties to unite in procuring an Act to enable the Grand Junction to come
over the River Mersey at Marsh Gate and join the Liverpool & Manchester at Huyton, thereby saving Ten miles'. The total shares of both companies was 47,911. The
Grand Junction reserved a sum of £50,000 consisting of a depreciation fund, surplus
to 30 Jun 1844 and the surplus for the remainder of 1844. The Duke of Sutherland
retained his original shares in the L & M. There were to be fifteen directors elected
according to the amount of capital in each company. They also agreed to make
changes in the stations and in the general management of the lines.—L & M Directors, *Minutes*, 18 Nov 1844.
[60] L & M Directors, *Report*, to Proprietors, 5 Dec 1844, p 1.

Kenyon & Leigh Junction Railways, and the North Union Railway, with its Branches and Engagements), and the Grand Junction Railway Company into one consolidated Company, on the terms above stated be and the same is hereby adopted and confirmed by this Meeting.[61]

The terms as understood by the proprietors were that the L & M and Grand Junction shares would be equal and that the Grand Junction company was free to create new £25 shares on its stock to date as an equaliser for the new £40 shares which the L & M had inaugurated shortly before the amalgamation agreements were drawn up.

With the approval of all the parties concerned, amalgamation was well on its way to becoming a reality. The proceedings moved with surprising speed, which seems to indicate that the necessity for amalgamation was a real one for the railways. The evolving 'railway mania' seemed to push the four railways together. Having agreed on the basic conditions for operating the various lines under the amalgamated system, the railways left the minute details to further discussion. One of these details was the make-up of the future Board of the amalgamated concern.[62] Since all the companies could not agree on the matter, the Grand Junction and L & M companies decided that the same committees which drew up the amalgamation agreements should decide the number of directors which would constitute the proposed Board. A related problem was the method of electing directors. The L & M suggested 'that the names of all Directors of the various Boards be inserted in the Act and the power of Proprietors of each Company to elect be retained in proportion to their respective capital'.[63] After much discussion, the number of directors was finally agreed on. The Duke of Sutherland would elect two directors, the North Union Board two, the L & M Board $3\frac{44}{47}$ and the Grand Junction $9\frac{33}{47}$. [64] By the time this agreement had been reached the Bill was in progress, and a copy of it was sent to Mr Swift with instructions to

[61] L & M Proprietors, *Minutes*, Special General Meeting, 10 Dec 1844.

[62] The committee ran the railways as a 'working union' until the Act of amalgamation would be passed. This is another indication of the anxiety of the parties involved to get the amalgamated concern into operation and profit from the investments.

[63] L & M Directors, *Minutes*, 21 Apr and 24 Apr 1845.

[64] L & M Directors, *Minutes*, 5 May and 8 May 1845. The following regulations were set up for the directors of the amalgamated company: three directors would go out of office by rotation every five years except those directors appointed by the Duke of Sutherland; the directors could be re-elected immediately; the first and second directors of the North Union company had to be residents of that line, and the Duke of Sutherland was not to sell his 1,000 original shares.

L

change the amalgamation Bill so as to include the arrangement for the number of directors.

On 17 March 1845, plans were set in motion to have the Bill for amalgamation presented to the House of Commons. The legal details were to be handled by Clay, Swift & Company. Since the L & M already had a Bill for extensions before Parliament, it was first felt that the amalgamation clause could be attached to the extension Bill. But, it was later decided to push the amalgamation Bill through independently. By April 1845, the Bill was drawn up, approved by all the companies and placed before the House of Commons.[65]

Some opposition sprang up against the Bill and the idea of amalgamation. Mr James Loch, MP, objected to the clause which indicated that the Duke of Sutherland's 1,000 shares were involved in the transfer. His objections were quieted by the assurance of the Duke, through George Loch, L & M director, that he would retain his 1,000 original shares in the company.[66] Henry Booth, treasurer, reported to L & M directors that he had received notice from two proprietors that they were against the proposed amalgamation.[67] In Commons, Mr Milner Gibson demonstrated that a clause in the L & M Railway Bill allowed the railway to amalgamate with other companies without applying to Parliament. Sir George Clark was of the opinion that the L & M would have the power to establish a monopoly against the interest of the public. To stop this he proposed a Bill that would:

... declare, that not withstanding the indefinite powers granted in several Railway Bills to lease or transfer their railways, it should not be lawful to do so unless the Bill under which the parties acted contained a clause specifying the parties authorized to make such a transfer, and the companies to whom it was to be made.[68]

Other than this, there was little or no opposition to the proposed amalgamation of the four railways.

The Amalgamation Bill was reported passed through Commons on 28 July 1845. The objections concerning monopoly brought forward

[65] L & M Directors, *Minutes*, 17 Mar, 24 Mar, 7 Apr, 28 Apr, and 30 Apr 1845.
[66] L & M Directors, *Minutes*, 12 May 1845 (committee only).
[67] L & M Directors, *Minutes*, 19 May 1845 (committee only). In July 1845, the Grand Junction directors reminded the L & M directors that if the latter agreed to build a branch line with the Birkenhead, Manchester & Cheshire Junction company, the amalgamation agreement would be broken. Even if the proposed amalgamation were not approved, the Grand Junction wanted to maintain friendly relations with the L & M .—L & M Directors, *Minutes*, 7 Jul 1845.
[68] *Hansard*, III Ser. LXXII, (1845), 620–1.

by Sir George Clark were also discussed, and it was agreed among the L & M directors to conciliate Clark and the Board of Trade by adding the required clauses, but at the same time making sure these were favourable to the L & M.[69] The changes were made and the directors still hoped that the Bill might get passed before Parliament adjourned. In early August 1845 their hopes appeared to grow dim but were raised again on hearing that the Bill had been read a second time. Two days later Mr Lawrence reported that the Preamble of the Amalgamation Bill 'was declared to be proved'[70] and finally, on 8 August 1845, the Bill was approved. It read in part as follows:

> . . . that from and immediately after the passing of this Act the several and respective Persons and Corporations who immediately before the passing of this Act were Proprietors of Shares in the Capital or Joint Stocks of the Liverpool and Manchester Railway Company, and the Bolton and Leigh Railway Company, or either of them, and their executors, administrators, Successors and Assigns respectively, shall be and they are hereby united and incorporated with the Grand Junction Railway Company.[71]

The powers, granted to the L & M in the Act, were to be carried out by the Grand Junction company. Each £100 L & M share was equal to a £100 share in the increased capital and joint stock of the Grand Junction company; and to qualify for a director of the 'new' company, an individual had to have at least £500 in shares.

Still further amalgamation took place in November 1845, when the Grand Junction company and the London & Birmingham Railway met to draw up the necessary agreements. Charles Lawrence, former L & M chairman, presided. On 16 July 1846, by an Act of Parliament, the London & Birmingham, Manchester & Birmingham, and the Grand Junction were consolidated under the title of London & North Western.[72]

[69] *Manchester Guardian*, 2 Aug 1845, p 7; L & M Directors, *Minutes*, 4 Aug 1845.

[70] L & M Directors, *Minutes*, 28 Jul 1845.

[71] 8 & 9 Victoria, *c.* cxcviii, 8 Aug 1845. The directors of the amalgamated concern were listed in the Act as follows: George Loch and Joseph Langton were appointed by the Duke of Sutherland; Charles Lawrence, William Rotheram, Joseph Hornby, John Cropper Jr., John Moss, Robertson Gladstone, George Grant, Hardman Earle, Joseph Sandars, Thomas Moss, George Hall Lawrence, Thomas Booth and Lewin Mozley. Before the Act for Amalgamation was obtained, the Kenyon & Leigh sold out to the Bolton & Leigh for £38,750; this explains the absence of the former in the Act.—L & M Directors, *Minutes*, 16 Jun 1845. For detailed explanations of amalgamation see *Manchester Guardian*, 14 Aug 1845, p 5, and Clapham, *Railway Age*, p 394.

[72] *Manchester Guardian*, 8 Nov 1845, p 7; Marshall, *One Hundred Years*, p 25.

L*

We have now reviewed in some detail operations on the L & M. From the outset, the operational success of the line was evident. However, as the railway grew in experience it developed a valuable legacy for transportation companies of the future. One of the outstanding elements in the L & M was the willingness of its directors to try new ideas. They constantly sought to improve methods of operation with a view to a safer, efficient and economical means of transport. The L & M likewise demonstrates that a shrewd handling of finance, along with a liberal attitude towards the paying public, paid off in terms of income and customer satisfaction. This was the key to the L & M concept of 'mass transit', and the steady, profitable income of the company indicates the wisdom of such a policy, a policy that might well be adopted by twentieth-century carriers. Finally, in the area of technology, the L & M demonstrated a willingness to accept, and work with, inventions. Because a thing worked successfully, it did not mean that it could not be improved. Tradition had no part to play in the technology of the L & M. 'The Grand British Experimental Railway' remained such among its contemporaries, and can still be regarded as such.

Appendixes

APPENDIX A

L&M receipts and net profits, September 1832 to June 1845 from *Directors' Reports*

Half-Year Ending:	Passengers			Receipts Freight			Coal			Net Profits		
	£	s	d	£	s	d	£	s	d	£	s	d
16 Sep 1830–31 Dec 1830										14,432	19	5
30 Jun 1831	43,600	7	5	21,875	0	1	218	6	2	30,314	9	10
31 Dec 1831	58,229	5	0	31,085	18	4	692	10	7	40,783	3	7
										71,097	13	5
30 Jun 1832	40,044	14	7	32,477	14	0	2,184	7	6	28,048	4	9
31 Dec 1832	43,120	6	11	34,977	12	7	2,804	3	4	32,623	14	0
										60,661	18	9
30 Jun 1833	44,130	17	2	39,301	17	3	2,638	15	9	33,171	1	1
31 Dec 1833	54,685	6	11	39,957	16	8	2,591	6	6	40,884	8	4
										74,055	9	5
30 Jun 1834	50,770	16	11	41,087	19	5	2,925	15	11	34,691	16	4
31 Dec 1834	60,292	7	4	41,197	18	6	3,408	16	4	40,346	6	7
										75,038	2	11
30 Jun 1835	52,437	3	4	43,631	1	4	3,406	11	4	37,660	9	10
31 Dec 1835	67,897	19	2	46,375	15	8	3,682	8	8	45,960	10	2
										73,621	0	0
30 Jun 1836	57,914	2	5	47,441	1	1	4,000	8	4	39,402	2	7
31 Dec 1836	75,986	13	9	45,742	16	4	3,550	10	4	45,651	5	9
										85,053	8	4

Half-Year Ending:	Passengers £ s d	Receipts Freight £ s d	Coal £ s d	Net Profits £ s d
30 Jun 1837	59,956 4 6	42,689 13 4	3,296 18 2	35,762 6 7
31 Dec 1837	73,869 11 5	43,406 19 0	2,771 17 8	47,148 11 1
				82,720 17 8
30 Jun 1838	61,776 17 1	58,122 4 0	3,711 8 2	46,556 0 11
31 Dec 1838	79,177 3 2	54,215 7 0	3,201 0 6	55,714 12 2
				102,270 13 1
30 Jun 1839	67,691 18 7	52,964 13 0	3,157 15 1	48,211 19 7
31 Dec 1839	85,425 16 9	57,194 17 7	3,127 13 2	62,968 12 6
				111,180 12 1
30 Jun 1840	70,980 6 1	52,476 1 4	3,018 2 3	59,471 4 7
31 Dec 1840	81,713 3 2	54,901 4 10	2,709 0 7	70,629 1 7
				131,100 6 2
30 Jun 1841	70,288 2 11	53,615 16 5	3,308 0 4	64,019 2 11
31 Dec 1841	80,549 14 7	53,974 19 11	3,006 3 4	67,450 12 3
				131,469 15 2
30 Jun 1842	65,639 2 0	45,367 7 1	3,070 6 7	54,496 2 10
31 Dec 1842	72,641 2 7	48,779 17 2	2,825 1 7	63,696 10 9
				118,192 13 7
30 Jun 1843	60,752 11 2	45,245 12 0	2,962 6 11	57,062 11 7
31 Dec 1843	69,407 2 4	48,412 2 11	3,211 19 3	63,338 14 4
				120,401 5 11
30 Jun 1844	61,916 18 1	51,786 14 9	3,855 18 4	60,320 3 9
31 Dec 1844	77,596 16 0	59,673 8 4	4,062 5 10	76,367 8 8
				136,687 12 5
30 Jun 1845	71,169 9 5	57,603 2 5	5,351 19 7	68,514 2 4

APPENDIX B

Dividends declared by L & M proprietors at their General Meetings, 1832–45, from *Directors' Reports*

Half-Year Ending	Dividend £100 Shares		
	£	s	d
31 Dec 1831	4	10	0
30 Jun 1832	4	0	0
31 Dec 1832	4	4	0
30 Jun 1833	4	4	0
31 Dec 1833	4	10	0
30 Jun 1834	4	10	0
31 Dec 1834	4	10	0
30 Jun 1835	4	10	0
31 Dec 1835	5	0	0
30 Jun 1836	5	0	0
31 Dec 1836	5	0	0
30 Jun 1837	4	10	0
31 Dec 1837	5	0	0
30 Jun 1838	4	10	0
31 Dec 1838	5	0	0
30 Jun 1839	4	10	0
31 Dec 1839	5	0	0
30 Jun 1840	5	0	0
31 Dec 1840	5	0	0
30 Jun 1841	5	0	0
31 Dec 1841	5	0	0
30 Jun 1842	5	0	0
31 Dec 1842	5	0	0
30 Jun 1843	5	0	0
31 Dec 1843	5	0	0
30 Jun 1844	5	0	0
31 Dec 1844	4	10	0
30 Jun 1845	5	0	0

APPENDIX C

Quoted values of Liverpool & Manchester Railway Company
£100 Shares on the Liverpool and London markets,
January 1831–September 1845
Market Prices only cited

Sources: (1) *Liverpool Mercury* (for Liverpool Prices, weekly, 1831, 1835)
(2) Tuck, *Shareholder's Manual* (for London Prices, half-yearly, 1839–45)
(3) *Gentleman's Magazine* (for London Prices, monthly, 1831–40)
(4) *Liverpool Merchantile Gazette* (for Liverpool Prices, weekly, 1844–45)
(5) *Manchester Guardian* (for Liverpool Prices, weekly, 1838–43)

		£			£
6 Jan 1831	(1)	190	23 Jan 1832	(3)	205
13 Jan 1831	(1)	190	21 Feb 1832	(3)	200
20 Jan 1831	(1)	190	21 Apr 1832	(3)	200
27 Jan 1831	(1)	190	28 May 1832	(3)	200
1 Feb 1831	(3)	176	19 Jun 1832	(3)	199
3 Feb 1831	(1)	190	27 Jul 1832	(3)	..
10 Feb 1831	(1)	190	27 Aug 1832	(3)	180
17 Feb 1831	(1)	186	24 Sep 1832	(3)	180
1 Mar 1831	(3)	185	27 Oct 1832	(3)	180
17 Mar 1831	(1)	186	19 Nov 1832	(3)	180
24 Mar 1831	(1)	190	19 Dec 1832	(3)	181
31 Mar 1831	(1)	190	28 Jan 1833	(3)	182
1 Apr 1831	(3)	186	23 Feb 1833	(3)	183
14 Apr 1831	(1)	190	21 Mar 1833	(3)	188
1 May 1831	(3)	186	21 Apr 1833	(3)	188
12 May 1831	(1)	190	23 May 1833	(3)	188
19 May 1831	(1)	190	21 Jun 1833	(3)	188
26 May 1831	(1)	190	21 Jul 1833	(3)	210
1 Jun 1831	(3)	195	28 Aug 1833	(3)	210
2 Jun 1831	(1)	190	23 Sep 1833	(3)	210
9 Jun 1831	(1)	190	28 Oct 1833	(3)	210
16 Jun 1831	(1)	195	25 Nov 1833	(3)	208
30 Jun 1831	(1)	180	27 Dec 1833	(3)	205
1 Jul 1831	(3)	185	27 Jan 1834	(3)	205
28 Jul 1831	(1)	180	24 Feb 1834	(3)	200
1 Aug 1831	(3)	190	26 Mar 1834	(3)	199
11 Aug 1831	(1)	190	24 Apr 1834	(3)	199
25 Aug 1831	(1)	190	26 May 1834	(3)	199
1 Sep 1831	(3)	190	23 Jun 1834	(3)	200
22 Sep 1831	(1)	190	25 Jul 1834	(3)	200
29 Sep 1831	(1)	190	22 Aug 1834	(3)	200
1 Oct 1831	(3)	205	22 Sep 1834	(3)	198
6 Oct 1831	(1)	190	27 Oct 1834	(3)	198
20 Oct 1831	(1)	200	24 Nov 1834	(3)	198
27 Oct 1831	(1)	205	8 Jan 1835	(1)	195
1 Nov 1831	(3)	205	15 Jan 1835	(1)	195
1 Dec 1831	(3)	210	26 Jan 1835	(3)	196

		£			£
29 Jan 1835	(1)	194	26 Jan 1838	(3)	197
23 Feb 1835	(3)	192	23 Feb 1838		197
23 Mar 1835	(3)	192	26 Mar 1838	(3)	200
2 Apr 1835	(1)	192	23 Apr 1838	(3)	200
16 Apr 1835	(1)	193	28 Apr 1838	(5)	200
24 Apr 1835	(3)	192	8 May 1838	(5)	200
21 May 1835	(1)	200	11 May 1838	(5)	201
25 May 1835	(3)	199	25 May 1838	(3)	204
18 Jun 1835	(1)	200	26 May 1838	(5)	204
26 Jun 1835	(3)	199	15 Jun 1838	(5)	206
9 Jul 1835	(1)	200	20 Jun 1838	(3)	206
24 Jul 1835	(1)	200	27 Jul 1838	(3)	206
27 Jul 1835	(3)	199	3 Aug 1838	(5)	196
7 Aug 1835	(1)	197	10 Aug 1838	(5)	201
14 Aug 1835	(1)	197	25 Aug 1838	(5)	201
24 Aug 1835	(3)	197	27 Aug 1838	(3)	200
3 Sep 1835	(1)	197	21 Sep 1838	(3)	200
10 Sep 1835	(1)	198	22 Sep 1838	(5)	201
17 Sep 1835	(1)	198	27 Sep 1838	(5)	201
21 Sep 1835	(3)	195	19 Oct 1838	(5)	201
24 Sep 1835	(1)	198	26 Oct 1838	(3)	200
23 Oct 1835	(1)	204	2 Nov 1838	(5)	204
26 Oct 1835	(3)	195	9 Nov 1838	(5)	204
30 Oct 1835	(1)	210	16 Nov 1838	(5)	204
6 Nov 1835	(1)	210	26 Nov 1838	(3)	204
13 Nov 1835	(1)	211	7 Dec 1838	(5)	204
20 Nov 1835	(1)	212	22 Dec 1838	(3)	203
23 Nov 1835	(3)	195	28 Dec 1838	(5)	204
4 Dec 1835	(1)	216	1 Jan 1839	(2)	203
11 Dec 1835	(1)	216	25 Jan 1839	(3)	204
25 Dec 1835	(1)	220	25 Feb 1839	(3)	200
25 Jan 1836	(3)	220	25 Mar 1939	(3)	200
22 Feb 1836	(3)	245	26 Apr 1839	(3)	193
28 Mar 1836	(3)	245	27 May 1839	(3)	193
25 Apr 1836	(3)	295	24 Jun 1839	(3)	193
23 May 1836	(3)	280	1 Jul 1839	(2)	194
20 Jun 1836	(3)	265	26 Jul 1839	(3)	196
25 Jul 1836	(3)	265	26 Aug 1839	(3)	190
26 Aug 1836	(3)	290	23 Sep 1839	(3)	187
26 Sep 1836	(3)	290	25 Oct 1839	(3)	185
24 Oct 1836	(3)	290	22 Nov 1839	(3)	185
25 Nov 1836	(3)	290	23 Dec 1839	(3)	183
26 Dec 1836	(3)	290	1 Jan 1840	(2)	182
27 Jan 1837	(3)	220	17 Jan 1840	(5)	183
24 Feb 1837	(3)	207	27 Jan 1840	(3)	183
24 Mar 1837	(3)	203	30 Jan 1840	(5)	190
26 Apr 1837	(3)	202	14 Feb 1840	(5)	190
21 May 1837	(3)	204	21 Feb 1840	(3)	183
26 Jun 1837	(3)	204	13 Mar 1840	(5)	184
24 Jul 1837	(3)	207	27 Mar 1840	(5)	183
23 Oct 1837	(3)	200	27 Mar 1840	(3)	183
27 Nov 1837	(3)	196	16 Apr 1840	(5)	183
23 Dec 1837	(3)	197	24 Apr 1840	(3)	183

		£			£
1 May 1840	(5)	184	1 Jul 1843	(2)	199
25 May 1840	(3)	183	21 Jul 1843	(5)	199
26 Jun 1840	(5)	186	4 Aug 1843	(5)	199
26 Jun 1840	(3)	185	22 Sep 1843	(5)	198
1 Jul 1840	(2)	191	11 Nov 1843	(5)	210
10 Jul 1840	(5)	193	2 Dec 1843	(5)	209
24 Jul 1840	(5)	193	7 Dec 1843	(5)	211
28 Jul 1840	(3)	185	30 Dec 1843	(5)	228
2 Oct 1840	(5)	186	1 Jan 1844	(2)	229
1 Jan 1841	(2)	186	15 Jan 1844	(4)	224
8 Jan 1841	(5)	$186\frac{1}{2}$	29 Jan 1844	(4)	219
15 Jan 1841	(5)	$185\frac{1}{2}$	12 Feb 1844	(4)	225
26 Feb 1841	(5)	186	26 Feb 1844	(4)	$221\frac{1}{2}$
16 Apr 1841	(5)	200	11 Mar 1844	(4)	224
23 Apr 1841	(5)	200	25 Mar 1844	(4)	226
14 May 1841	(5)	199	15 Apr 1844	(4)	226
4 Jun 1841	(5)	199	29 Apr 1844	(4)	$221\frac{3}{4}$
1 Jul 1841	(2)	198	13 May 1844	(4)	224
13 Aug 1841	(5)	195	27 May 1844	(4)	222
8 Oct 1841	(5)	195	24 Jun 1844	(4)	223
22 Oct 1841	(5)	197	8 Jul 1844	(4)	231
26 Nov 1841	(5)	$196\frac{1}{2}$	22 Jul 1844	(4)	231
1 Jan 1842	(2)	196	29 Jul 1844	(4)	225
7 Jan 1842	(5)	198	5 Aug 1844	(4)	235
21 Jan 1842	(5)	$197\frac{1}{2}$	19 Aug 1844	(4)	201
11 Feb 1842	(5)	191	26 Aug 1844	(4)	213
25 Feb 1842	(5)	$190\frac{3}{4}$	9 Sep 1844	(4)	200
29 Mar 1842	(5)	173	30 Sep 1844	(4)	203
29 Apr 1842	(5)	$187\frac{1}{2}$	14 Oct 1844	(4)	202
1 Jul 1842	(2)	185	21 Oct 1844	(4)	201
15 Jul 1842	(5)	185	11 Nov 1844	(4)	202
22 Jul 1842	(5)	184	25 Nov 1844	(4)	204
26 Aug 1842	(5)	176	9 Dec 1844	(4)	212
15 Nov 1842	(5)	180	23 Dec 1844	(4)	209
18 Nov 1842	(5)	180	1 Jan 1845	(2)	217
6 Dec 1842	(5)	192	13 Jan 1845	(4)	218
9 Dec 1842	(5)	192	27 Jan 1845	(4)	220
20 Dec 1842	(5)	190	17 Feb 1845	(4)	$213\frac{1}{2}$
23 Dec 1842	(5)	190	3 Mar 1845	(4)	202
1 Jan 1843	(2)	191	24 Mar 1845	(4)	208
21 Jan 1843	(5)	191	14 Apr 1845	(4)	205
4 Feb 1843	(5)	191	5 May 1845	(4)	203
25 Feb 1843	(5)	$192\frac{1}{2}$	2 Jun 1845	(4)	211
11 Mar 1843	(5)	205	30 Jun 1845	(4)	215
15 Apr 1843	(5)	$200\frac{1}{2}$	14 Jul 1845	(4)	213
22 Apr 1843	(5)	201	4 Aug 1845	(4)	214
27 May 1843	(5)	199	25 Aug 1845	(4)	212
10 Jun 1843	(5)	199	2 Sep 1845	(4)	$211\frac{1}{2}$
17 Jun 1843	(5)	198			

APPENDIX D

Acts authorising Liverpool & Manchester Railway company to raise funds

	Capital in Joint Stock £	Loan £	Total £
1 William IV, c. li, 22 April 1831	159,375		159,375
2 William IV, c. xlvi, 23 May 1832		200,000	200,000
7 William IV, c. xxvii, 5 May 1837		400,000	400,000
2 Victoria, c. xli, 14 June 1839		208,000	208,000
8 & 9 Victoria, c. xcciii, 21 July 1845	805,000		805,000

APPENDIX E

An Index of locomotives operated over the Liverpool & Manchester Railway
C. F. Dendy Marshall, *Centenary History*, pp 75–77.

Name	Date	Builder	Type	Cylinders
Rocket	Oct 1829	Stephenson	0–2–2	8 × 17
Meteor	Jan 1830	Stephenson	0–2–2	10 × 16
Comet	Jan 1830	Stephenson	0–2–2	10 × 16
Arrow	Jan 1830	Stephenson	0–2–2	10 × 16
Dart	Feb 1830	Stephenson	0–2–2	11 × 16
Phoenix	Jun 1830	Stephenson	0–2–2	11 × 16
North Star	Aug 1830	Stephenson	0–2–2	11 × 16
Northumbrian	Aug 1830	Stephenson	2–2–0	11 × 16
Planet	Oct 1830	Stephenson	0–2–2	11 × 16
Majestic	Nov 1830	Stephenson	2–2–0	11 × 16
Mercury	Jan 1831	Stephenson	2–2–0	11 × 16
Mars	Jan 1831	Stephenson	2–2–0	11 × 16
Samson	Feb 1831	Stephenson	0–4–0	14 × 16
Jupiter	Feb 1831	Stephenson	2–2–0	11 × 16
Goliath	Mar 1831	Stephenson	0–4–0	14 × 16
Saturn	Apr 1831	Stephenson	2–2–0	11 × 16
Sun	Apr 1831	Stephenson	2–2–0	11 × 16
Venus	Apr 1831	Stephenson	2–2–0	11 × 16
Vulcan	May 1831	Fenton, Murray	2–2–0	11 × 16
Etna	Jun 1831	Stephenson	2–2–0	11 × 16
Fury	Aug 1831	Fenton, Murray	2–2–0	11 × 16
Victory	Sep 1831	Stephenson	2–2–0	11 × 16
Atlas	Oct 1831	Stephenson	0–4–0	12 × 16
Vesta	Nov 1831	Stephenson	2–2–0	11 × 16
Milo	Mar 1832	Stephenson	0–4–0	12 × 16
Liver	Apr 1832	Bury	2–2–0	11 × 16
Pluto	Aug 1832	Stephenson	2–2–0	12 × 16
Caledonian	Aug 1832	Galloway	0–4–0	12 × 16

Name	Date	Builder	Type	Cylinders
Ajax	Nov 1832	Stephenson	2–2–0	11 × 18
Leeds	Jan 1833	Fenton, Murray	2–2–0	11 × 16
Firefly	Mar 1833	Stephenson	2–2–0	11 × 18
Experiment	Mar 1833	Sharp, Roberts	2–2–0	13½ × 16?
Patentee	Mar 1834	Stephenson	2–2–2	11 × 18
Titan	Sep 1834	Tayleur	0–4–0	11 × 20
Orion	Oct 1834	Tayleur	0–4–0	11 × 20
Swiftsure	Oct 1834	Forrester	2–2–0	11 × 18
Rapid	Dec 1835	Tayleur	2–2–2	12 × 18
Speedwell	Dec 1835	Tayleur	2–2–2	12 × 18
Hercules	Dec 1835	Mather, Dixon	0–4–2	15 × 16
Eclipse	Dec 1835	Tayleur	0–4–0	12 × 18
Star	Feb 1836	Tayleur	2–2–0	14 × 12
York	Jan 1836	Tayleur	0–4–2	12 × 18
Vesuvius	Feb 1836	Haigh Foundry	2–2–2	12½ × 16
Thunderer	Feb 1836	Mather, Dixon	0–4–2	15 × 16
Lightning	Jun 1836	Haigh Foundry	2–2–2	12½ × 16
Cyclops	Jun 1836	Haigh Foundry	2–2–2	12½ × 16
Milo*	Nov 1836	Tayleur	2–2–2	14 × 12
Dart*	Dec 1836	Mather, Dixon	2–2–2	14 × 12
Phoenix*	Dec 1836	Tayleur	2–2–2	14 × 12
Majestic*	Dec 1836	Tayleur	2–2–2	14 × 12
Etna*	Jan 1837	Tayleur	2–2–2	14 × 12
Arrow*	Feb 1837	Mather, Dixon	2–2–2	14 × 12
Sun*	Mar 1837	Hawthorn	2–2–2	14 × 12
Meteor*	Mar 1837	Mather, Dixon	2–2–2	14 × 12
Comet*	Mar 1837	Mather, Dixon	2–2–2	14 × 12
Vesta*	Mar 1837	Hawthorn	2–2–2	14 × 12
Lion	Mar 1838	Todd, K & L	0–4–2	12 × 18
Tiger	Mar 1838	Todd, K & L	0–4–2	12 × 18
Rokeby	Mar 1838	Rothwell	2–2–2	11 × 18
Roderic	Mar 1838	Rothwell	2–2–2	11 × 18
Mammoth	Mar 1839	Banks	0–4–2	12 × 18
Leopard	Mar 1839	Todd, K & L	2–2–2	11½ × 18
Mastadon	Mar 1839	Banks	0–4–2	12 × 18
Panther	Mar 1839	Todd, K & L	2–2–2	11½ × 18
Elephant	Mar 1839	Todd, K & L	0–4–2	14 × 20
Samson*	Mar 1839	Hick	0–4–2	11 × 20
Buffalo	Mar 1839	Todd, K & L	0–4–2	14 × 20
Goliath*	Mar 1839	Hick	0–4–2	11 × 20
Swallow	Sep 1841	L & M Railway	2–2–2	12 × 18
Martin	Jan 1842	L & M Railway	2–2–2	12 × 18
Kingfisher	Sep 1841	L & M Railway	2–2–2	12 × 18
Heron	Nov 1841	L & M Railway	2–2–2	12 × 18
Pelican	Dec 1841	L & M Railway	2–2–2	12 × 18
Ostrich	Mar 1842	L & M Railway	2–2–2	12 × 18
Owl	Mar 1842	L & M Railway	2–4–0	13 × 20
Bat	Jun 1842	L & M Railway	2–4–0	13 × 20
Stork	May 1842	L & M Railway	2–2–2	12 × 18
Crane	Oct 1842	L & M Railway	2–2–2	12 × 18
Swan	Oct 1842	L & M Railway	2–2–2	12 × 18
Cygnet	Dec 1842	L & M Railway	2–2–2	12 × 18
Atlas*	Nov 1842	L & M Railway	0–4–2	12 × 18

Name	Date	Builder	Type	Cylinders
Pheasant	Jan 1843	L & M Railway	2–2–2	12 × 18
Partridge	Jun 1843	L & M Railway	2–2–2	12 × 18
Bittern	Apr 1843	L & M Railway	2–4–0	13 × 20
Lapwing	Oct 1843	L & M Railway	2–4–0	13 × 20
Raven	Dec 1843	L & M Railway	2–4–0	13 × 20
Crow	Jan 1844	L & M Railway	2–4–0	13 × 20
Redwing	Mar 1844	L & M Railway	2–2–2	12 × 18
Woodlark	Mar 1844	L & M Railway	2–2–2	12 × 18
Penguin	Jan 1845	L & M Railway	2–1–0	13 × 20
Petrel	Jul 1844	L & M Railway	2–1–0	13 × 20
Linnet	Jul 1845	L & M Railway	2–2–2	12 × 18
Goldfinch	Jul 1845	L & M Railway	2–2–2	12 × 18
Bullfinch	Jul 1845	L & M Railway	2–2–2	12 × 18
Chaffinch	Jun 1845	L & M Railway	2–2–2–	12 × 18
Starling	Jul 1845	L & M Railway	2–2–2	12 × 18

* Indicates name used a second time.

APPENDIX F

A Detailed Description of the Joint Railway Station, Hunt's Bank
Manchester Guardian, 19 August 1843, p 6.

The station, by which we mean the lines with their sidings, turntables, and arrival and departure platforms for both companies, will be
the largest in England, surpassing even that at Derby, in point of
extent. It covers a distance from Hunt's Bank to Ducie bridge of 852
feet, with an average width of 130 feet; having five main lines of rails
from end to end, three of which are appropriated for the main lines,
and two are sidings for goods. In addition to this there are other sidings
for goods; and the departure lines for the two railways are also
sidings, on the south side of the other rails. To the length of 700 feet
from Great Ducie street, the station will be covered with an iron
roofing, erected in three compartments, the centre one being 59 feet
6 inches span; that on the north side 28 feet, that on the south side 26
feet 3 inches. This roofing with a length of 700 feet, and an entire width
of about 114 feet, will form the largest extent of railway roofing in the
Kingdom, being little short of 80,000 square feet of roofing. This
immense roof will be supported by the north boundary wall of the
station, and by a number of iron columns. During the day, the station
will be well lighted by skylights in the roof, and, during the night, by
a series of gas lamps, fitted with burners for the beautiful 'Rose light'.

M

On the north side, the station will be bounded by a lofty stone wall, forming also a retaining wall, for the approach road from Hunt's Bank. The walls bounding this approach road will be surmounted by ornamental cast-iron railing, instead of stone parapets.

All the arrival and departure platforms are, as at Derby, on the same side of the rails; viz. on the south side. The arrival platform for the Liverpool line is between the station-house and Ducie street; and to this there is a covered way for carriages; one-half of the southerly roof projecting over the arrival platform, so as to protect the passengers effectually from the weather in getting in and out of the carriages. The platforms are very large and convenient. That in front of the building is 24 feet wide (of which each company occupies half) and this is continued toward Liverpool, past the west end of the building, to a length of 184 feet, by 12 feet wide; being, in fact, a continuation of the Liverpool departure platform. Towards Leeds, the platform is continued for 120 feet, by 12 feet wide; being also a continuation of the Leeds departure platform. The length of each departure platform is about 320 feet. The total length of the several arrival and departure platforms exceeds a thousand lineal feet. At the end of the station is a place where horses and carriages, for conveyance by railway, going to or arriving from the east or west, may be embarked or landed with every facility; and near are series of turn-tables into the sidings, which are on the north side of the main lines. On that side of the station, there is also to be a large covered shed, to and from which the sidings will convey spare carriages. The arriving passengers who prefer walking to their destination, instead of going along the approach-road to Hunt's Bank, may descend a flight of steps near the line, which saves the 'detour' into Great Ducie street. Such is the joint station, so far as regards the line itself, its approaches and roofing. But we must now notice

THE STATION-HOUSE

which is placed on the centre of the south side of the station, and has two fronts; the north to the railway, and the south to the carriage way on the approach, and facing also the back of Chetham College. This handsome building, designed in what is termed the Roman Doric style, is only one storey in height above the ground, and is about 266 feet long by 36 feet in width. The material used in its erection is a description of wall stone, much used in the West Riding of Yorkshire, though we believe this is the first instance of its use for building in this town or neighbourhood. It is procured at Brighouse, and is usually called 'parrpoint:' it is, in fact, a flagstone, broken into small blocks, which are uniform and good colour. The westerly half of this building, and indeed the whole station, will be occupied by the Liverpool and Manchester Railway Company; the other half, to the east, by the Manchester and Leeds Railway Company. Approaching the south front of the station by the inclined plane, the visitor finds himself opposite its centre, which projects a little from the line of the building, and in which is the refreshment saloon for the first- and second-class passengers, with ladies' waiting rooms &c. This centre presents a frontage of about 60 feet; the freshment saloon is lighted with handsome circular headed windows, with stone pilasters and dressings, and surmounted by an elegant cornice, about the centre of which is placed a large clock. To the right and left respectively are the booking-offices of the two companies, having entrances under a covered way, supported by brackets nine feet six inches long. The substitution of these for pillars is an improvement in convenience, as pillars are often in the way of the doors of cabs or coaches drawing up, which these brackets leave the whole covered way clear. At the east and west end of the buildings are the offices of the station masters, and the parcel offices, which project to the same face as the central portion of the building, with handsome doorways and cornices to correspond. A parapet surmounts the whole length of the building.

Internally, the large central refreshment room will be of the dimensions of 40 feet 3 inches by 22 feet 2 inches. It contains also a space for a bar &c. 40 feet 3 inches by 11 feet 3 inches. This room will have two entrance doors, both from the railway platform; one for the Liverpool and the other for the Leeds passengers. This saloon is for the first- and second-class passengers only. A door at each end opens into the ladies' waiting rooms &c. These waiting rooms have also doors of egress direct to the railway platform. The saloon itself will be the gentlemen's waiting room. Below this refreshment room on the basement storey, will be that for third-class passengers, which is to be of similar size, and will be approached by stone steps from the railway platform; it will have a bar and every convenience and accommodation suitable for that class of passengers; and in the basement storey are also kitchens &c., wine and spirit cellars, ale and porter stores &c. Between the upper refreshment room and the wings, are the large and convenient booking offices; there being two for the Leeds Railway Company, viz. one 50 feet 1 inch by 22 feet 9 inches for the first- and second-class passengers; and another of similar dimensions for third-class passengers. . . . Between the booking offices and the parcel offices on each side, there is to be a waiting lobby and other conveniences for second- or third-class passengers. The two wings at the extreme ends of the building are to be occupied as the parcel offices, and the offices of the station-masters of the two companies. Beneath these, in the basement storey, are rooms for porters, in which to wait and take their meals, during their hours of attendance at the station.

Bibliography

I. CONTEMPORARY MATERIALS

A. Public Documents

1. Parliamentary Documents

(a) Parliamentary Debates
Hansard, III ser, XIV (1832), 1300–1: 9 August 1832.
Hansard, III ser, LXI (1842), 344: 20 July 1842.
Hansard, III ser, LXXXII (1845), 620–1: 17 July 1845.

(b) Committee Reports
(1) Reports of Select Committees on Railway Matters
Great Britain, Parliament, House of Lords, *Second Report from the Select Committee of the House of Lords Appointed to Inquire and to Report Whether Any Danger by Fire Is Likely to Arise from Locomotive Engines Being Used on Railroads Passing through Narrow Streets; with the Minutes of Evidence, and an Index.* Ordered printed 7 July 1836.

—, —, House of Lords, *Report from the Select Committee of the House of Lords Appointed to Consider of the Bill Intituled 'An Act to repeal such Portions of all Acts as impose prohibitory TOLLS on STEAM CARRIAGES, and to substitute other Tolls on an equitable Footing with Horse Carriages;' and to Report to the House, with the Minutes of Evidence and an Index.* Ordered printed 19 July 1836.

—, —, House of Commons, *Report from the Select Committee on Railroad Communication; Together With the Minutes of Evidence and an Index.* Ordered printed 28 March 1838.

—, —, House of Commons, *First Report from the Select Committee on Railways Together with the Minutes of Evidence, and Appendix.* Ordered printed 26 April 1839.

—, —, House of Commons, *Second Report from the Select Committee on Railways Together With Minutes of Evidence, and Appendix.* Ordered printed 9 August 1839.

185

Great Britain, Parliament, House of Commons, *Fifth Report from the Select Committee on Railway Communication; Together with the Minutes of Evidence Taken before Them, and an Appendix, and Index*. Ordered printed 10 July 1840.

—, —, House of Commons, *Report from the Select Committee on Railways Appointed to consider whether it is desirable for the Public Safety to vest a Discretionary Power of issuing Regulations for the Prevention of Accidents upon Railways, in the Board of Trade; and if so, under what Conditions and Limitations; Together with the Minutes of Evidence Taken Before Them, and an Appendix, and Index*. Ordered printed 27 May 1841.

—, —, House of Commons, *Report from the Select Committee on Atmospheric Railways; Together with the Minutes of Evidence, Appendix and Index*. Ordered printed 24 April 1845.

(c) Statutes: Public Local and Personal Acts

George IV, c. lvi, An Act for making and maintaining a Railway from the Borough of *Wigan* to the *Liverpool* and *Manchester* Railway in the Borough of *Newton* in the County Palatine of *Lancaster*, and collateral Branches to communicate therewith, 29 May 1830.

1 William IV, c. li, An Act for Amending and Enlarging the Powers and Provisions of the several Acts relating to the *Liverpool* and *Manchester* Railway, 22 April 1831.

2 William IV, c. xlvi, An Act for enabling the *Liverpool* and *Manchester* Railway Company to make a Branch Railway; and for Amending and Enlarging the Powers and Provisions of the several Acts relating to such Railway, 23 May 1832.

7 William IV, c. xxvii, An Act for enabling the *Liverpool* and *Manchester* Railway Company to raise more Money, and for Amending and Enlarging the Powers and Provisions of the several Acts relating to the said Railway, 5 May 1837.

1 & 2 Victoria, c. xcviii, An Act to provide for the Conveyance of the Mails by Railways, 14 August 1838.

2 Victoria, c. xli, An Act for enabling the *Liverpool* and *Manchester* Railway Company to extend the Line of the said Railway, and for Amending and Enlarging the

Powers and Provisions of the several Acts relating to such Railways, 14 June 1839.

3 & 4 Victoria, c. xcvii, An Act for regulating Railways, 10 August 1840.

5 & 6 Victoria, c. cviii, An Act for better enabling the *Liverpool* and *Manchester* Railway Company to extend the Line of the said Railway, and for Amending and Enlarging the Powers and Provisions of the several Acts relating to such Railway, 30 July 1842.

5 & 6 Victoria, c. lv, An Act for the better Regulation of Railways and for the Conveyance of Troops, 30 July 1842.

5 & 6 Victoria, c. lxxix, An Act to repeal the Duties payable on Stage Carriages and on Passengers Conveyed upon Railways, and certain other Stamp Duties in Great Britain, and to grant other duties in lieu thereof; and also to Amend the Laws relating to Stamp Duties, 5 August 1842.

7 & 8 Victoria, c. lxxv, An Act to attach certain conditions to the Construction of future Railroads Authorized or to be Authorized by any Act of the present or succeeding Sessions of Parliament; and for other Purposes in relation to Railways, 9 August 1844.

8 & 9 Victoria, c. xcciii, An Act for enabling the *Liverpool* and *Manchester* Railway Company to extend and enlarge the said Railway, and to make certain Branch Railways; and for Amending and Enlarging the Powers of the several Acts relating to the said Railway, 21 July 1845.

8 & 9 Victoria, c. cxi, An Act for making a Railway to connect the *Manchester* and *Birmingham* and *Liverpool* and *Manchester* Railways in the Parish of *Manchester*, and also to *Altrincham* in the County of *Chester*, to be called 'The *Manchester* South Junction and *Altrincham* Railway', 21 July 1845.

8 & 9 Victoria, c. xcvi, An Act to restrict the Powers of selling or leasing Railways contained in certain Acts of Parliament relating to such Railways, 4 August 1845.

8 & 9 Victoria, c. cxcviii, An Act for consolidating the *Bolton* and *Leigh*, the *Kenyon* and *Leigh* Junction, the *Liverpool* and *Manchester*, and the Grand Junction Railway Companies, 8 August 1845.

(*d*) Journals
    (1) Great Britain, Parliament, Journal of the House of Commons, 1830–45.
    (2) Great Britain, Parliament, Journal of the House of Lords, 1830–45.

(*e*) Miscellaneous
    Great Britain, Parliament, House of Commons, *Return: Reports, Returns, etc. Relative to Railways*. Ordered printed 8 March 1841.
    —, —, House of Commons, *A Lithographed Plan or Plans of the Carriage or Carriages either already sanctioned, recommended, or most approved of by the Railway Department of the Board of Trade, for the Conveyance of Third Class Passengers under the Penny a Mile Clause of the Railway Act;—Also, a Statement, in detail, showing the Number of Passengers the above Carriage or Carriages are constructed to hold, with the Length, Breadth, and Height of the same, and the Sizes and Situations of the Spaces provided for admitting Air and Light, and whether Glass is used in any and in which of the Said Spaces;—Also, a Copy of the Rules and Regulations, if any, which the Railway Department of the Board of Trade have issued or recommended for carrying out the Law applicable to the Carriages on those Railways which come under the Penny a Mile Clause; and stating whether the Locking of any of the Doors of these Carriages is in Practice; and also various Destinations, the entire Time on the Road, and the Distance travelled in each case respectively.* Ordered printed 27 June 1845.
    Erickson, Edgar L. ed., 'British Sessional Papers, House of Commons', Urbana, Illinois, University of Illinois (microprint edition).

2. Liverpool & Manchester Railway Company Documents
    (*a*) Minutes of Meetings, Reports and Miscellaneous held by the British Transport Commission
        (1) Minutes, Board of Directors Meetings, 1826–45.
        (2) Minutes, Proprietors Meetings, 1830–45.
        (3) Minutes, Sub-Committee Meetings, 1832–45.
        (4) 'Answer of the Directors to an article in the *Edinburgh Review* for October 1832'. (Pamphlet.)

(5) Copy of report from John Dixon, Railway Office, Manchester, 29 June 1835, to Chairman of the Grand Junction Railway.
(6) Record of Locomotive Performance and Fuel Consumption, 1839–40.
(7) Disbursements Accounts, 1833–45.
(8) List of Proprietors, about 1844–5.
(9) Directors' reports to Proprietors and accounts (printed), 1831–45.
(10) Miscellaneous Reports and Materials, 1830–45.

B.   Contemporary Published Works

1. General Historical Accounts
   (*a*) Canals and Railways

Priestly, Joseph, *Historical Account of the Navigable Rivers, Canals, and Railways of Great Britain, as a Reference to Nichols, Priestly & Walker's New Map of Inland Navigation, Derived from Original and Parliamentary Documents*, London, Longman, Rees, Orme, Brown & Green, 1831.

A Letter to a Friend containing Observations on the Comparative Merits of Canals and Railways, Occasioned by the Reports of the Committee of the Liverpool and Manchester Railway, London, Longman and Co., 1832.

Great Britain, Parliament, House of Lords, *Extracts from the Minutes of Evidence Given before the Committee of the Lords on the London and Birmingham Railway Bill*, London, Smith & Ebbs, 1832.

Cort, R., *Rail-Road Impositions Detected: or, Facts and Arguments To Prove that the Manchester and Liverpool Railway Has Not Paid One Per Cent Nett Profit; and That The Birmingham, Bristol, Southampton, Windsor, and Other Railways, Are and Must For Ever Be, Only Bubble Speculations*, London, W. Lake, 1834.

Freeling, Arthur, *The Grand Junction Railway Companion to Liverpool, Manchester, and Birmingham; and Liverpool, Manchester, and Birmingham Guide: Containing An Account of Everything Worth the Attention of the Traveller Upon the Line; Including a Complete Description of Every Part of the Railroad; of the Noblemen or Gentlemen's Seats which May*

Be Seen From It; and of the Towns and Villages of Importance in Its Neighbourhood, Liverpool, Henry Lacey, 1837.

Mudge, Richard Z., *Observations on Railways, with Reference to Utility, Profit, and the Obvious Necessity for a National System*, London, James Gardner, 1837.

Whishaw, Francis, *Analysis of Railways: Consisting of a Series of Reports on the Twelve Hundred Miles of Projected Railways in England and Wales, Now before Parliament: Together with Those Which Have Been Abandoned for the Present Session: to Which Are Added, a Table of Distances from the Proposed London Termini to Eight Well-known Places in the Metropolis: a Table Exhibiting the Length, Cost, Tunnelling, Curves, etc., of Each of the Railways for Which Bills Are Now in Progress Through Parliament; with a Glossary; and Other Useful Information*, London, John Weale, 1837.

The Roads and Railroads, Vehicles, and Modes of Travelling, of Ancient and Modern Countries, with accounts of Bridges, Tunnels and Canals, in Various Parts of the World, London, John W. Parker, 1839.

Bradshaw's Railway Companion, containing The Times of Departure, Fares etc., of the Railways in England, and also Hackney Coach Fares from the Principal Railway Stations, Illustrated with Maps of the Country Through Which the Railways Pass, and Plans of London, Birmingham, Leeds, Liverpool, and Manchester, Manchester, Bradshaw & Blacklock, 1840.

Brees, Samuel C., *Second Series of Railway Practice: A Collection of Working Plans and Practical Details of Construction in the Public Works of the Most Celebrated Engineers*, London, John Williams, 1840.

Whishaw, Francis, *The Railways of Great Britain and Ireland Practically Described and Illustrated*, London, John Weale, 1842.

Tuck, Henry, *The Railway Shareholders' Manual; or Practical Guide to the Railways of Great Britain, Completed, in Progress. and Projected, Forming an Entire Railway Synopsis, Indispensable to all Interested in Railway Locomotion*, ed 5, London, Effingham Wilson, 1845.

Clarke, Hyde, *Contributions to Railway Statistics in 1845*, London, John Weale, 1846.

Ritchie, Robert, *Railways: Their Rise, Progress, and Construc-*

tion; with Remarks on Railway Accidents, and Proposals for Their Prevention, London, Longman, Brown, Green & Longmans, 1846.

Salt, Samuel, *Facts and Figures, Principally Relating to Railways and Commerce*, London, Longman, Brown, Green & Longmans, 1848.

Martin, R. M., *Railways–Past, Present, & Prospective*, ed 2, London, W. H. Smith, 1849.

Scrivenor, Harry, *The Railways of the United Kingdom Statistically Considered, in Relation to Their Extent, Capital, Amalgamations, Debentures, Financial Position; Acts of Parliament by Which Regulated, Creation and Appropriation of Shares, Calls, Dividends, and Various Other Minor Particulars; Concisely Arranged from Solely Authentic Documents; Together with the Railway Accounts, Rendered Upon a Uniform Plan*, London, Smith, Elder, 1849.

Chadwick, Sir Edwin, ed, *Papers Read Before the Statistical Society of Manchester on the Demoralisation and Injuries occasioned by the Want of Proper Regulations of Labourers Engaged in the Construction of Railways*, Manchester, Simms and Dinham, n.d.

Churton, Edward, *The Railroad Book of England: Historical, Topographical, and Picturesque; Descriptive of the Cities, Towns, County Seats, and Other Subjects of Local History With a Brief Sketch of the Lines in Scotland and England*, London, Edward Churton, 1851.

Francis, John, *A History of the English Railway; Its Social Relations and Revelations, 1820–1845*, 2 vols, London, Longman, Brown, Green & Longmans, 1851.

(b) The Steam Engine and the Steam Locomotive

Galloway, Elijah, *History and Progress of the Steam Engine: with a Practical Investigation of Its Structure and Application*, London, Thomas Kelly, 1832.

2. Technical Treatises

(a) Canals and Railways

Page, Frederick, *A Letter to a Friend, Containing Observations on the Comparative Merits of Canals and Railways, Occasioned by the Reports of the Committees of the Liverpool and Manchester Railway*, ed 2, Longman, London, 1832.

Wood, Nicholas, *A Practical Treatise on Rail-roads, and Interior Communication In General. Containing an Account of the Performances of the Different Locomotive Engines at and subsequent to the Liverpool Contest; Upwards of Two Hundred and Sixty Experiments; with Tables of Comparative Value of Canals and Rail-roads, and the Power of the Present Locomotive Engines*, First American, from the second English, edition, Philadelphia, Carey & Lea, 1832.

Badnall, Richard, *A Treatise on Railway Improvements, Explanatory of the Chief Difficulties and Inconveniences Which At Present Attend the General Adoption of Railways, and the Means by Which These Objections May Be Overcome; as Proved by a Series of Interesting Experiments. To Which Are Added, Various Remarks on the Operation and Effect of Locomotive Power*, London, Sherwood, Gilbert & Piper, 1833.

Grahame, Thomas, *A Treatise on Internal Intercourse and Communication in Civilised States and Particularly in Great Britain*, London, Longman, Rees, Orme, Brown, Green & Longmans, 1834.

Fairbairn, Henry, *Treatise on the Political Economy of Railroads; in Which the New Mode of Locomotion Is Considered in its Influence Upon the Affairs of Nations*, London, 1836.

Herbert, Luke, *A Practical Treatise on Rail-roads and Locomotive Engines, for the Use of Engineers, Mechanics, and Others; in Which the Mechanical Construction of Edge, Tram, Suspension, and All Other Railways, and the Various Locomotive Carriages, Designed for Rail and Common Roads, Are Described in Chronological Order, Accompanied by an Analysis of the Whole: Including an Explanation of Every Patent that Has Hitherto Been Granted in England for Improvements in the Mechanism of Locomotion*, London, Thomas Kelly, 1837.

Wood, Nicholas, *A Practical Treatise on Rail-roads, and Interior Communication in General. Containing Numerous Experiments on the Powers of the Improved Locomotive Engines: And Tables of the Comparative Cost of Conveyance on Canals, Railways, and Turnpike Roads*, ed 3, London, Longman, Orme, Brown, Green & Longmans, 1838.

Lecount, Lieut. Peter, *A Practical Treatise on Railways, Explaining Their Construction and Management, with Numerous*

Woodcuts and Ten Plates; Being the Article 'Rail-Ways' in the Seventh Edition of the Encyclopedia Britannica, with Additional Details, Edinburgh, Adam & Charles Black, 1839.

(b) The Steam Engine and the Steam Locomotive

Rankine, David, *A Popular Exposition of the Effect of Forces Applied to Draught with Illustrations of the Principles of Action, and Tables on the Performance of Horses and of Locomotive Engines on Railways. And an Appendix Containing the Results of Some Experiments on Friction*, Glasgow, John Smith, 1828.

Gordon, Alexander, *An Historical and Practical Treatise upon Elementary Locomotion, by means of Steam Carriage on Common Roads, etc.*, London, B. Steuart, 1832.

Lardner, Rev. Dionysius, *Lectures on the Steam-engine, in which Its Construction and Operation are Familiarly Explained: with a Sketch of Its Invention and Progressive Improvement and an Account of the Present State of the Liverpool Railway, and the Performances on It; and of Steam Carriages on Turnpike Roads*, London, John Taylor, 1832.

Gordon, Alexander, *A Treatise upon Elemental Locomotion, and Interior Communication, Wherein Are Explained and Illustrated, the History, Practice, and Prospects of Steam Carriages; and the Comparative Value of Turnpike Roads, Railways, and Canals*, ed. 2, London, Thomas Tegg, 1834.

Grahame, Thomas, *Essays and Letters on Subjects Conducive to the Improvement and Extension of Inland Communication and Transport*, Westminster, Vacher, 1835.

Lardner, Rev. Dionysius, *The Steam Engine Familiarly Explained and Illustrated; with an Historical Sketch of Its Invention and Progressive Improvement; Its Application to Navigation and Railways; with Plain Maxims for Railway Speculators*, ed 6, London, Taylor & Walton, 1836.

de Pambour, F. M. Guyonneau, *A Practical Treatise on Locomotive Engines Upon Railways. . . . With Practical Tables, Giving at once the Results of the Formulae; Founded Upon a Great Many New Experiments Made on a large scale, in a daily practice on the Liverpool and Manchester Railway, with many different Engines and Considerable trains of Carriages, etc.*, New York, D. K. Minor and George C. Schaeffer, 1836.

3. Pamphlets on Railways

Gray, Thomas, *Observations on a General Iron Rail-way, or Land Steam-Conveyance: To Supersede the Necessity of Horses in All Public Vehicles; Showing Its Vast Superiority in Every Respect, over all the Present Pitiful Methods of Conveyance by Turnpike Roads, Canals, and Coasting-Traders, Containing Every Species of Information Relative to Railroads and Loco-Motive Engines*, ed 5, London, Baldwin, Cradock & Joy, 1825.

[Baltimore and Ohio Railroad Company], *Experiments on Railroads in England, Illustrative of the Safety, Economy and Speed of Transportation, Which This System, As Now Improved, Is Capable of Affording*, Baltimore, William Woody, 1829.

Allen, Horatio, *Reports to the Board of Directors of the South Carolina Canal and Railroad Company*, Charleston, J. S. Burges, 1831.

4. Technical Reports on the Liverpool & Manchester Railway

Stephenson, Robert, and Locke, Joseph, *Observations on the Comparative Merits of Locomotive and Fixed Engines, as Applied to Railways*, Philadelphia, Carey & Lea, 1831.

Walker, James, *Report to the Directors of the Liverpool and Manchester Rail-way on the Comparative Merits of Locomotive and Fixed Engines, as a Moving Power*, Philadelphia, Carey & Lea, 1831.

Report of John Farey and Joshua Field: Respecting Boilers for Steam Engines, Liverpool, E. Smith, 1833.

5. Histories of the Liverpool & Manchester Railway

Booth, Henry, *An Account of the Liverpool and Manchester Railway, Comprising a History of the Parliamentary Proceedings, Preparatory to the Passing of the Act, a Description of the Railway, in an Excursion from Liverpool to Manchester and a Popular Illustration of the Mechanical Principles Applicable to Railways. Also, An Abstract of the Expenditure from the Commencement of the Undertaking, With Observations on the Same*, Liverpool, Wales and Baines, 1830.

Bethell, Wm., *Bethell's Broad Sheet, No. 1; History of the Rise and Progress of the Liverpool & Manchester Railway; with a Detail of the Difficulties and Expenses Attendant on the*

Completion of That Stupendous National Undertaking, and a Descriptive Sketch of the Scenery on the Line of the Road, Liverpool, Wm. Bethell, (1830).

Kirwan, Joseph, *A Descriptive and Historical Account of the Liverpool and Manchester Railway, from Its First Projection to the Present Time, Containing All the Facts and Information That Have Yet Appeared on the Subject, with Numerous Interesting and Curious Original Details, Estimates of Expenses, &c. &c.*, ed 2, London, Simpkin & Marshall, 1831.

A History and Description of the Liverpool & Manchester Railway, Liverpool, Thomas Taylor, 1832.

6. Descriptions of the Liverpool & Manchester Railway

Walker, James Scott, *An Accurate Description of the Liverpool and Manchester Railway, the Tunnel, the Bridges, and Other Works throughout the Line; an Account of the Opening of the Rail-way, and the Melancholy Accident Which Occurred; a Short Memoir of the Late Right Hon. Wm. Huskisson, and Particulars of the Funeral Procession, &c. with a Map of the Line, and a View of the Bridge over Water Street, Manchester*, ed 2, Liverpool, J. F. Cannell, 1830; ed 3, 1831.

Shaw, Isaac, *A New and Complete Work of the Liverpool and Manchester Railway*, Liverpool, I. Shaw, 1831.

Notre, A., *Description of the Rail Road from Liverpool to Manchester. By P. Moreau, Engineer. Together with a History of Rail Roads, and Matters Concerned Therewith, Compiled by A. Notre, from the Works of Messers. Wood and Stephenson, and from Information Furnished by the Latter*, trans. by J. C. Stocker, Jr., Boston, Hilliard, Gray, 1833.

A Tourist, *The Railway Companion, Describing an Excursion Along the Liverpool Line, Accompanied With a Succinct and Popular History of the Rise and Progress of Railroads*, London, Effingham Wilson and James Fraser, 1833.

Descriptive Catalogue of the Panoramic Exhibition of the Manchester and Liverpool Railroad, Containing 15,000 square feet of Canvas, Now Exhibiting Illustrated with Twelve Lithographic Views, Taken on the spot, by Artists of Acknowledged Talent, London, E. Colyer, Printer, 1835.

Cornish, James, *Cornish's Guide and Companion to the Grand*

Junction and the Liverpool and Manchester Railways, Containing also the Stranger's Guide to Liverpool and Manchester, and an Account of Birmingham and All the Towns on or near the Line, Together with Every Thing Worthy the Notice of the Traveller on the Road; the Company's Charges from One Station to Another; their Regulations; Time of Departure and Arrival of Each Train, &c., &c., ed 3, London, S. Cornish, 1838.

Osborne's Guide to the Grand Junction, Or Birmingham, Liverpool and Manchester Railway, with the Topography of the Country through Which the Line Passes, and Complete Guides to the Towns of Birmingham, Liverpool and Manchester, ed 2, Birmingham, E. C. & W. Osborne, 1838.

7. Atlases and Maps

Greenwood, C. & J., *Atlas of the Counties of England, from Actual Surveys Made from the Years of 1817 to 1833,* London, Greenwood, 1834.

Bell, James, *Maps of England and Wales,* Glasgow, Arch. Fullarton, 1836.

Hall, Sidney, *A New British Atlas; Comprising a Series of 54 Maps. Constructed from the Most Recent Surveys,* London, Chapman & Hall, 1836.

Walker, J. & C., *To Her Most Excellent Majesty Queen Victoria, and to Her Royal Highness the Duchess of Kent, This British Atlas Comprising Separate Maps of Every County in England, Each Riding in Yorkshire and North & South Wales, Showing the Roads, Railways, Canals, Parks, Boundaries of Boroughs &c. Compiled from the Maps of the Board of Ordinance and Other Trigonometrical Surveys, Is, with Their Gracious Permission Most Respectfully Dedicated by Their Very Humble & Devoted Servants,* London, Longman, Rees, 1838.

Pigot & Co., *British Atlas, Comprising the Counties of England, (Upon Which are Laid Down All Railways Completed and in Progress), with Separate Large Sheet Maps of England and Wales, Ireland and Scotland, and a Circular One of the Country round London,* London, Pigot & Slater, 1842.

Hall, Sidney, *A Travelling County Atlas; with All the Railroads Accurately Laid Down, and the Boundaries Coloured,* London, Chapman & Hall, 1846.

8. Collections of Statutes

> *A Collection of the Local and Personal Acts, Declared Public and To Be Judically Noticed*, London, George Eyre and Andrew Spottiswoode, 1830–45.
>
> *A Collection of the Public General Statutes*, London, Owen Richards, Law Bookseller and Publisher, 1830–45.
>
> Simons, N. ed., *The Statutes of The United Kingdom of Great Britain and Ireland With Notes and References*, London, George Eyre and Andrew Spottiswoode, 1830–45.

9. Parliamentary Procedure

> Halcombe, John, *A Practical Treatise of Passing Private Bills Through Both Houses of Parliament, Containing Full Directions for Members Who Have Charge of Private Bills, and for Solicitors, &c., with a Supplement, Correcting the Practice to the Commencement of the Session 1838, and Appendices, Containing the Standing Orders, and Tables of Fees, of Lords and Commons*, London, S. Sweet, 1838.
>
> Frere, Charles, *A Treatise on the Practice of Committees of the House of Commons, with Reference Especially to Private Bills*, Westminster, James Bigg, 1846.

10. Reference Works

> *Arcana of Science and Art: or, an Annual Register of Popular Inventions and Improvements, Abridged from the Transactions of Public Societies, and from Scientific Journals, British and Foreign, of the Past Year*, London, John Limbird, 1830.
>
> Brewster, David, *The Edinburgh Encyclopaedia*, 18 vols, Edinburgh, William Blackwood, 1830.
>
> Pritchard, Andrew, English Patents; *Being a Register of All Those Granted for Inventions in the Arts, Manufactures, Chemistry, Agriculture, etc., etc., during the First Forty-five Years of the Present Century*, London, Whittaker, 1847.
>
> Crabb, George, *A Technical Dictionary; or, A Dictionary Explaining the Terms Used in All Arts and Sciences*, London, W. Maxwell, 1851.

11. Miscellaneous

> Wheeler, James, *Manchester: Its Political, Social and Commercial History, Ancient and Modern*, London, Whittaker & Co, 1836.

N

C. *Contemporary Newspaper Materials*

1. Lancashire Newspapers
   Liverpool Mercury. 1830, 1835.
   Myer's Merchantile Advertiser, (Liverpool). 1829–32.
   Liverpool Merchantile Gazette. 1844–5.
   Manchester Guardian. 1830–45.
2. Other British Newspapers
   The (London) *Times.* 1831–45.

II. RECENT MATERIALS

A. *Economics*

1. General Economic Histories of Great Britain
   Checkland, Sydney G., *The Rise of Industrial Society in England 1815–1885*, London, Longmans, 1964.
   Clapham, John Harold, *The Early Railway Age, 1820–1850* (Vol I of *An Economic History of Modern Britain*), Cambridge, University Press, 1926.
   Fay, C. R., *Great Britain from Adam Smith to the Present Day: An Economic and Social Survey*, New York, Longmans, Green, 1928.
   Gayer, Arthur D., Rostow, W. W., and Schwartz, Anna Jacobson, *The Growth and Fluctuation of the British Economy, 1790-1850: An Historical, Statistical, and Theoretical Study of Britain's Economic Development*, 2 vols, Oxford, Clarendon Press, 1953.
   Jenks, Leland Hamilton, *The Migration of British Capital To 1875*, London, Alfred A. Knopf, 1938.

2. Accounts of Transportation Economics
   Acworth, Sir William Mitchell, and Stephenson, W. T., *The Elements of Railway Economics*, Oxford, The Clarendon Press, 1924.
   Beckman, Martin, McGuire, C. B., and Winsten, Christopher B., *Studies in the Economics of Transportation*, London, Oxford University Press, 1956.
   Penfold, Charles, *Practical Remarks Upon the Principle of Rating Railway Gas and Water Companies*, ed. 3, London, Robert Baldwin, 1857.
   Poole, Braithwaite, *The Economy of Railways as a Means of Transit, Comprising the Classification of the Traffic, in Relation to the Most*

Appropriate Speeds for the Conveyance of Passengers and Merchandise, London, William Clowes & Sons, 1856.

Reed, M. C., ed., *Railways in the Victorian Economy*. New York, Augustus Kelly, 1968.

Savage, Christopher I., *An Economic History of Transport*, London, Hutchinson University Library, 1961.

B. *General Histories of British Transportation*

Acworth, W. M., *The Railways of England*, ed 3, London, John Murray, 1889; ed 5, 1900.

Allen, Cecil John, *Railways of Britain*, London, Thomas Nelson & Sons, 1958.

Barman, Christian Augustus, *Early British Railways*, Harmondsworth, Penguin Books, 1950.

Boulton, William Henry, *The Railways of Britain, Their History, Construction and Working*, London, Sampson Low, 1950.

Carter, Ernest F., *Britain's Railway Liveries: Colours, Crests and Linings, 1825–1948*, London, Burke, 1952.

Chattaway, E. D., *Railways: Their Capital and Dividends, with Statistics of Their Working in Great Britain and Ireland, &c., &c.*, London, John Weals, 1855–6.

Clinker, C. R. comp., *Railways of the West Midlands: A Chronology, 1808–1954*, London, The Stephenson Locomotive Society, n.d.

Dolfus, Charles, and de Geoffry, Edgar, *Historie de la Locomotion Terrestre Les Chemins de Fer*, Paris, 13 rue Saint-Georges, 1935.

Ellis, C. Hamilton, *Nineteenth Century Railway Carriages In the British Isles—from the Eighteen-thirties to the Nineteen-hundreds*, London, Modern Transport Publishing Co, 1949.

Elton, Arthur, *British Railways*, London, Collins, 1947.

Gordon, William John, *Our Home Railways: How They Began and How They Are Worked*, 2 vols, London, Frederick Warne, 1910.

Jackman, William T., *The Development of Transportation in Modern England*, 2nd ed., London, F. Cass, 1962.

Lee, Charles E., *The Evolution of Railways*, London, Railway Gazette, 1937.

—, —, *The Centenary of 'Bradshaw,'* London, Railway Gazette, 1940.

—, —, *Passenger Class Distinction*, London, Railway Gazette, 1946.

Lewin, Henry Grote, *Early British Railways: A Short History of Their Origin and Development 1801–1844*, London, Locomotive Publishing, 1926.

—, —, *The Railway Mania and Its Aftermath 1845–1852*, 2d ed., Newton Abbot, David and Charles, 1968.

Marshall, C. F. Dendy, *One Hundred Years of Railways, from Liverpool and Manchester to London Midland and Scottish*, London, London Midland & Scottish Railway, 1930.

—, —, *A History of British Railways Down to the Year 1830*, London, Oxford University, 1938.

Newbold, J. T. Walton, *The Railways, 1825–1925*, London, Labour Publishing, 1925.

Nock, O. S., *The Railways of Britain*, London, B. T. Batsford, 1947.

—, —, *British Trains, Past and Present*, London, B. T. Batsford, 1951.

—, —, *The Railway Engineers*, London, B. T. Batsford, 1955.

—, —, *Branch Lines*, London, B. T. Batsford, 1957.

O'Dell, Andrew C., *Railways and Geography*, London, Hutchinson's University Library, 1956.

Pangborn, J. G., *The World's Railways: Historical, Descriptive, Illustrative*, New York, Winchell Printing, 1904.

Pendleton, John, *Our Railways: Their Origin, Development, Incident and Romance*, 2 vols. London, Cassell, 1894.

Robbins, Michael, *The Railway Age*, London, Routledge & Kegan Paul, 1962.

Rolt, Lionel Thomas Caswell, *Red For Danger: A History of Railway Accidents and Railway Safety Precautions*, London, The Bodley Head, 1955.

Sherrington, C. E. R., *The Economics of Rail Transport in Great Britain*, 2 vols, New York, Longmans, Green, 1928.

—, —, *A Hundred Years of Inland Transport 1830-1933*, London, Duckworth, 1934.

Simnett, William Edward, *Railway Amalgamation in Great Britain*, London, Railway Gazette, 1923.

Tatford, Barrington, *The Story of British Railways*, London, Sampson Low, Marston, 1946.

Williams, Frederick S., *Our Iron Roads: Their History, Construction and Social Influences*, London, Ingram Cooke, 1852.

C. Histories of Individual Railways

1. Liverpool & Manchester Railway
   (a) Published

   Carlson, Robert E., *The Liverpool & Manchester Railway Project, 1821–1831*, Newton Abbot, David & Charles, 1969.

Grieve, C. M., 'A Short History of the Liverpool and Manchester Railway', in *The Book and Programme of the Liverpool and Manchester Railway Centenary*, Liverpool, 1930, pp 33–43.

Holt, G. O., *A Short History of the Liverpool & Manchester Railway*, Railway & Canal Historical Society, 1955.

Marshall, C. F. Dendy, *Centenary History of the Liverpool & Manchester Railway; (to which is appended a transcript of the relevant portions of Rastrick's 'Rainhill' Notebook)*, London, Locomotive Publishing, 1930.

Pike, Richard, ed., *Romance of the Liverpool and Manchester Railway, as Described by Fanny Kemble (The Celebrated Actress), Mr. C. F. Adams, Lord Brougham, and Other Contemporary Writers*, Manchester, John Heywood, (1885).

Veitch, George Stead, *The Struggle for the Liverpool and Manchester Railway*, Liverpool, Daily Post Printers, 1930.

2. Other Railways
   (*a*) Published
   Greville, Maurice D., and Holt, Geoffrey O., *The Lancaster and Preston Junction Railway*, Newton Abbot, David & Charles, 1961.

   McDermott, Edward Terence, *History of the Great Western Railway*, 2 vols (vol 1 in 2 pts), London, Great Western Railway, 1927.

   MacLean, John S., *The Newcastle & Carlisle Railway, 1825–1862; The First Railway Across Britain*, Newcastle upon Tyne, R. Robinson, 1948.

   Steel, Wilfred L., *The History of the London & North Western Railway*, The Railway and Travel Monthly, 1914.

   (*b*) Unpublished
   Ciaburri, Robert L., 'The Manchester, Bolton & Bury Railway Project, 1831–1839'. Unpublished Master's thesis, Department of History, University of Pittsburgh, 1958.

D. *Histories of Steam Locomotion*

Ahrons, Ernest Leopold, *The British Steam Railway Locomotive, 1825–1925*, London, Locomotive Publishing, 1927.

Clark, Daniel Kinnear, *On The Improvement of Railway Locomotive Stock, and The Reduction of Working Expenses*, London, William Clowes, 1857.

Dow, George, *British Steam Horses*, London, Phoenix House, 1950.

Marshall, C. F. Dendy, *Two Essays in Early Locomotive History. I. The First Hundred Railway Engines. II. British Locomotives in North America*, London, Locomotive Publishing, 1928.

—, —, *Early British Locomotives: A Supplement to the First of the Author's 'Two Essays in Early Locomotive History'*. London, Locomotive Publishing, 1939.

—, —, *A History of Railway Locomotives Down to the End of the Year 1831*, London, Locomotive Publishing, 1953.

Nock, Oswald Stevens, *Steam Locomotive. A Retrospect of the Work of Eight Great Locomotive Engineers*, London, British Transport Commission, 1955.

Sekon, G. A., *The Evolution of the Steam Locomotive (1803 to 1898)*, Railway Publishing, 1899.

Stretton, Clement E., *The Locomotive Engine and Its Development. A Popular Treatise on the Gradual Improvements Made in Railway Engines between 1803–1903*, ed 6, London, Crosby Lockwood, 1903.

Thurston, Robert H., *A History of the Growth of the Steam Engine*, ed 6, London, Oxford University Press, 1939.

Warren, J. G. H., *A Century of Locomotive Building by Robert Stephenson & Co., 1823–1923*, Newcastle upon Tyne, Andrew Reid, 1923.

Westcott, Gerald Francis, comp., *The British Railway Locomotive. A Brief Pictorial History of the First Fifty Years of the British Steam Railway Locomotive, 1803–1853*, London, Her Majesty's Stationary Office, 1958.

Young, Robert, *Timothy Hackworth and the Locomotive*, London, Locomotive Publishing, 1923.

E.   Histories of Liverpool and Manchester

1. Liverpool

Baines, Thomas, *History of the Commerce and Town of Liverpool, and of the Rise of Manufacturing Industry in the Adjoining Counties*, London, Longman, Brown, Green & Longman, 1852.

Muir, Ramsay, *A History of Municipal Government in Liverpool from the Earliest Times to the Municipal Reform Act of 1835*, 2 pts, Liverpool, University Press, 1906.

—, —, *A History of Liverpool*, ed 2, Liverpool, University Press 1907.

Parkinson, C. Northcote, *The Rise of the Port of Liverpool*, Liverpool, University Press, 1952.

Picton, James Allanson, *Memorials of Liverpool, Historical and*

Topographical: Including A History of the Dock Estate, 2 vols, London, Longmans, Green, 1875.

White, Brian D., *A History of the Corporation of Liverpool, 1835–1914*, Liverpool, The University Press, 1951.

2. Manchester

Axon, William E. A., *The Annals of Manchester: A Chronological Record from the Earliest Times to the End of 1885*, Manchester, John Heywood, 1886.

Redford, Arthur, *et al., Manchester Merchants and Foreign Trade, 1794–1858*, Manchester, University Press, 1934.

Reilly, John, *The History of Manchester*, Manchester, John Gray Bell, 1861.

Slugg, Josiah Thomas, *Reminiscences of Manchester Fifty Years Ago*, Manchester, J. E. Cornish, 1881.

F.   Biographical Works

Hough, Richard, *Six Great Railwaymen: Stephenson, Hudson, Deniso n Huish, Stephen, Gresley*, London, Hamish Hamilton, 1955.

Jeaffreson, J. C., *The Life of Robert Stephenson, F.R.S., With Descriptive Chapters on Some of His Most Important Professional Works by William Pole, F.R.S.*, ed 2, 2 vols, London, Longmans, Green, Reader & Dyer, 1866.

Lambert, Richard Stanton, *The Railway King, 1800–1871*, London, George Allen and Unwin Ltd., 1934.

Macaulay, Thomas Babington, *et al., New Biographies of Illustrious Men*, Boston, Whittemore, Niles & Hall, 1857.

Melville, Lewis, ed, *The Huskisson Papers*, New York, Richard R. Smith, 1931.

Morley, John, *The Life of William Ewart Gladstone*, new ed, 3 vols in 2, New York, Macmillan, 1911.

P(aine), E.M.S., *The Two James's and The Two Stephensons; or The Earliest History of Passenger Transit on Railways*, London, G. Phipps, 1861.

Rolt, L. T. C., *Great Engineers*, London, G. Bell & Sons, 1962.

Rolt, L. T. C., *The Railway Revolution, George and Robert Stephenson*, New York, St Martins Press, 1960.

Rowland, John, *George Stephenson, Creator of Britain's Railways*, London, Odhams Press, 1954.

Smiles, Robert, *Memoir of the Late Henry Booth, of the Liverpool and*

Manchester, and afterwards of the London and North-western Railway, London, Wyman, 1869.

Smiles, Samuel, *The Life of George Stephenson and of His son Robert Stephenson; comprising also A History of the Invention and Introduction of the Railway Locomotive,* ed 8, New York, Harper, 1868.

Vignoles, Olinthus, J., *Life of Charles Blacker Vignoles, F.R.S., F.R.A.S., M.R.I.A., &c. Soldier and Civil Engineer. Formerly Lieutenant in H.M. 1st Royals. Past-President of Institution of Civil Engineers, A Reminiscence of Early Railway History,* London, Longmans, Green, 1889.

G. Parliamentary Procedure

Clifford, Frederick, *A History of Private Bill Legislation,* 2 vols, London, Butterworths, 1885–7.

May, Thomas Erskine, *A Practical Treatise on the Law, Privileges, Proceedings, and Usage of Parliament,* ed 4, London, Butterworths, 1859.

Norris, W., *Parliamentary Costs. Analysis and Particulars of a Solicitor's Bill of Costs in Respect of Obtaining a Railway Act,* London, P. S. King, n.d.

Webster, Edward, *Parliamentary Costs Relative to Private Bills, Election Petitions, and Appeal Causes, Together with Allowances to Witnesses,* London, Stevens & Norton, 1859.

Williams, O. Cyprian, *The Historical Development of Private Bill Procedure and Standing Orders in the House of Commons,* 2 vols, London, H.M. Stationary Office, 1948–9.

H. Reference Works

1. Published

Encyclopaedia Britannica, ed 9, 1875.

Encyclopaedia Britannica, ed 14, 1958.

Great Britain, Parliament, House of Commons, *General Index to The Accounts and Papers Reports of Commissioners Estimates &c. &c. Printed by Order of the House of Commons or Presented by Command. 1801–1852,* London, H.M. Stationary Office, 1938.

—, —, *House of Lords, A General Index to the Sessional Papers Printed by Order of the House of Lords, or Presented by Special Command: From the Union With Ireland To the Termination of the Seventeenth Parliament of the United Kingdom,* London, George E. Eyre and William Spottiswoode, 1859.

—, —, House of Commons, *Index To Local and Personal Acts Consisting of Classified Lists of the Local and Personal and Private Acts and Special Orders and Special Procedure Orders. 1801–1947*, London, H.M. Stationary Office, 1949.

City of Liverpool Library Museum and Arts Committee, *Liverpool Prints and Documents Catalogue of Maps Plans Views Portraits Memoirs Literature &c. in the Reference Library Relating to Liverpool and Serving to Illustrate Its History Biography Administration Commerce and General Condition and Progress from Earliest Times*, Liverpool, 1908.

City of Liverpool Library Museum and Arts Committee, *The Centenary of the Liverpool and Manchester Railway, 1830–1930: A List of Printed & Illustrated Material in the Reference Library*, Liverpool, 1930.

Ford, G., and Ford P., *A Guide to Parliamentary Papers: What they Are: How to Find Them: How to Use Them*, Oxford, Basil Blackwell, 1955.

Haskell, Daniel C., *A Tentative Check List of Early European Railway Literature, 1831-1848*, Boston, Baker Library, Harvard Graduate School of Business Administration, 1955.

Stephen, Sir Leslie, and Lee, Sir Sidney, eds, *The Dictionary of National Biography, from the Earliest Times to 1900*, 21 vols, London, Oxford, 1917.

Thompson, Slason, ed, *The Railway Library, 1912: A Collection of Noteworthy Addresses and Papers, Mostly Delivered or Published During the Year Named*, Chicago, Stromberg, Allen, 1913.

A Bibliography of Parliamentary Debates of Great Britain, London, H.M. Stationary Office, 1956.

Catalogue of the William Barclay Parsons Collection, New York, The New York Public Library, 1941.

Early Railway Pamphlets, 1825–1900 (Gladstone Library Pamphlet Collection Subject Lists No. 1), London, Gladstone Library, 1938.

Index to Signal Literature, Bethlehem, Pennsylvania, Times Publishing Co., 1911.

London Times: Reports, Statements, Letters, &c., Relative to the Liverpool and Manchester Railway, Manchester, Charles Sever, Printer, 1879.

The Pioneer Period of European Railroads: A Tribute to Thomas W. Streeter, Boston, Baker Library, Harvard Graduate School of Business Administration, 1946.

Tercentenary Handlist of English & Welsh Newspapers, Magazines &
Reviews, (1620–1920), London, The Times, 1920.

2. Unpublished
Day, Mary B., comp., 'A Selected Reading List on the History of
Railroads', Chicago, Library of the Museum of Science and
Industry, 1952. (Mimeographed.)

Index